Brown Bros. photo from "MAMBA'S DAUGHTERS"

Brown Bros. photo from
"PINKY"

SOME GREAT MOMENTS IN ETHEL WATERS' LIFE

photo by Bob Golby
from the Whitehead, Rea,
Martineau production
"THE MEMBER
OF THE WEDDING"

Anton Bruehl photo
from *Vanity Fair*
"AS THOUSANDS
CHEER"

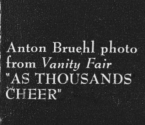

Talk With Ethel Waters

By HARVEY BREIT

the other things
mind. Oh, I can get
angry and curse a little (of
Lord look the oth

Where the Blues Begin

His Eye Is on the Sparrow (278 pp.) —*Ethel Waters, with Charles Samuels*—Doubleday ($3).

"I never was a child.

"I never was coddled, or liked, or understood by my family.

"I never felt I belonged.

"I was always an outsider.

"I was born out of wedlock, but that had nothing to do with all this. To people like mine, a thing like that just didn't mean much.

"Nobody brought me up."

So begins *His Eye Is on the Sparrow*, the autobiography of Singer-Actress Ethel Waters. It is surely one of the frankest self-revelations ever to see print, a combination of depressing sordidness and one proud Negro's piled-up resentment against the experience of white discrimination. It is also, just as surely, an American success story. It is often vulgar to the point of endangering sympathy for its narrator. It is crudely ghost-written in a mixture of Broadway pressagentry, dubious religiosity and chip-on-shoulder sensationalism. It also has a final ring of truth that may account for its being a March selection of the Book-of-the-Month Club.

Errands to Run. Ethel Waters was born in Chester, Pa., the daughter of a Negro girl who was raped at the age of twelve. As she remembers her childhood, it was a continuous round of poverty, filth, lust and violence. By the time she

Anton Bruehl—*Vanity Fair*
ETHEL WATERS
Offstage, bitterness.

was seven, she had an adult's knowledge of sex. Farmed out by her child-mother and her grandmother to a succession of relatives, she had a childhood "almost like a series of one-night stands."

When her people moved to Philadelphia, it was to the red-light district, where Ethel, not yet six, picked up money running errands for prostitutes; she still has "great respect" for them as "kind and generous" people. Hunger also drove her to become "a very good child thief," and at eleven, "I had trouble getting men to leave me alone."

Image to Cuddle. But before that, something else had happened. At her Roman Catholic school, she was taken into the church, and through *His Eye Is on the Sparrow* runs a strong if naive faith: "The Catholic religion gives you a beautiful image to cuddle. I who have always believed in an eye for an eye and a tooth for a tooth try to get God in my corner."

Most of Actress Waters' book is an engagement-by-engagement account of how she went from shimmy dancer and blues

TIME, MARCH 12, 1951

singer in mean Negro dives to better things on stage & screen. But it is edged with appalling descriptions of racial discrimination, freely spiced with a man-by-man record of her long, disastrous and violent love life. A great actress, she has nothing important to say about acting. A vital human being, buffeted by life even in success, Ethel Waters never lets her bitterness get far offstage. But it is a story worth having for the truths it has to tell about the millions of her race who never got top billing.

HIS EYE IS ON THE SPARROW

HIS EYE

$\mathcal{I}$s ON THE $\mathcal{S}$PARROW

an autobiography by

ETHEL WATERS

with CHARLES SAMUELS

DOUBLEDAY & COMPANY, INC.

Garden City, New York, 1951

The first stanza of "Chinese Blues,"
is by Fred D. Moore, music by Oscar Gardner;
reprinted by permission of the copyright owners, Melrose Music Corp.
"His Eye Is on the Sparrow" is copyright 1906, renewal 1934,
by The Rodeheaver Co. Used by permission.

HIS EYE IS ON THE SPARROW

1

I never was a child.

I never was coddled, or liked, or understood by my family.

I never felt I belonged.

I was always an outsider.

I was born out of wedlock, but that had nothing to do with all this. To people like mine a thing like that just didn't mean much.

Nobody brought me up.

I just ran wild as a little girl. I was bad, always a leader of the street gang in stealing and general hell-raising. By the time I was seven I knew all about sex and life in the raw. I could outcurse any stevedore and took a sadistic pleasure in shocking people.

My mixed blood explains this, partly, I think.

My maternal great-grandfather was Albert Harris, a native of India. My great-grandmother was a slave, but very fair, and Albert Harris had to buy her from her owner before he could marry her. That made their five children freeborn, according to the law.

But his daughter, Sarah Harris, who was my grandmother, often told me how her father, on hearing there were white strangers in the neighborhood, would take down his shotgun and go out on the porch. With the shotgun across his knees, he'd sit there for hours, watching her, her brother, and three sisters as they played in the yard. He kept the shotgun loaded and ready, to make sure that none of them would be carried off by white men to be sold into slavery.

Slavery had been abolished, but these white men were still making money by kidnaping little Negro children. They'd put the Negro boys and girls on ships and send them off to sections of the United States where slavery was still being practiced in spite of the law.

My grandmother was always called Sally. When she was eleven years old a white family that had taken a fancy to her wanted to bring her North, to Pennsylvania, and put her into service there. But the law then read that no person of Negro blood could be taken out of Maryland until after he proved himself intelligent and competent.

So these white people sent my grandmother to a school run by a Professor Loomis, and for a whole year they paid for her instruction there. She passed all the tests and was taken to Pennsylvania.

When she was only thirteen she married my grandfather, Louis Anderson, who was nicknamed Honey. Still only a kid himself at the time, Honey had been one of the youngest drum majors in the Civil War. His whole family was well-esteemed in Germantown, Pennsylvania, where they had been associated for many years with the Cox Coal Company.

Three children were born of this marriage: Viola, Charlie, and Louise, my mother. But Honey Anderson was a hard drinker, and he and my grandmother separated when the children were small. From that time on the entire burden of taking care of the three children fell on her, Sally Anderson. In the years that followed she had romances with various men and had another child by one of them. This was Edith, who was nicknamed Ching.

My grandmother was anything but promiscuous. She was hard-working and honest, liked her little nip now and then, but hated drunkenness. Sally could fight like a sonofabitch. She had a fiery temper, and there was a terrible pride in her. We were always the poor relatives in our family, but she wouldn't ask nor accept favors from anyone. I am proud of being her granddaughter.

All her life she was puzzled by the four children she had brought into the world. She neither liked nor understood the way they lived.

Sally was intelligent but, except for Ching, her children were of the slow-thinking, dumb-animal type. Ching was the brilliant one and had silky hair and copper-colored skin. She was about five feet tall, attractive, and had lots of life and laughter in her. All my life I've dreaded being around people who can't laugh. But I could always laugh with Ching and have a good time with her.

Vi, the eldest of the four, was agitative. She could sing beautifully, like all the women in my family. But she had an insane temper. All the women in my family had tempers like hers.

Charlie, my uncle, was woman-simple, but harmless. Things just didn't matter much to Charlie. He could whistle and sold newspapers on the street corners. He was always falling in love with all the women he met. Charlie was weak, and any woman he loved could get him to do anything. She could tell him, "Go home and steal your sister's shoes." And Charlie would do it. Vi's shoes, Ching's money, a dress of my mother's that the woman he loved had seen her wearing. His family meant nothing to him. But Charlie did love children, and I was always a child to him.

We'd seldom see Charlie, and whenever he did come around we'd start locking up everything in sight. He'd steal jewelry, clothing, shoes, anything he could lay his hands on. If there was any food in the house he'd sit down and eat it all up.

My aunts, my mother, and Charlie had to bring themselves up. Mom (when I say that I mean my grandmother; when I was very small I called my mother Louise and later on Momweeze), in order to pay the rent in the rickety shanties where her children lived, was forced to take jobs where she had to sleep in. So her children raised themselves.

They lived in an alley, and the boys were around the house all the time. When my grandmother was home on her day off they'd watch for her to leave and then would return.

Louise, my mother, took no part in any of this. She was religious and at all times had Christian learning. She was always where there was a church meeting, and wanted to be an evangelist. She went to church instead of with the boys. She shut out of her mind everything worldly.

One of the boys who would come around to that rickety home in the alley was John Waters, my father. There was a saying used then when anyone wanted to ask if a girl was a virgin. They would say, "Is she broke in yet?"

One day John Waters asked Vi, "Is Louise broke in yet?" Vi told him my mother wasn't broke in. Vi was the eldest, and Mom had left her in charge of the others. But she plotted this whole thing out with John Waters, who was dark brown in color though he had white blood. Vi told him to come around on a day when she was sure my grandmother wouldn't be home.

So John Waters, my father, came back one day and forced my mother to submit to him. She tried to fight him, but he raped her, holding a knife. She was only twelve and didn't know what it was all about, but she had to give in to him. And that is how I was conceived.

My mother always hated and resented my father and never afterward would have anything to do with him. It was just that one time with them.

Nobody suspicioned anything was wrong at the time. And my mother wouldn't tell, she being so hurt and bitter and hardly understanding herself what was happening inside her body. It was Sally who finally noticed the change in her, the bulge that was beginning to show under her dress.

Mom just couldn't understand how such a thing could have happened. "Not to Louise," she kept saying. "Not to Louise. Louise has always been so meek and good, going to church all the time."

Then my grandmother beat and upbraided my mother. Not because my mother had done wrong and was going to have a baby, but because Mom thought she had been sly.

That's when Vi came forward and interfered. She told my grandmother, Sally Anderson, just how it had happened. Sally took my mother and Vi to see my other grandmother, Mrs. Lydia Waters. She was Dutch, a member of the Timbers family in Gettysburg. As far as I could ever find out she was a white woman who married a dark brown Negro. But I am not sure of this. Her skin was a snowy white, but it is possible that she might have had some colored blood. She lived—after her marriage, anyway—as a Negro and among Negro people. And I never heard of her spoken about as white. She was accepted by her Negro neighbors as one of them.

Lydia Waters was in good circumstances. She denied the whole thing. "My son just wouldn't do a thing like that."

It seems that, of all her children, my father was the one Lydia Waters loved best and took the most pleasure in.

The contempt of Mrs. Waters upset Mom more than anything else. Along with her awful pride, she'd always despised "dictys," which is the name my people have for those who look down on others and consider themselves superior to plebeian folks.

My white grandmother then called my father into the room. He admitted having sex relations with my mother. I guess he felt ashamed and sorry. But his account of the circumstances differed from Vi's and hers. He denied using physical force.

Sally Anderson stood up. "I don't want him ever to cross my door again," she said. "We don't want nothing more to do with him."

She meant it. It never occurred to her to try to compel John Waters to marry my mother. She was more interested in getting the facts straight. What was important to her was finding out whether or not Louise had been sly and deceitful. She was convinced now, even though he denied it, that John Waters had forced my mother to give in to him.

That was the end of it as far as Sally was concerned. She never, after I was born, asked or wanted my father or his family to contribute to my support. Until the end of Sally Anderson's life, she would fly into an uncontrollable fury if the name Waters was even mentioned in our home. For this reason I never used my name while I was growing up.

When I was born it was at my great-aunt Ida's home in Chester, near Philadelphia. Sally Anderson was working in a house in Chester, so she'd arranged for my mother to stay with her sister nearby.

My mother was alone in the house when I came into the world at 9:15 A.M. on October 31, 1900. She was alone because I arrived unexpectedly.

There was no doctor or midwife. The woman next door was a Hunky lady, and she came in on hearing my mother cry out in pain. It was this woman who delivered me. She notified my grandmother, who got excused from work for the day. I was a little baby when Sally arrived, and she always said I was very bright and alert even at that early age.

I hope this will eliminate all of the questions about my age that have been raised since I became prominent as an actress. When I first went on the stage I was seventeen and under the legal age for performers, and my mother had to sign a paper saying I was four years older than I was. But October 31, 1900, was the date, Chester, Pennsylvania, the place, which makes me, I trust, an American citizen.

As soon as I was born my grandmother took over, my mother being only a child herself, a child under thirteen and utterly bewildered. The church people had turned on her and cast her out. She, being so slow and stubborn, had kept quiet. She never wanted me, and my coming almost killed her. All alone she had stood the gaff and the ridicule, and everything stayed bottled up inside of her. So it was natural for her to resent me, the child she had conceived against her will and desire.

After I was born everybody could see that I was a spitting-image

Waters. My uncle, Harry Waters, would sneak down to our alley shanty to get a look at me. So would other members of the Waters family. But they had to do that with the connivance of my aunts, who didn't share my grandmother's resentment. Sally Anderson would have been furious if she had known that any of my father's relatives had entered her home. So they had to come while she was out working.

When my grandmother, Lydia Waters, heard how much I resembled her family, she hurriedly married my father off to another girl whom she considered more respectable. My half brothers from this marriage are only a little younger than I.

My mother also got married, shortly after my birth, to Norman Howard, a handsome, light-colored man. All the women in my family inclined to light-colored men, though I never did.

Norman Howard was a stoker, or an engineer, or something like that on the railway in Chester. Even after her marriage my mother left me in the hands of my grandmother. She had a daughter by Norman Howard, my half sister Genevieve, who is only fifteen months younger than I am.

I was about three years old when my father died. He was poisoned by another woman. My father was a pianist, a playboy, and everybody was crazy about him and his music. But just the same, this woman poisoned him out of jealousy.

I can't remember ever seeing my father while he was alive. I never heard that he ever sneaked downtown, like other members of his family, to see me when I was a baby.

But I can remember being told by my aunts that he was dead. They took me to his home to see him. When we went in, it seemed to tear the mourners' hearts out to see me. I looked so much like them.

"How could this family deny this darling child?" they said, and made a big fuss over me.

I was always a smart child. Though I was only three years old, I remember being in that place and seeing all those people. I even remember the conversation before I was taken in to see my father in his coffin.

"Do you know why you're here, Ethel?"

"Yes."

"Why?"

"To see my father. He's dead."

I wasn't afraid when I was taken in to see him. I knew there was a man in the big box, but that didn't scare me. What impressed me most was the setting, the white shroud, the flowers, the drapes.

I didn't go to the funeral. Knowing my grandmother would be coming home soon, my aunts rushed me back there so she wouldn't find out where they'd taken me. They were afraid of what Sally Anderson would do if she learned they'd taken me to the home of a Waters.

Soon after I was born the stork visited our home twice. Ching had two children—Myrtle and Tom. Myrtle didn't live long enough to walk. Because my grandmother was away working so much the responsibility of taking care of us fell on Vi and Ching. But they had their own lives to live and liked to go out. So we had to bring ourselves up. My aunts would take in washing and ironing and would work out by the day. But they would never, as my grandmother and later my mother did, take jobs as houseworkers where they had to sleep in. That would have prevented them from going out every night.

The main thing that Vi and Ching taught Tom and me when we were so little was to know our names and address. I was not Ethel Waters then. I was Ethel Perry. As a girl, I always used the name of the man my grandmother was in love with.

Left to our own devices, little Tom and I often went out, hand in hand, adventuring. We were always getting lost and being found by policemen who would take us to the station house. They'd feed us candy and lots of other stuff.

When we lived on Waverly Street I'd tell them, "Diksteen, Diksteen Waverly." We got lost so often that after a while the policemen didn't ask, just took us to 1616 Waverly.

Tom also died when I was three. He'd been living with relatives over in Chester. When my grandmother heard that he was dead she took me to the house in Chester on a streetcar.

She was in a hurry to get there. She must also have been full of distress and grief because she forgot that I was with her, and hurried ahead of me, walking faster than my little legs could carry me.

I could see her up ahead, moving down the street and then going into the house. By the time I got up the steps she was inside. I knocked on the door. When no one opened it I knocked again and again.

Among Negroes it is a bad omen when someone knocks on the door of a house where a person has died. My aunts came to the door and looked out through the glass panel that covered the upper half of it.

They couldn't see me because I was so little.

So I kept knocking. They kept coming to the door and looking out. "Who's that?" they said nervously. "Who in hell is knocking on the door?"

Finally my grandmother remembered that I'd been with her. She came out and drew me inside.

It was carefully explained to me that Tom was dead and cold and that he was lying in a black box in the next room. But I kept sneaking in there and trying to get him up to play with me.

My family didn't have the money to have him embalmed. Instead ice had been packed around his body. When my grandmother and aunts would miss me they'd run into the room where Tom was laid out and find me there. The last time they caught me trying to eat a piece of ice I'd taken out of the coffin. After that they locked the door so I couldn't get in again.

Afterward they consulted the doctor who had attended Tom through his last illness, meningitis. He told them that the ice I'd put into my mouth was just like any other ice, and uncontaminated. He said I couldn't catch the disease that had killed Tom.

My grandmother, Sally Anderson, had three sisters and a brother. Three of the four—Elizabeth, George, and Margaret—were snobbish and had little to do with us. Aunt Ida, whom we called Ide, was closest to Mom. Whenever things got tough I was sent over to live with Ide for a while.

My whole childhood was almost like a series of one-night stands. I was shuttled about among relatives, boarded out, continually being moved around to Camden, Chester, and Philadelphia homes.

For some reason Mom, who was so disappointed in her own children, tried to cling to me. But her world was really in the kitchen with the white families she worked for.

In her whole life Mom never earned more than five or six dollars a week. Being without a husband, it was hard for her to find any place at all for us to live, a place she could afford. And even then she never got a chance to live with my aunts and me, could only visit us on her day off. Being with white people so much, she stopped living colored, thinking colored.

What broke Mom's heart was realizing that her children knew nothing and cared nothing about the better side of life. From the white people she worked for she had learned there could be a nice side. But Vi and Ching and Charlie took no interest in that. Mom might as well have tried to read poetry to cows. I think she saw I was different, even when I was very small, nothing like them.

Almost always, when Mom would come to the bleak and dreary household she was trying to keep together, she'd find it full of men, with Vi or Ching, or both of them, out stiff.

She would bitch and fight my aunts, trying to force her way of life on them—and they resisted. Mom had intelligence, but she never understood that people don't like to be prodded and ordered about and made to live somebody else's way. So always, when she came home, there was hell and confusion.

We all used to dread her day off, and the girls, my aunts, would tense up as the hour for recriminations and fighting approached.

Mom traced all her troubles to her unhappy marriage with Honey Anderson. She thought that Vi and Ching took to drink because their fathers were liquorheads. And always it hurt her that she couldn't stay there and straighten out their harum-scarum lives.

She, Mom, was the greatest influence of my childhood. What she wanted to do, and desperately, was save me from the vice, lust, and drinking that was all about me—and to keep me whole and unharmed as a human being.

Mom never accepted our dismal surroundings or felt they were good enough for her. She was passionate, almost fanatical, on the subject of personal cleanliness. Each time she came home she'd instruct me in the whole ritual of bodily care.

We never had a bathtub. Mom would bathe me in the wooden or tin washtub in the kitchen, or in a big lard can we had. After scrubbing me she'd inspect my hair. Then she'd bend down and smell me all over.

Sally Anderson fought a never-ending war against bedbugs. We called them chinches, and they were all over the place, hard-biting armies in constant battle formation, in the bed slats, the pillows and the woodwork, the bedding.

Mom never routed the chinches, though she worked ceaselessly to wipe them out. She'd wash everything with carbolic acid and other disinfectants. Twice I suffered bad burns: once when I put my hand out into the carbolic acid while sleeping; once when I moved my head and the carbolic acid burned my face.

When the incessant attentions of the bedbugs prevented me from sleeping Mom would put me on the floor, spreading newspapers all around me. The theory was that chinches were illiterates who wouldn't cross newspapers with printed words on them. But our chinches were Rhodes scholars; they could read English, French, Spanish, and Sanskrit. At any rate, the newspapers never stopped them.

I had better luck outwitting the rats who usually stayed outside of our houses. Women would encounter them when they went out to the water hydrant in the yard and would have to fight them. But I never did.

The rats would sometimes get into our closets. When I opened the door and came across one I'd freeze up, petrify with fear. I'd stand there, paralyzed by terror, and look into the face of the rat. He would watch me, alert and antagonistic. But if I didn't move, didn't attack him, he would slink away, as though disgusted at being disturbed and having his rat business interrupted. It was only after he'd disappeared that I'd unfreeze enough to scream. And these rat-infested, bedbug-plagued shanties were all the home Sally Anderson ever had to go to when she left the spotless, clean houses of her white employers.

Frantic with defeat down through the years, Mom never quit on me. My great regret is that she didn't live long enough to share some of the money and the comforts my work in show business has brought me.

I would keep her now in my big house in California. She could sit out in the sun, have her meals in bed, warm always and with all worry far away. But the money, as often happens, came too late to do little Sally Anderson any good.

Wherever Mom worked—in Philadelphia, Camden, or Chester—she boarded or bunked me near her so she could come to me quickly if I needed her. Again and again the pathetic little homes she set up for us broke up. There was only Mom to keep them going, and her work kept her away too much of the time for that.

Following Tom's death, I lived with Ide for a while, then was moved in with Vi, who was living in Camden with John Bassett, whom I called Uncle Bassett. He was a good provider and a family man. It was in this home that I realized for the first time the make-shift way we'd been living and that there was another better and more settled way to live.

With Vi and Uncle Bassett I learned what it was to have three squares a day and a bed to sleep in. Until I went to their house I'd just sleep anywhere—on the floor, a broken-down couch, two chairs, an ironing board—anywhere at all.

I had a probing mind and an elephant memory. I was already tall for my age and could outcurse any sailor. I knew that I was a bastard and what that meant.

I've never in my whole life, by the way, minded in the least being a bastard. I've always found it can work both ways. If I wanted pity, I got it because I am illegitimate. And when I didn't want it and was mean and nasty, I always could say:

"Well, what can you expect of an old bastard like me?"

Now Vi was fly, and Uncle Bassett was very jealous of her. She'd bring men into the house or skip over to Philadelphia while he was working. Above everything else, she schooled me never to talk about anything I knew or saw.

Uncle Bassett was never able to pick anything out of me. I wouldn't talk, no matter how many piggy-back rides he gave me, nor on the promise of toys and candy. Little as I was, I knew how to keep my mouth shut—and I never got myself in Dutch by talking.

While I lived at their house I would play with another kid who lived on the other side of the street, across the car tracks. I always re-sented the ding-dong noise the streetcars made as they came along. I particularly resented having to wait until that big, noisy car passed be-fore I crossed the street. I'd been told a thousand times to look both ways and wait for the cars to go by, but one day I decided to disregard the advice.

So I just dashed in front of it. The cowcatcher in front of the trol-ley car hit me and I was hurled to the opposite curb, knocking out two teeth and cutting my chin.

I had a paper bag clutched in my hand. There were two pennies in it that I'd been given to buy sourballs. I held on tightly to that paper bag. A boy picked me up, but even with my teeth knocked out, I didn't let go of the bag with the two pennies in it. I didn't tell the boy what was in the bag because I knew he'd take the pennies away from me.

My getting run over turned out to be a bad thing for Vi. It happened on one of those days when she had skipped over to Philadelphia. That she wasn't there to take care of me made Uncle Bassett suspicion that there was something wrong. He slapped her. That made Vi mad, and she beat the devil out of me. So first I had the accident, and then I got beat because Vi had been found out.

But Vi was very pleased with me when the adjusters for the transit company came to question me about the accident. Nothing they could do or say made me change my story that it was "Car 81" that had hit me. I knew numbers because I had made Vi teach me to tell time. The adjusters kept showing me different numbers, and I knew them all because I could tell time. "Car 81, it was," I kept saying. The company had to pay my family money for the accident.

Around that time I had another near accident. I was out with Uncle Bassett when we came to the railway crossing. The gates were down, and I had always been told not to cross the tracks when the gates were down. But that day I broke away from Uncle Bassett, who had only a chance to yell "Heh!" when the train rushed down upon me. I jumped off the track just in the nick, but the wind that locomotive made in passing blew me right down the sandy embankment. And I got beat for that too.

I was about four when Vi got me put into the kindergarten.The teachers said I was "the cutest thing, a little sweetheart." But it was in that first school that I found out how other people could hurt you. The kids tried to sneer at me but quickly found out that I could defend myself. I might have looked angelic, but what came out of my mouth would have shocked any New York taxi driver.

Even then, at four and five, I was beginning to sprout. I was so huge that my people were having trouble about me on the streetcars. The conductors insisted I was at least seven and wanted three cents, half fare, paid for me. We had a hard time talking them out of that. I spoke right up along with my aunts. Whatever else I was, I was never timid.

Often when my aunts wanted to go out at night they'd give me a couple of drinks of sweetened whisky and water before I went to sleep to make sure I wouldn't wake up while they were gone.

It was about that time that I began to have peculiar dreams at night. In my room in Uncle Bassett's house there was a picture of the Rock of Ages. It always fascinated me, and when I'd go to sleep I'd dream about it. In the dream I would be going down a long road that always ended up on the rock in the water, with me among the people clinging to it.

During these first years of my life my family was never settled anywhere, in one place, for long enough for me to go to church. But I was taught to say my prayers every night. I got a whipping when I failed to memorize them.

I was told that God was up there in heaven watching me. I would look up and try to see Him. When things went wrong with me I'd get mad at Him because He was falling down on His job of looking after me. I fought with Him plenty, had plenty of fault to find with Him as a little girl.

There was one emotional outlet my people always had when they had the blues. That was singing. I'd listen, fascinated by the stories told in the songs. Later, when I sang those same old songs, both folk songs and popular numbers, on the stage or on the radio, they gained nationwide attention. In 1949, when I appeared on the Tex and Jinx program, I sang some of those songs, humming the parts where I didn't remember the lines. I got letters from people all over the country who sent me the words I'd forgotten. They'd remembered the old songs all those years and kept them in their minds like treasures.

My whole family could sing. Vi had a sweet, soft voice. Ching's was bell-like and resonant, Louise's rich and warm. One of the first pieces I remember Vi singing was "I Don't Want to Play in Your Yard." Ching's favorites were "There'll Come a Time" and "Volunteer Organist."

But in the beginning it was always the story told in the song that enchanted me. I'd ask one of them, "Tell me a story," when I was little, and they'd sing it.

My family and the other families who lived in those alley homes harmonized without any instruments to accompany them. There were musicians in the neighborhood, fellows who played the banjo, mandolin, guitar, and the bells (sometimes one man would play all of them). But they played at parties and sometimes on street corners. And we never had the money for a party. There were always people in the house, but that wasn't for any party.

Then, of course, there was the hurdy-gurdy man. We kids would dance to the music he made and sing the words of the songs that came out of his tired, battered street organ.

I can remember coming home some days when Vi would be drunk. She'd be sitting there with a bottle, all alone and feeling her blues. And she'd start to sing, softly and sweetly.

But singing and dancing were nothing among us colored people. They came natural as breathing.

I was five when I made my first public appearance as an entertainer. That was on a child program put on in a small Protestant church in Philadelphia. I was living at the time with Aunt Ching and one of my numerous unkies, as I called those transient uncles of mine.

I was billed as Baby Star. In my act I had to recite a short piece and also sing a little song which went like this:

> *I am dying for some one to love me,*
> *Some one to call my own.*
> *Some one to stay with me all of the time*
> *For I'm tired of living alone.*

Aunt Ching had worked hard and done a wonderful job of rehearsing me. On the night of my debut she was seated right in front of the stage so she could prompt me.

Everything went along fine until I got near the end of the song. But then I got scared, and Ching realized it. So she began to make gestures to remind me of the words in the last two lines—putting her hands under her cheek and nodding her head. I sang along, fitting the words to her gestures, as follows:

> *I am dying for some one to love me,*
> *And some one to call my own,*
> *And some one to sleep with me all night long*
> *For I'm tired of sleeping alone.*

Again and again I was called back for encores. I was a sensational success in my very first appearance on stage, screen, or radio.

2

I did have one childhood home for more than a few weeks. It was a three-room shanty in an alley just off Clifton Street. Prostitution was legal in Philadelphia then, and Clifton Street, located in the old Bloody Eighth Ward, lay in the heart of the red-light district.

There was always something interesting to watch in that lively neighborhood. Every night the whores, black and white, paraded up and down Clifton Street. They all wore the same outfit, a regular uniform consisting of a voile skirt with taffeta underneath, cork-heeled shoes, a black velvet neckband, and big whores' hoop earrings. Of course their unmistakable trade-mark was their hip-wriggling walk.

I was not yet six years old when we moved there and seven when we left, but I had one hell of a time for myself in that plague spot of vice and crime. I came to know well the street whores, the ladies in the sporting houses, their pimps, the pickpockets, shoplifters, and other thieves who lived all around us. I played with the thieves' children and the sporting women's trick babies. It was they who taught me how to steal.

Things at home didn't change much, but I remember that little alley home as the heaven on earth of my childhood. For once we were all together in a whole house—Vi, Ching, Charlie, me, Mom on her days off. And after a while Louise also came to live with us.

We stayed in Clifton Street for fifteen months. That was the only time I could feel that I had a family that wasn't continually disrupting and belonged in one neighborhood. My family kept on squabbling, but I lived more in the street than at home.

All of us dead-end kids ran errands for the whores. Some of them were good for as much as fifteen, twenty, or twenty-five cents in tips.

We spent most of our earnings on candy and food. You could buy a frankfurter for three cents at a street stand, yat-gaw-mein cost a nickel in the Chinese joints, and for a dime you could get a whole plate of fish and French-fried potatoes at a food stand called See Willie's.

A bunch of us would often sleep all night out on the street, over the warm iron gratings of bakeries or laundries. Our families didn't care where we were, and these nesting places, when you put your coat under you, were no more uncomfortable than the broken-down beds with treacherous springs or the bedbug-infested pallets we had at home. Being so large for my age, I was accepted as an equal by older boys and girls. My biggest asset as a street child in the tenderloin was my ability to keep my mouth shut.

Along with a few other Clifton Street youngsters I acted as a semi-official lookout girl for the sporting houses. Though prostitution was a legalized business, there were occasional police raids. These came when church groups bore down heavily on the authorities or after one body too many, stabbed, shot, or cut up very untidily, had been found in some dark alley.

Any of us slum children could smell out a cop even though he was a John, a plain-clothes man. These brilliant sleuths never suspicioned that we were tipsters for the whole whoring industry. Usually we'd be playing some singing game on the street when we spotted a cop, a game like Here Come Two Dudes A-Riding or the one that begins:

> "King William was King James's son,
> Upon his breast he wore a star,
> And that was called . . ."

On smelling out the common enemy, we boys and girls in the know would start to shout the songs, accenting certain phrases. If we happened to be playing a singing game we'd whistle the agreed-on tune. The other kids, even those who weren't lookouts, would innocently imitate us, and in no time at all the whole neighborhood would be alerted. The street women would disappear, the lights would go out, and the doors would be locked in the sporting houses.

Some of the friendlier policemen tried to be nice to us, but that got them nowhere. It was an unwritten law among us not to accept candy from cops or have anything to do with them. It was the only law that was never broken on Clifton Street.

The Bloody Eighth at that time was not exclusively a Negro slum. We had plenty of white neighbors, Hunkies and Jews, and some Chinese. The few respectable families, white and black, forced by circumstances to live in that slum kept to themselves as much as possible.

I didn't know much about color then. There was no racial prejudice at all in that big melting pot running over with vice and crime, violence, poverty, and corruption. I never was made to feel like an outcast on Clifton Street. All of us, whites, blacks, and yellows, were outcasts there together and having a fine time among ourselves.

Anyway, racial prejudice couldn't have existed in that neighborhood where vice was the most important business. The white and Negro street whores worked together, lived and slept together. The two men who owned and protected most of them were Lovey Joe and Rosebud, both of them Negroes. It was not considered unusual for a colored prostitute to have a trick baby white as a lily.

I've always had great respect for whores. The many I've known were kind and generous. Some of them supported whole families and kept at their trade for years to send their trick babies through college. I never knew a prostitute who did harm to anyone but herself. I except, of course, the whores who are real criminals and use knockout drops and bring men to their rooms to be robbed, beaten, and blackmailed.

No woman in my immediate family ever turned to prostitution. Neither were they saints. Sometimes they lived with men they weren't married to. This is true of my mother and my two aunts, Vi and Ching. And they never saw anything wrong in getting what presents they could from their men—shoes for themselves or for me, clothes, or money.

My grandmother hated the idea of my growing up in the red-light district and strongly disapproved of prostitution. But there was nothing she could do about it. The alley shanty was the best home she could find or afford.

And Mom had no objection at all to doing the weekly laundry of the prostitutes. However, they had to address her respectfully as Mrs. Perry or she wouldn't take their work. Mom used that name all of the years she was in love with Pop Sam Perry, who was a huckster and had his own little vegetable wagon. Vi and Ching also insisted that their prostitute customers treat them with dignity and respect.

We had one family link, though, with prostitution. This was Blanche, one of Mom's nieces, who was only seven or eight years older than I. Though Mom shook her head over Blanche's way of life, she was always strongly biased in her favor because she was our relative.

Being hardly more than a child herself, Blanche often played with me, read me stories, and sang little songs with me. Her beauty fascinated me. I loved her. There was a great camaraderie between us, and that young prostitute gave me some of the attention and warm affection I was starving for. Whenever I tipped off the sporting world that the cops were just around the corner I felt I was doing it for Blanche and her friends.

Mom herself always did Blanche's laundry, and I delivered it each week. In her room I saw the equipment used by a woman in her profession. I never commented or asked questions about it but used my eyes and my ears. I never was a child to pretend ignorance to learn more about something that aroused my curiosity.

Blanche soon decided that she could trust me completely. Lovey Joe, the pimp, a huge, kindly man, was her sweetheart, and she'd send messages to him through me. Whenever they quarreled Lovey Joe would find me on the street and give me notes to deliver to Blanche. Afterward he was always able to sweet-talk himself back into her affections.

Later Blanche got into the habit of sending me to the druggist with a sealed envelope. He'd give me bichloride of mercury, blue ointment, and larkspur. Blanche had syphilis which we called the Pox. She had a horrible sore on her upper leg that eventually became so painful she couldn't bear to bathe it herself. So I would wash it for her, apply the medicines, and help her pull on the specially made stocking she had to wear.

Blanche was in and out of my life until I was twelve. In the last stages of her life, and still not twenty years old, she took to sniffing coke and using the bang needles to forget the pain. From that same drugstore I got the dope she had to have.

I never have forgotten that sweet, lovely-looking, and enchanting Blanche and what it was like to watch her decay and rot before my eyes. I'd see her at night, all dressed up and gay, and then the next day so ripped and pounded by pain.

The prettiest sight in that whole neighborhood came at dusk when the lights were turned on in the sporting houses. I'd stand on the street and look in with awe at the rich, highly polished furniture and the beautiful women sitting at the windows wearing low-cut evening gowns or kimonos. Some of them put on aprons.

But there was Blanche—and others. Prostitution and dope never could afterward tempt me. Blanche, poor soul, did more to keep me straight in the tough years to come than any person I ever knew. I also never have touched liquor except for medicinal purposes because I saw as a child what whisky and gin can do to people. I don't smoke because cigarettes are forever associated in my mind with the drinking and chaos there. I don't gamble because I know what trouble *that* can bring.

Whatever moral qualities I have, come, I'm afraid, from all the sordidness and evil I observed firsthand as a child. However, I do not wish to exaggerate the impact on me of the evil that constantly surrounded me when I was little. I was tough always and, like all slum kids, was able quickly to adjust myself to any and all situations.

God's hand must have closed over me very early in life, making me tough and headstrong and resilient. It is His hand that has carried me safely down the long, dark road I've had to follow since.

In crowded slum homes one's sex education begins very early indeed. Mine began when I was about three and sleeping in the same room, often in the same bed, with my aunts and my transient "uncles." I wasn't fully aware of what was going on but resented it. By the time I was seven I was repelled by every aspect of sex.

Being so enormous for my age, I didn't escape the attentions of the fully grown men in the neighborhood who liked little girls. The first thing that I discovered about sporting men, society's despised pimps, was that they had a much more moral attitude toward kids than many of the squares around Clifton Street.

Lovey Joe, Rosebud, and the others had a strict "Hands off!" code with little girls. I think they would have beaten to death any other pimp who molested one of us youngsters.

Actually, being such a wised-up child, I don't think I was ever in too much danger from degenerates. Nobody was handing me any package. My vile tongue was my shield, my toughness my armor. With my gutter vocabulary and my aggressiveness I outshocked the odd ones. When I wanted to tell anyone off I began with the four-letter words.

I like to think I am remembered with a horrified head-to-toe shudder by at least one fully grown man who lived in the old Bloody Eighth Ward.

When he made a grab for me I closed my fist and slammed it down hard on the anatomical feature he most treasured. I put him out of amorous action, I imagine, for weeks.

Through my mother, this temporarily disabled child lover complained to Mom that I had slugged him under the belt when he tried to pat me in a paternal manner.

After questioning me Sally accepted my interpretation of the incident and sent this message to the wounded gent: "I'll cut your throat if you ever come near Ethel again."

When Louise joined us in Clifton Street it was because she'd been having a little woman trouble. Pop Norman chased the women—and vice versa. One of Pop Norman's bright flames became so bold and giddy with infatuation that she came to Louise's house to flaunt her intimacy with my stepfather.

I've mentioned that Louise, like my aunts, Mom, and me, had an insanely violent temper. No matter what she had done, she afterward knew neither remorse nor pity.

My mother and the bright flame tangled. During the fight Louise picked up a railroad spike and beat the other woman so badly with it that she had to be taken to the hospital. Louise left Genevieve, my stepsister, with Norman's parents and came to live with us. She stayed until the Chester police lost interest in the case.

I'd always been told that Louise was my mother. That hadn't meant anything to me because I always called my grandmother Mom and felt so much closer to her. But when Louise moved into the shanty I began to realize she was my mother and came to like her. But she never liked me. She merely tolerated me.

Yet once, while in Clifton Street, I did feel she cared for me with a mother's affection. When I was six I suffered an attack of typhoid fever and double pneumonia and was taken to the Pennsylvania Hospital, where Louise was working as an attendant. When the doctors there told Louise I might die, some of the long-repressed maternal love seemed to come to life in her. She spent as much time as she could at my bedside. Every time I opened my eyes Louise seemed to be there, looking down on me with tenderness and apprehension.

Sally Anderson had always inclined to the Catholic faith. When she learned that I might not survive my illness Mom sent for Father Healey of St. Peter Claver R.C. Church. He baptized and anointed me.

After I recovered, Louise went back into her shell, ignoring me as much as possible. She always lavished all her mother's love on Genevieve. If she couldn't love me, I suppose it was because I was the living reminder of the most frightening day of her life.

We had no Sunday things on Clifton Street. The stores and other businesses were open as on every other day. The nearest we came to religious observance of the Sabbath was listening to street preachers. And none of us dead-end kids knew what it was like to go off with the family on a Sunday picnic or to the bathing beaches.

Pop Sam Perry was always kind to me and would take me for a walk sometimes on Sunday. "Dress Ethel up," he'd say, "I want to take her out." Hand in hand, we'd walk through the bleak, dreary streets, looking into the shopwindows and ending up with a visit to an ice cream parlor.

Whenever Pop Sam Perry had an argument with Mom I knew enough to keep away from her. When things weren't going well in Mom's love life she seemed to take it out on me.

But at all other times I was her favorite. For me there was one pleasant feature about her militant weekly home-comings. Mom always came home with "cold functions" for me.

In those days most of the white people who had Negro servants preferred to throw leftover food in the garbage pail rather than give it to the people who worked so hard for them around the house.

Early in her life Mom figured out a way to outwit her white bosses. She sewed little pockets in an apron and filled the pockets with neatly done up parcels of food—sandwiches, pieces of pie or cake, sugar, and eggs. Then when she was ready to take her day off on Thursday she'd put on the heavily laden apron under her petticoat. Mom could sneak any kind of food out of her boss's house except soup.

The parcels were my "cold functions." When I was very little I'd pull up her dress and dive under it, yelling, "What did you bring me this time, Mom? What did you bring me?" Mom always got a big thrill out of that.

Sometimes, on days when she wasn't coming home, she worried about me not getting enough to eat. Whenever she could she'd fix up a parcel of food for me and leave it on a post or the garbage pail of the house where she was working, and I'd come out and get it.

But I can never remember Mom kissing or hugging me. She wasn't demonstrative, and I think she feared that Vi and Ching would resent her showing affection and make my life a living hell while she was out working. Vi, more than Ching, was always jealous of the way Mom tried to take care of me.

Being a tough-minded and realistic child, I can't say that Mom's home-comings gave me any great pleasure, despite the delicious "cold functions."

Only on the rare occasions when she found my aunts sober was there peace in the house. But almost always she'd come home and find them high—nasty and horrible on gin that cost ten cents a pint. Mom would bitch, chase their men friends out, then resume bitching and sometimes hit my aunts.

Fortunately, neither Vi nor Ching dared fight back. They seemed to realize, even when they were drunk, that Mom's terrible temper would drive her on and on until she'd killed or crippled them.

Once, though, Ching, the easier-going one, did try hitting back. In her towering rage Mom bit a whole piece of flesh out of Ching's arm. Police questioned Ching when she was taken to the hospital, but she refused to tell who had bitten her. The next day I found my aunt's chunk of severed flesh on the floor.

Mom had the curious idea that she could keep me out of mischief by continually sending me on errands or by telling me to take a walk in the park. Hating the neighborhood as violently as she did, she always pulled the shades down low and wouldn't look out on the alley even if she heard an explosion out there. This permitted me to play in peace with children she disapproved of, right in front of my own door.

It was natural for children of the shoplifters and pickpockets to follow in their parents' footsteps. But, oddly enough, I never knew of a trick baby of a whore turning to prostitution. They learned from their own mothers, as I had from my cousin Blanche, how big the pay-off is in suffering and misery.

These kids were older than me. They accepted me as an equal, not only because I was hep and so big for my age, but because they were awed by my atomic delivery of the King's profanity. Some of these words they had never heard before. Generously, with the children who were my friends, I shared my encyclopedic knowledge of bad words, offering precise definitions of what each term meant. I also saw fit to punish my enemies by refusing them this valuable information. Sometimes we initiates would stand on the street screaming curses at the top of our voices.

The older boys and girls who were my friends sometimes went into the darker alleys at night to make fumbling sex experiments. I was always happy to be their lookout, though I took no such pride in this as I did in singing and whistling warnings to the neighborhood brothels and street women. I myself made no such experiments. The other kids did largely out of curiosity. Usually, once their curiosity was satisfied, they quit experimenting, finding it more fun to steal and play street games. Sex didn't interest me. There was nothing about it I didn't know.

I got my kindergarten course in thievery when the pickpockets' kids showed me how to swipe bags of rolls and bottles of milk from doorsteps and porches. I displayed such adeptness that I soon was helping them raid stores of food. Before long I became their leader. In the end we stole so much that we exhausted the looting possibilities of the whole neighborhood and had to fan out into other sections for action.

I stole because I was always hungry. I'm still always hungry, now that I come to think of it. Whenever I remember the old days on Clifton Street I develop a lumberjack appetite. And I think of those days often. We never felt there was anything wrong in stealing. We never thought anything about it at all. We were hungry. I still don't know what's wrong about a kid stealing when he's hungry.

When my grandmother wasn't home I seldom sat down to a fully prepared meal. My aunts lived on liquor and seldom felt like eating much.

But after they found out that I was the best child thief in the Bloody Eighth Ward my aunts occasionally decided that a cooked meal wouldn't kill them.

Whenever this happened they'd send me out with a quarter. If there was no cash in the house they'd have me gather up all the empty whisky and beer bottles in the shanty and return them. If there were not enough empties to get twenty-five cents for I'd be sent to the pawnshop to borrow a quarter on a new pair of shoes some admirer had given Vi or Ching.

Once I had the quarter, I was ready to go shopping and stealing. First I'd buy wood for three cents and charcoal for a nickel. Walking into the bakery, I'd order a loaf of yesterday's bread, which also cost three cents. When the man turned to get the bread from a shelf I'd slip a half dozen cinnamon buns into my big shopping bag.

In the butcher shop I'd ask for three cents' worth of cat or dog meat. The butchers on Clifton Street only had to look at my big hungry eyes to know that I didn't want the meat for any pet animal. They'd give me plenty of good scraps fit for human consumption.

Swiping plenty of fresh vegetables was the easiest job of all. If the owner was inside the store I'd just take my choice of the potatoes, onions, carrots, and peas lying on the stands outside his shop. If he was outside I'd order three cents' worth of salt or something else I knew he kept in the rear of his store. By the time he'd come out with it I'd have my bag full of vegetables covered up by the package of meat.

My ability to go out with a quarter and come back with a whole dinner—and some change—delighted my aunts. They never tired of praising my prowess.

I was a very good child thief.

I was never caught.

I only stopped stealing some years later while I was living in Chester. One day I went out, carrying a parasol, to the five-and-dime store. Because of its wide variety of merchandise this was the kind of store I most enjoyed robbing.

Everything I took—hair ribbons, Hershey bars, toys, and trinkets of all sorts—I dropped into my parasol. But when I came out of the store it was raining like mad. I couldn't open the parasol because all my loot would have fallen out.

I had to walk all the way home in the teeming rain, carrying the closed parasol. Everyone I met looked at it, then at me, as though I were crazy. Soaked to the skin, I indignantly decided petty larceny didn't pay if it made me get that wet.

Thereafter I only stole things once in a while to find out whether I still retained my magic touch.

I had a second cousin, Eli, who had a dim-witted brother named Herman whose chief distinction was that he took fits.

Herman was very fond of his aunt Sally and often came around to see her on her day off. But because we moved so often he couldn't ever remember just where we lived. He couldn't keep our name straight, either, as Mom changed that with each new sweetheart she acquired.

Determinedly he'd come into the approximate neighborhood and start looking for us in the first alley he saw. Knocking on the door of a shanty, he'd yell:

"Does a woman named Aunt Sally Anderson live in this here alley?"

Told that she didn't, Herman would shriek, "Well, then, does a woman named Aunt Sally Brown live in this here alley?"

If the answer was still no, Herman would fly into a rage and howl in a frustrated voice:

"Does a woman named Aunt Sally Perry live here?"

When it proved to be the wrong alley Herman would patiently go on to the next alley, and the next, hopping up and down in exasperation, until he came to ours. Mom would hear him, open our door, and call out:

"Here we are, Herman. For heaven's sake, come in, before you disgrace me."

Eli, his brother, was a smiling, friendly man who would steal thunder and grab at lightning. Whenever he paid us a visit, we'd have to keep our eyes open or he'd clean out the joint. Nothing was too big or too small for Eli to make off with. He'd move out the furniture and take pictures right off the wall. We always welcomed him but had to keep watching him all the time he was in the house.

Once Eli came so late at night we wouldn't let him in. Ching told Vi that was inhospitable. Vi said, "Well, if I let him in who is gonna sit up all night to watch him?" None of us resented Eli's stealing. We knew he just couldn't help it.

And one Christmas morning when there was nothing to eat in the house the smiling Eli appeared on Mom's doorstep with a whole roast pig under his coat, complete with baked apples and potatoes. None of us was rude enough to ask him where he'd stolen it. But even as we ate the dinner he'd swiped we had to watch Eli or he would have stolen the clothes off our backs.

Eli, who couldn't stop stealing, did a lot of time later. I think he died in prison.

Besides scrubbing me every time she came home, Mom took other measures to safeguard my health. Each fall, when I put on my red flannel underwear, she'd pin a rag with sticky white pine tar on it to the part covering my chest. It smelled terrible. She pinned another rag, smeared with the same tar, on my nightgown, which meant I had to sleep with it.

She also hung a little bag of asafetida around my neck. The combination of the two dreadful odors was almost unbearable, but I had to carry it with me from late September until spring. The asafetida was to cure child complaints, and the sticky white pine tar was supposed to ward off lung ailments. In the spring she made me take sulphur and cream of tartar and drink sassafras tea, believing they thinned one's blood.

There were no free clinics then for people like us, or if there were any we never heard of them. Mom's health measures were well intended, but they sure made me miserable.

Our home in Clifton Street broke up when I got diphtheria. Louise had moved to a furnished room quite a distance away. Mom one day sent me there on an errand, telling me to stay overnight. When I woke up in the morning I was sick. Mom heard that the Philadelphia health authorities were planning to quarantine the house. She hurried out and took me to the home of Aunt Ide, who'd moved to North Chester. Mom could have been sent to jail for that, so it was just as well that we got out of the city of Philadelphia for a while.

While in Clifton Street I went to the Friends School. But the important part of my education I acquired on the streets. I've never regretted having been a child in the red-light district. In Clifton Street I came to know, to understand, and to accept life in the raw and in all its ugliness.

3

Aunt Ide's house in North Chester was in a semi-rural neighborhood. When I woke up there in the morning I could smell the trees and the grass and hear birds singing.

In the school I went to there I met a better class of children. I considered them morons because they obeyed their parents.

But I was too smart to tip my mitt. I didn't boast that I'd been a smart child thief and the trusted errand girl of whores and pimps. I even managed not to swear—except when provoked beyond endurance.

What irked me about the peaceful life in North Chester was the routine, having set times for eating, going to bed, and getting up. I'd become accustomed to living like a little animal, foraging for my own food, sleeping where and when I pleased. I had not known there was any way to live except frantically, flamboyantly, and depending on nobody else for survival.

The teachers in the North Chester school were nice to me. They were surprised at how well I could count and read. My elephant memory and gift for mimicry astonished them. I was best in my class in elocution. Each day our teacher would tell us a story and ask for a volunteer to repeat it.

Big Ethel's hand would always be the first to shoot up. I'd tell the story back to the teacher as though I'd been memorizing it for a week. The only times I fell from grace in that school were during the art lessons.

I could never draw worth a damn. Our teacher would select a "live subject" for the day, and it would always be some pudgy boy or girl.

I'd pray hard to be chosen the live subject because that would get me out of the drawing part. But I never was picked.

I was very eager to excel in everything and I'd carefully draw the first line. But it would always come out wobbly. I'd erase it, then nervously draw the line again and have to erase it once more. Before I could even get started there would be a hole in the paper. This would infuriate me so that I'd shriek out a four-letter word.

The shocked teacher always kept me after school. She'd make me write the profane word five hundred times as punishment. The next day I would have to go before the whole school and apologize. "Boys and girls," I'd say, "I'm sorry I said——" Automatically I'd repeat the word. That afternoon I'd have to write it five hundred times more. I apologized so much to that school that everybody got sick of the whole thing.

I wasn't permitted to remain long in bucolic North Chester. Mom soon got a little place for us in the rear of a Jewish family's house in Philadelphia. Their back yard was my front yard, and I played with the two children, but mostly with the little Jewish boy who was about my age.

Every afternoon our games in the yard were interrupted by the arrival of the rabbi who was giving him Hebrew lessons. The Jewish boy hated to stop playing with me to learn the ancient prayers and chants. But I was intrigued by the strange sounds. I'd stand under the window by the hour, listening, without, of course, understanding a single word.

Because of my phonographic ear I could repeat the words, syllable for syllable, afterward. The rabbi heard about this and had me say some of the Hebraic prayers for him. He mistook my mimicry for genius and constantly was reproaching his student for not being as good a scholar as the little Negro girl who had never taken one lesson in Hebrew.

When the Jewish boy and I quarreled he'd call me nigger and I'd say he was a kike. If I ran out of insults I'd jeeringly shout at him the Hebrew chants and prayers he had so much trouble with.

About this time I discovered a wonderful way to stun grownups. If I'd meet a stranger on the street I'd say:

"You look itchy. What's the matter? You got the crabs?"

Coming from a child, this always was a blockbuster, and I got much sadistic pleasure from observing the reaction of the staggered strangers.

I saw my first stage shows when I was eight, and without any permission from my grandmother, for she was very strict with me. The shows were vaudeville, put on in the little store-front theaters along South Street. These were like nickelodeons and had tiny stages and folding chairs. Admission cost ten cents, with a few front rows at twenty-five cents. I always stayed to see these shows over and over again, until the manager put me out.

When I got home I'd imitate the performers who'd done anything I liked. I'd sing their songs as they'd sung them, songs like "Lovie Joe," "That Ever Loving Man," and "Barber Shop Chord."

On having a fight with Mom, as I've said, Louise would snatch me away to live with her in Chester. Beginning when I was eight, she had another reason for this besides hurting Mom. It occurred to her that she could make some money by putting me out to work. She'd do this even if she could get only fifteen cents by having me work all day. She also taught me to set bread for her neighbors. She'd get twenty-five cents from each woman, and I'd make as much as a dollar and a half for her on a Saturday night. But setting bread is hard work, and my wrists would swell up like balloons.

I was just eight years old the time Louise hired me out to a white woman who lived in West Chester. This woman gave me the filthiest, most disgusting jobs around the house to do. When I refused to do them she threatened to beat me.

"If you ever tried to beat me," I told her, "I would kill your baby."

"How would you kill him?" she asked.

"I'd just pick him up and take him downstairs. Going down the steps, I'd let myself stumble so he'd fall on his head. That would kill him, I guess."

The white woman didn't beat me. But she fired me. I had to come back to Chester on the milk train next morning.

My imagination always seemed to flower most lushly when I was threatening people. One reason I quickly became a leader of the bad kids wherever I moved was because I could dream up frightening stories. In Philadelphia I had a friend, Sis, whom I kept in a state of terror by whispering to her the dark secrets of my past.

"Look out," I'd say, "I once killed another girl like you for not doing what I told her."

"How did you kill her?" asked Sis, her eyes big with fear.

"I stuck a needle in the top of her head. I pushed the needle all the way in. The hole closed up, so nobody ever found out she was murdered."

"Where was this?"

"In Camden," I said, knowing Sis could never check up if I made it Camden. "And you better keep watching the color of my eyes. If they change color, watch out. The days my eyes change color is when I murder people. I'll kill you, too, Sis, if you ever tell anyone that I'm a murderer."

Ever after that Sis was so in awe of me that I could get her to give me anything she had—an orange, a stick of candy, a ball. But I knew Sis would tell the other kids that I'd killed a girl and make them so scared they'd let me be their leader and do whatever I wanted.

I was a bad girl, all right. I wanted other people to like me but never made the slightest effort to win them over. I felt it was up to them to discover my remarkable qualities.

I didn't like white people, or even Negroes with light skins. Mom had never stopped drumming into me how badly my other grandmother had treated us.

Whenever I lived with Louise I made life a nightmare for my stepsister Genevieve, who was lighter in color than I and was treated much better by my mother.

"Yaller dog" and "yaller puppy" were my favorite names for Genevieve. But I'd warn her, "I'll kill you if you ever say I'm dark. Don't you ever dare say I'm blacker than you."

Whenever we ate together I'd quickly gobble up everything on my plate and then take away most of her food. She was too cowed to complain to Louise.

We usually slept on a cot so narrow that we had to sleep head and tail. Being taller than Genevieve, I'd pretend to be asleep and push my big toe in her face again and again.

I did love one thing about living with Louise: that was going to her little Protestant churches. I also loved shoes that shrieked and screeched and sometimes bought them at rummage sales. I was always the little pilgrim sitting demurely in the back pew of the church. And no matter what happened during the week, I managed to hold out a penny for the church collection.

When the plate came around I didn't put my penny on it; I waited. I knew that after the collection had all been gathered up the preacher would say with a smile:

"Now where is that penny? Who is going to give that extra penny that will start another buck on its way?"

That was my cue. I'd get up and strut to the pulpit, my shoes howling and whimpering, with my penny in my hand. As I went down the aisle I'd hear people say:

"Look at the little darling! Look at that darling little soldier of the Lord!"

I wanted to show off my shoes and my outfit. But I was sincere. I was glad to give my penny to the church.

Though imaginative, I stubbornly refused to lie to get out of punishment. This was due, I think, to a cute stunt I originated when my second teeth started to come in.

Always the child showman, eager to startle and amaze and demonstrate my courage, I forced all sorts of metal objects—safety pins, hairpins, and even nails—between my two upper front teeth. My admiring playmates imitated me, bringing down on my head the wrath of their parents. It also left a hole between my teeth, which I have to this day, and ruined my reputation as a truthful child.

My people call such a separation in one's teeth "the lie gap." Whenever I told an unusual story grownups would shake their heads and say, "Ethel, open your mouth!"

Then they'd look at my teeth and exclaim, "I knew it! There it is— the lie gap. She's a born liar!"

I was angered even more by what happened after they checked up on the story and found it to be true. Instead of apologizing for calling me a liar, they said I was "brazen and bold" and shouldn't tell such tales.

Resentfully I kept on telling the truth so no one could say that any lies were coming through my lie gap.

The greatest thing in my whole childhood happened to me when I was nine. Purely by accident I had a chance to walk for a little while in a clean and brightly shining world. In my dreams I'd found myself climbing up stairs to a light that I never managed to reach. Now in my real life I reached that light and also the Rock of Ages in the picture on the wall of Uncle Bassett's house. In other childish dreams, as you'll remember, I had seen myself clinging with the others to the rock, surrounded by boiling, leaping waves.

The rock and the light I found was the Catholic Church.

Moving about so much, I'd used up all the public schools in the district, exhausted the whole list. Someone told Mom that a new Catholic school for white and Negro children had just been opened at Ninth and Pine streets, and she entered me there.

The school was in a neat brownstone house that had been a private home. I went there, determined to hate my teachers and to lose no time establishing myself as a holy terror. But from the beginning the nuns were so patient and understanding that I couldn't cope with them, couldn't hate them.

The first thing I noticed was that they expected you to answer "Yes, Sister," or "No, Sister," when they asked you a question. I'd already learned that if you didn't say "ma'am" when addressing any white woman you, as a Negro, were liable to have your block knocked off. "Sister" was the friendlier term Negroes used among themselves.

I soon came to love the instruction periods in which our teacher, Sister Mary Louise Agnes, told us little stories about the Boy Jesus, and told them beautifully. The Boy Jesus in the stories was my age and, as I listened, it was as though He was growing up with me. I was moved deeply when she told me how close Mary was to Jesus, and that you could ask Her for things and she'd ask Jesus to see that you got them.

There was a statue in our classroom of Mother Mary and the Infant Jesus. Sister Mary Louise Agnes told us that any good child would be rewarded by being allowed for a whole week to kneel alone, close to the statue, and say his prayers.

"I want to pray in front of the statue, all by myself, right now," I told the white nun.

"There are other little girls ahead of you, Ethel," she explained. "But if you are good your turn will come."

Even though I couldn't believe her, that fixed me. It was impossible for me to visualize myself, a battered and buffeted bad girl, being allowed to pray so close to the image of the Virgin and the Boy Jesus, so close and all alone. Some way would be found to gyp me.

Yet I couldn't be quite sure of that. The warm and friendly atmosphere of the little school was changing the standards by which I judged the world. I'd never before known the consideration and patience the nuns were showing me as they tried so gently to help me adjust myself.

The only possible way to find out was by behaving myself.

I did, and after only a few weeks I got my chance.

I could hardly believe it.

As soon as the week was up I asked Sister Mary Louise Agnes, "Why can't I pray all next week before the Sacred Image? That's what I want."

"You'll have another chance, Ethel. Just keep on being a good girl. But first the others must have their turn."

Convinced I'd not be cheated, I was hooked into permanent good behavior. I loved every hour in that school—except the lunch hour, when we all went downstairs to the recreation room in the basement to eat.

The trouble was that I seldom had any lunch. If there was anything in the house to eat it would be some stale old cakes. I was afraid to bring them, knowing the other kids—who had sandwiches, fruit, fresh cake, hard-boiled eggs—would make fun of me. That would make me fly at them. And when I had nothing I couldn't sit there and watch them eat.

To get out of my dilemma I began to act up a little, always just before the lunch period, so I'd be kept upstairs. But I never slid on discipline enough to endanger my chance of praying again all alone before the Sacred Image.

The nuns noticed and guessed what I was doing. They began to send me on little errands each morning. That gave them an excuse to ask me to eat the noontime meal with them. I gladly accepted their food for what it seemed to be, pay for the errands I had done.

Mom at the time was working in a house away over at the other end of Philadelphia. She was able to give me a hot evening meal there sometimes. After school I'd walk what seemed endless miles to see her and have dinner.

On other afternoons I was given a good meal by the bartenders in our neighborhood. My two aunts were such good customers in those bars that the bartenders seemed to suspicion that I wasn't getting enough to eat.

They'd call to me as I passed their places and let me into the dining room in the rear through the ladies' entrance. Nobody else would be eating there at the time, and the saloonkeepers gave me a big plate of whatever was left over from lunch. I'd sit all alone at a table in the big room, eating that fine food.

Several times the sisters asked me about my parents. I always had the right evasive answers ready—my grandmother worked out, my mother had married again and lived over in Chester, so my two aunts were taking care of me.

Gradually I was becoming more and more of a Catholic. But when the soft-voiced nun first suggested I go to confession I told her, "I can't go to confession, Sister."

"Why not, Ethel?"

"I just couldn't tell the father all the bad things I've done." I was thinking of all the stealing, fighting, and cursing I'd done.

"Why not, Ethel?" persisted Sister Mary Louise Agnes.

"I have to tell him the truth if I go to confession. It would be a sin if I lied to the father. I can't tell him the truth, Sister, I just can't."

I was afraid that any full and honest confession from me would shock the priest so that he'd fall right out of his box onto the marble floor of the church. In the end, though, Sister Mary Louise Agnes and the other little white nuns talked me into taking a chance.

The very least I expected was that the father would be so appalled at hearing about all I'd done—and this from the mouth of a very young child—that he'd tell me never to come back.

I went, but that first confession of mine took hours. Yet all the priest said on hearing me out was:

"I understand, my child. You must not swear any more. You must not do these other things ever again."

My penance that first day was saying ten Hail Marys and five Our Fathers before each of the fourteen Stations of the Cross in the church. You just won't cheat on a thing like that when you're a child. I stayed in that church, saying penance, darn near all night. I tried not to be so bad a girl and was very proud of myself when I cut down my penance to a mere hour and a half after only a few weeks.

I would leave the school full of hope and feeling exalted.

Then I had to go home.

From eight in the morning until two each day I'd feel wanted, enriched by the affection of the nuns, and an accepted member of the human race.

But nothing had changed at home. Always it was the same: Vi or Ching drunk, nothing washed or clean, nothing in order, the smell of beer and smoked cigarettes all over the hovel. And the same tensions and recriminations, unchanging and unrelieved.

I had a cold, detached way of looking at my aunts that drove them half crazy with frustration. There was in me some great inner strength and a will power that I telegraphed to them in that look, in the very way I walked. They couldn't crush me, but their resentment made them try.

"You're late," Vi would say. "Where have you been, you dirty little sneak? You haven't been in school all this time."

"I've been in church, Vi."

"Don't you lie to me! You are a big-eyed, big-head slut!"

As long as I could, I wouldn't answer. But I'd look at Vi, and that look, blazing with defiance, would make her want to beat my brains out. Dozens of times I've had my lips beaten black and blue and bleeding because of that look.

So then I'd have to set God down in the corner. The place would start jumping with blows, curses, threats. I know now that it would have helped a lot if I could have prayed when those blows were falling. But I didn't know then that one could pray away from the church.

My aunts were not always drunk. Vi and Ching both had long spells when they didn't drink anything. The trouble was that they never stopped drinking at the same time. When Ching was sober, Vi was drunk. If it was Vi on the wagon, Ching would be crocked. They did not often get falling-down drunk. But neither was able to handle liquor, and they always seemed to drink just enough to make them horrible.

Their drunkenness, and the fury and the quarreling it brought out, was the one thing I could never accept. What saddened me most was knowing how nice they could be when sober, Ching particularly. If there had been no drinking we could have been the happiest little family in the world—even without money or anything but the barest necessities. All of us had a wonderful sense of humor and were full of fun and laughter.

Once I felt so bad about the drinking that I went to the officials of the Catholic school and asked to be put away. But they told me they couldn't place me in an orphanage because I had a mother and my aunts were taking care of me.

I never told them what it was like at home. I loved the people in that school, but I couldn't have taken their pity.

Louise never approved of my Catholicism and didn't let me stay in the school for very long. But I did return there intermittently during the two years that followed.

My mother never drank heavily. Old-fashioned religion was her refuge. I've always felt that I inherited her deeply religious feelings, but her conception of God was nothing like mine. Louise went in for the old backwoods, down-home religion, closely resembling that of the Holy Rollers and the Hard-Shell Baptists.

Louise painted God almost as an ogre. To her He was principally an avenging Spirit. Only a thin line was drawn between Him and the devil. My mother didn't make God ugly, but she sure made Him wrathful. I felt that God loved me as I loved Him. To me He was never a tyrant, an enemy just waiting to pounce if I made some mistake.

Mom always challenged Louise's whooping and hollering religion. "You don't have to holler so," she'd say. "God has very big ears. He can hear you even if you whisper."

Though Louise's religion was almost fanatical, she wasn't as strict with me as Mom. Even though she tried to work me hard as possible, I had more freedom living with her. For one thing, she was out many nights at the missions.

Louise had a habit of inviting whole families who had no homes of their own to move in with us. When the house was full our cot was moved into my mother's and Norman's room. But if we had no visitors Genevieve and I slept in a bed in the near room.

Life in Chester could be as uproarious as in Philadelphia, and sometimes there was plenty of comic relief. Norman was forever complaining that my mother's devotion to church affairs was interfering with the performance of her marital duties.

I didn't like Norman because he was light-colored. I knew he was running around with other women but never mentioned this to my mother, realizing it would only add to her unhappiness.

I tried hard to please her, but she never became as fond of me as she was of Genevieve, her legitimately born child. But Louise must have retained some smoldering maternal instinct toward me. When Norman hit her, she'd never fight him. Yet when I tried to take her part and he'd lift his hand to me, Louise would go for him like a tigress.

Louise was so scrawny and starved-looking that once the Chester health authorities feared she might be tubercular. They asked her to bring Genevieve and me to their offices so we, too, could be examined. To build us up they allotted us two dozen eggs a week and six quarts of milk daily.

My stepsister and I immediately went into the retail dairy-products business. We sold our free eggs and milk to the entire neighborhood at bargain prices and earned plenty of pocket money.

Often we were invited to parties where we also had a fight about who got the biggest plate of ice cream. Sometimes the other kids wanted to go home with us. We never let them come in. We'd given glowing descriptions of our furniture and didn't want them to find out how little stuff we really had.

There was another reason: We never knew when Pop Norman would bring up in the conversation the matter of not getting sufficient satisfaction out of his married life. The subject was such an obsession with him that he'd start grumbling about it no matter who was in the house.

I have always been psychic. The walls of any room I walk into talk to me. Louise claimed this was because she had seen an apparition while she was carrying me.

One night she went to sleep with the light on in her room. She was all alone in the house. When she sensed something in the room she opened her eyes. A strange man in a brown suit was standing near her bed. Transfixed, she stared at him, and he came closer and closer. Louise had always heard that looking at a ghost drew him toward you and that if you closed your eyes you broke the spell. But she was too frightened to close her eyes.

Louise was about to faint with terror when a friend of the family passed by outside and called in to ask why the light was on so late. Louise told him to come in. That broke the spell—the ghost vanished.

Next day neighbors told my mother that her description of the apparition fitted a gambler who had been murdered in that same room not long before. His throat had been slashed from ear to ear. He had never been known to wear anything but a brown suit.

Though such stories about ghosts fascinated me, I never saw one while I was a child. This vastly disappointed me, as I didn't believe they could hurt you physically. I knew they could hurt you mentally, but only if you were afraid of them.

Of our family, Vi was the most mystic one. Vi had second sight, could read cards and foretell the future. This was credited to her being born with a caul over her head.

Vi didn't think highly of her supernatural gifts. But if you worked on her you could get her to read cards and foretell your future.

For a while Vi was staying with us in Chester. She was sleeping in the back room with Genevieve. I was on the cot in my parents' room.

After we had quieted down there was a knock on the door. It turned out to be a dreary droop who was ambitious to be Vi's boy friend and wished to talk with her. Climbing out of bed, Vi went down to talk to her wobbly-minded admirer. He went away after a while, and she came upstairs. At the head of the steps she stopped short on seeing a man, just outside our door, wearing long winter underwear. Believing it was Norman trying to eavesdrop on her, she yelled:

"What are you standing out here in the hall for, Norman?"

There was no answer, and Vi raised her voice even more, waking up the whole household. "What in heaven's name you talking about, Vi?" asked my mother. "It ain't Norman out there in the hall. Norman is right here beside me in the bed."

Vi came in, shrugging her shoulders, and told what she'd seen. "I wonder who that feller in the long underwear was, then," she said, and got back into bed with Genevieve. My parents tried to go to sleep again. Louise wanted to sleep over the sheet and Norman wanted to sleep under the sheet, so there was one hell of a disturbance before they got settled.

Then, just as all was quiet, I announced that I had to get up to do what refined children call number one. I wasn't too eager because I'd just listened to Vi's account of her meeting with the mysterious fellow in the long underwear just outside. I had to be coaxed before I consented to use the chamber pot.

As I was about to do this a big picture fell off the wall. The sudden noise frightened me so that I collapsed on the chamber pot and broke it. Then I really started to wail.

This again awoke Norman, who decided to get out of bed and investigate. But when he put his foot on the floor he howled. Putting his foot down again in another spot, he howled louder.

"That man in the long underwear is still around, making trouble," he said between curses. "Now he's spilled water all over the floor."

There was pandemonium, with me screaming, Genevieve joining in, and Norman bitterly complaining about having the house flooded by mischief-making ghosts.

It was dawn before we all got back to sleep. The following day Louise told the neighbors about Vi's ghost, and they said a man built like Pop Norman had died under mysterious circumstances in our house a few years before. When his body was found he was wearing long woolen underwear.

Louise's and Pop Norman's reconciliations were always brief, and the next place I was moved to was a broken-down furnished room that Ching had in Philadelphia. It was on the third floor of a tenement, and from our window you could see the house in front, which seemed to be beautifully furnished.

A Negro policeman named Smith lived there with his wife, who looked white, and their little girl. Ching and Vi, who soon moved in with us, became so curious about the Smiths' elegant furniture that I told them I'd find out all about it for them.

"No one in this colored neighborhood will play with that kid because they think her mother is white," I said. "She'll be glad to play with me and invite me inside her house."

When the policeman's wife Elsie did ask me into the house, I was overwhelmed by the Smiths' three floors of furniture. They even had a piano, which was an unheard-of luxury in our neighborhood in a private home.

One day Elsie asked me my last name.

"It's Perry," I told her. "I don't like my stepfather, so I don't use his name. But I'm really a bastard," I went on cheerfully, "and my right name is Waters."

"Waters!"

I explained that my father was Johnny Waters but that neither he nor his family had ever acknowledged me. Mrs. Smith said no more, but a couple of days later she called me in and burst into tears.

"I'm your second cousin, Ethel," she said, explaining that her mother was the sister of my white grandmother, Lydia Waters. "And your grandmother wants to see you."

But Trix Waters, my stepmother and John Waters' widow, came down first to look me over. After that, with my aunts' permission, I was taken to Lydia Waters' big home uptown.

She seemed sad on seeing me, but I wasn't much moved. The resemblance I bore her was unmistakable, but my chief feeling was one of not wishing her to touch me. She offered me nothing, but that didn't matter. Sally Anderson would not have permitted me to accept help from a Waters.

As I talked to my white grandmother in her luxurious home I knew

I would have to go on as before, taking the chaos, the discomforts, and bickerings all in my stride.

Yet even when I felt most like an outsider I was never alone. I belonged to the great misery class and knew it. I was learning to eat cat meat and to enjoy it better than roast pork.

Besides, I was a Catholic now. I felt that God would always be with me, helping as I battled my way through that wasteland of violent emotions and exploding egos in which I was growing up.

4

By the time I was eleven I was so big that I had trouble getting men to leave me alone. Several times Mom sent me to a doctor who examined me to find out if I was still a virgin. The doctor said I was but "might be going into a decline." This meant tuberculosis, so Mom gave me porter, beer, and ale to stimulate my appetite, milk being too dear for us to buy.

My grandmother also decided it was time I had some wholesome amusement. She took me to Pop Grey, an old friend of hers, who ran a respectable dance hall on South Street. Even though I was so much under the legal age he agreed to let me attend evening sessions at his place.

Admission cost fifty cents, but before long Pop offered to let me in free if I'd give his other girl customers dancing lessons. I won many prizes in dancing contests put on at Grey's. Besides the usual one-steps and waltzes, we did square dances and all the schottisches and quadrilles that have lately become so popular all over again.

I could always dance for hours without getting tired. The year before (I was ten but looked fifteen) I made Mabel, a girl friend of mine, take me to the Saturday-night dances at another hall in a dimly lighted place over a stable. Mabel was a little bit of a thing, but at fourteen she was as developed as she'd ever be.

To those Saturday-night dances I'd wear the high-heeled shoes I'd found at rummage sales. Though my hair reached to my waist, I'd put it up and pack it with rats, which were very fashionable just then.

I'd make my eyebrows bigger by using burnt cork. For cheek rouge I rubbed the red dye from crepe shelving paper into my face, topping it off with talcum powder. Proudly I hung whores' hoop earrings in my pierced ears and, for a last touch of class, tied a black velvet ribbon around my neck.

With my bucket-shaped head on a long, scrawny neck, topped by the mountain of built-up black hair, I'd hobble off to the dance on my rickety high-heeled shoes. I never doubted that I was the best-dressed girl there.

I kept believing that, even after I heard a woman friend tell Louise: "I saw a freak at the dance last Saturday night. She looked just like your Ethel." It was me she'd seen, of course, but she couldn't believe her eyes.

Fortunately, my mother didn't catch on and I was able to keep going to those wonderful Saturday-night dances, feeling always like the belle of the ball and a dream girl in my outlandish getup.

The last little place Mom was able to set up for us was in an alley off Kater Street. This was in a semi-red-light district of Philadelphia. In some ways it was even tougher than Clifton Street. Whenever I entered the alley on my way home I walked to the shanty with my face turned to the wall. This was the only way I could avoid seeing the whores emptying the pockets of sailors and other men who were making love to them right in the open.

The common toilet in the alley had to be locked inside and out. The outside lock kept out the hookers and their customers. The inside lock was for the protection of me and the other young girls who lived in the alley.

Kater Street was almost the end of the road for Mom. When she got home she was so tired and groaning with her many aches and pains. But her children—Vi, Charlie, Ching, and Louise—were still plaguing her.

I felt very sorry for Mom, but I didn't let that interrupt my mischief-making. Across a fence from our shanty was the back yard of a restaurant called the Busy Bee. Every chance I got I gathered up garbage and other refuse and threw it into the baskets of potatoes, lettuce, and other vegetables which lay exposed in the yard.

Going into the house, I'd wait patiently at the window for the restaurant men to come out of the kitchen to get the baskets. When they saw my garbage on their nice clean vegetables they'd cry out in anguish:

"What's this? What sonsofbitches have been here? Dammit to hell what stuff is this?"

Utterly charmed by my ability to throw them into a frenzy, I'd then go out and ask people I met on the street, "What restaurant do you eat in?"

If they replied, "The Busy Bee," I'd laugh with joy until I became hysterical. Puzzled, they'd always want to know what I was laughing at. But giving them only a pitying look, I'd walk on until I met someone else who said he patronized the Busy Bee. Then I would get hysterical all over again.

In Kater Street I learned another lesson you'll never find in the book called *What Every Young Girl Should Know*, a lesson about opium and the sort of people who smoke it.

Back in Clifton Street I'd learned a little about the other narcotics —cocaine, morphine, and heroin. And I'd heard my aunts call Harry, a friend of my mother's and a sneak thief, a junkie. But I'd never known quite what that meant. When I thought of Harry, "the junkie," I remembered his high and flighty eyes.

While we were on Kater Street my aunts were again earning their drinking money by doing the sporting women's laundry. They sent me out to get and deliver the wash. Whenever I took the weekly bundle to a customer I called Miss Hazel I had to wait a long time after knocking on her door before it was opened. And her eyes, like Harry's, were high and flighty. Sometimes there was a curious smell—an odor like yeast—in the hall.

One day when Miss Hazel asked me to do some errands for her I said, "That funny smell ain't in the hallway today."

"What funny smell?"

I described it.

Miss Hazel nodded. "Ethel," she said, "any time you notice that in the hallway, let me know—ring my bell three times. That will be our signal. Okay?"

Unknowingly I'd saved her from a police raid. The yeasty smell was the odor of opium cooking. Miss Hazel hadn't known it was escaping from her rooms into the hallway.

After that she felt more free with me. She'd let me into her room, something she'd never done before. I didn't comment on what I saw there—wet towels and sheets spread across the windows and the door, silent, sleepy-looking people in the room, the little lamp sitting on the floor.

Before very long Miss Hazel trusted me to the point of asking me to stay with her when she smoked alone. She paid me a dollar just for stroking her temples while she smoked.

Sometimes her boy friend would come in, take off his coat, lie down, and smoke. Miss Hazel knew how to prepare and cook the stuff. The little black opium pellets looked like pine tar. She'd put her head in my lap as she lay down to smoke.

"These are my kicks," Miss Hazel would say.

I never forgot that dark room, the wet sheets hanging over the door, or that yeasty smell. I never forgot watching the torment of Miss Hazel and her friends when they couldn't get dope. My aunts were like that when they couldn't get liquor. They'd become frantic, would get the shakes, be thrown into utter chaos. And what they were going mad for was fifteen minutes of artificial stimulation.

Going around with girls of fourteen or fifteen when I was eleven, I was continually embarrassed because they had breasts and I was as flat as a board. I made many experiments with falsies, which I had seen prostitutes wearing. My luck was bad; half the time one falsie would be up around my shoulder and the other down on my hip.

The other girls never stopped talking about their sweethearts, so I invented a boy friend for myself. He was handsome, loaded with money, generous, and out of his mind about me. He was also strictly anonymous, and that was what I appreciated most about him. I had no boy friend and I wanted none. All I wanted was to talk about him.

These girls were of a better class than I'd known before, but hotly interested in sex. Often as I walked home from school with them one would suggest, "Let's stop in this place."

The place would be the home or the store of some middle-aged man who had a yen for young girls. The moment I saw him I'd dig him, dig the place, dig the situation. I'd watch, showing no surprise as the man fondled the young girls, played with their childlike breasts, and slapped them over the behind.

These older girls, knowing I was hep to sex, trusted me not to tell on them. But I must have had a chilling eye because none of the men ever touched me or even tried to.

Strong as a bull at eleven, I'd taken a job as cleaning woman for Giuseppe Donato, the sculptor. I got seventy-five cents a week for working after school for him. Besides cleaning up his studio, I kept his big stove full of egg coal. Mr. Donato predicted I'd have a pretty figure when I grew up.

With Mom so full of the misery, I thought a lot about her and all she'd tried to do for me. When fall came I decided to give her the only good Christmas she'd ever had.

By saving my money for months, I managed to amass five dollars. On Christmas Eve I bought a tiny tree, put it on the table, and decorated it. I also bought three fancy little glasses, the kind Mom liked, set them out in a row before the tree with a dollar bill stuck in each one. I didn't buy any food, knowing that Mom would come home with enough "cold functions" for dinner.

Ching was away, and there was only Vi at home. For weeks I'd begged her to be sober on this one Christmas Eve. "That will mean so much to Mom," I kept saying. "It will make her so happy."

But Vi wasn't there when Mom came in, tired and all beat up. When she saw the tree all decorated and the little glasses with the dollar bills in them, her whole face lighted up.

"This is nice, Ethel," she said. "This makes me feel good."

She sat down at the table, and I sat down on the other side. The idea that some of the family had thought of her this Christmas gave her a wonderful, warm thrill. It was nice for me, too, feeling close to her, talking to her so peacefully. I kept looking across the tiny tree at her smiling face.

We sat there, and it was as though Mom at last had the home and the family she wanted.

We sat there like that, feeling happy and lighthearted, until we heard Vi outside and let her in. She was drunk and bullish.

"Why did you have to get drunk this one day, Vi?" I asked her. "This one day I asked you to stay sober so Mom could have a nice Christmas."

Vi started calling me horrible names. I went over to the steps leading upstairs and sat down. I didn't answer her curses, just stared at her.

"Don't pay her no mind, Ethel," said Mom. "Leave her be. Let her get it all out of her system."

Vi fell into a chair and continued to upbraid and curse me. I said nothing, just kept watching her. Seeing something on the floor, Vi swayed down and picked it up. It was a hatchet. I didn't move but never took my eyes off her.

"Put down that hatchet, Vi," said Mom. "Put it down. Have you lost your mind?"

Vi pulled back her arm and threw the hatchet at me with all her strength. I didn't have time to fall out of the way, just managed to move my head sideways as it flew across the room. It went into the wall back of me with a quivering, zinging noise. It had gone over my shoulder, missing my head by inches.

I got up and jumped on Vi. I don't remember anything after that. I was temporarily insane and I must have choked and punched, kicked and gouged Vi in my maniacal fury. All I can remember after that was being pulled off Vi by Mom and a fat man who lived next door. He had rushed in on hearing Vi's screams. It was that fat man who pried my hands from Vi's throat and stopped me from killing her. I never would have let go by myself until she was dead.

Vi was unconscious, out. They gave her ammonia and smelling salts, then they carried her upstairs and put her on the bed. When Mom came downstairs again she found me in a daze and gave me some smelling salts too. Then came release—and hysterics.

Next day when I looked at Vi I got sick. Her face was nothing but bumps and lumps and all shades of purple and red and black. Her throat had deep black-and-blue dents where I'd clawed her.

I had almost killed her. But if I had killed her before Mom and the fat man interfered I wouldn't have been sorry. It was the first time I ever whipped Vi. She was scared stiff of me from then on. I never had to fight her again.

The one regret I had was that Mom's Christmas—like everything else in her life—had been spoiled.

My aunts and my mother were not ignorant women. They discussed people and things that happened with considerable intelligence and insight. But I could never get them to listen when I told them about what was happening at school or of anything else that concerned me. They just didn't care. Perhaps they were alienated from me because I was so different in every way from the three of them.

Yet I can't condemn them for that. For them, too, each day was a scuffle, a racking struggle to keep alive. When people are in that situation the problems of a child must seem very unimportant. All that counts is eating and keeping a roof over your head.

None of us felt we were underprivileged or victims of society. The families we knew were doing no better than we were, so the daily struggle seemed universal.

When Louise's father-in-law, Grandpa Howard, a nice old man, died, Mrs. Howard could no longer take care of Genevieve. Louise, whom I had started to call Momweeze, once more set up housekeeping, and I went to live with them in Chester. Before long Mom had to move in with us. She had become too weak to work. Pop Norman didn't want her there, but there was no other place for her to go. Though she was fading fast, she had only a broken-down couch to rest on.

Momweeze always was wonderful about getting things on the installment plan. In this place she even had an organ. Louise never once managed to pay all the installments on the furniture she had bought so optimistically. One week her house would be full, the next week bare. But we often got a lot of use out of the stuff before the finance company got discouraged about Louise being able to pay up and sent their men to take it away.

Sick as she was, Mom loved having an organ in the house. She'd ask me to pick out her favorite hymns with one finger on that little organ. One of these favorites was "His Eye Is on the Sparrow," the hymn I sing now for the second-act curtain in my Broadway play, *The Member of the Wedding*.

I was spending a lot of time now with Mom. I didn't think I'd have her much longer. But sometimes Genevieve and I would go at night to parlor socials. Seemingly, in Chester, I was taken for a show person and a celebrity, principally because I came from the great city of Philadelphia, a few miles away.

And I could dance, sing, and do the split. In Chester I was also known as the champion hip shaker, the best in the world. The boys were also nimble-hipped. What we most prided ourselves on was our pure prowess in quivering, muscle-rolling, and shaking. Among these amateurs I encountered professional jealousy for the first time—because I could not only dance with the boys but could dance alone. The other girls didn't like that.

Pop Norman was boss of that household most of the time, but not on Sunday. We all had to go to church on the Sabbath, no matter how much he rumbled and grumbled and jeered. At home, too, the whole religious ritual was observed.

Louise didn't object to my going to church and staying there the whole day. I didn't say anything about my Catholic leanings in these little Protestant churches I attended, fearing I'd be ridiculed and mocked. And I soon became aware of the differences in the various Protestant denominations.

When I went to a Baptist church I noticed that the officials let you know that they considered you highly intelligent for at least having seen the light. The Methodists never concealed their opinion that your judgment was excellent when you attended their meetings.

But what I learned from going to these churches was that other religions than mine held something that was worth while and exalting. I preferred the Methodist sect, which appeals to the inner spiritual sense, but also liked the free-swinging, uninhibited Baptist preachers.

I came to love and value the inner fire of a brimstone-and-hellfire preacher. I sensed that there was something splendid about this kind of religion that exploded in the pastor's heart, enabling him to reach you and make you believe.

There was much innocent romancing at Sunday school. We had the sweetest, dumbest instructors. They never suspicioned that we kids, particularly my older friends of fourteen and fifteen, used the hymns to send love messages back and forth. By choosing a certain hymn a girl could tell her boy friend she'd see him tonight or that she'd be at the dance on Wednesday.

My devotion to the spiritual side of life did not dent or alter my basically Jekyll and Hyde character. I was in deep fear that my shameful virginity would be discovered by the crowd that so admired my conversation, which was sophisticated—not to say gritty—at all times. My lack of breasts and other evidences of physical immaturity continued to embarrass me. Some of the boys called me slack-belly, for I was then a bean pole with the kind of shape that is considered fashionable today.

And this was my dilemma: Though I had no desire to lose my virginity, I also was determined to maintain my respected position as a worldly girl. However, I could foresee that the day might come soon when vulgar words and my intimate knowledge of the sex lives of other people might not get me by.

With my younger admirers the solution was simple because they were as inexperienced as I. And when the older couples, for instance, would go off down to the railway yards to make love and I'd offer to be their lookout, the little boy with me was only too glad just to assist me as lookout. Such kids were as reluctant as I was to reveal their innocence and ignorance of how to proceed.

Other, more enterprising young boys I held to a standoff with tall tales about my big shot uptown who was loaded with money and was so insanely jealous that he threatened to slash the throat of any man who even presumed to wink at me.

The older boys with whom I went on dancing sprees just laughed at such stories. So I was reduced to telling them that I was going with a little boy. Though I can hardly say they were intimidated, it did seem to enhance my desirability.

In fact, I was soon being grabbed at so persistently that I made Genevieve go to all the dances with me. I told her that she must never let me out of her sight for a second—no matter what the boys said or did. I couldn't think of any other way to avoid getting into a spot in which one of my ungentle admirers could force a showdown.

Genevieve, always quick to capitalize on the misfortunes of others, set a high price on her services. Before she would agree to become my human mustard plaster I had to promise her half of everything I had and was making by my after-school work.

But she earned all she got from me. No share cropper ever reaped a bigger harvest of insults and humiliations. They did everything but throw rocks at her. For once I was glad that my stepsister was such a greedy little girl. Genevieve never let go of my arm.

Meanwhile my education in life in the raw was continuing. In our house on Morton Street, Chester, the neighbors were friendly. The woman talk there was all obstetrical gossip and reminiscences.

The outstanding feminine personality on our block was a woman everyone called Aunt Kate. A big woman deep in her fifties, she was considered remarkable because she was always "full of babies," as we termed it.

Aunt Kate, the walking incubator, was still having children with the greatest of ease. After one or two slight labor pains she didn't even have to sneeze to bring her latest infant into the world. And early the next morning Aunt Kate would leap up from bed and eat ham and eggs for breakfast.

The other Morton Street housewives talked of little else but the babies they'd had or were about to have. One woman would boast, "My Joe weighed fourteen pounds when he was born, and he nearly killed me."

Another would say with equal pride, "My Hannah only weighed seven and a half pounds. Having her was the easiest thing that ever happened to me."

An unmarried girl who had a baby was said to have "stumped her toe."

I struck up a friendship with a pregnant woman who lived across the street from us. She told me she enjoyed my company "because you know so much about having babies."

I did know many things, such as rubbing an expectant mother's stomach with oil to loosen the muscles. And no details had been overlooked by the gossiping women who discussed so endlessly their childbearing feats in front of us youngsters.

When this woman had her baby she sent for me. I took over until the doctor arrived. I have never delivered a baby, but I'm sure I could. I saw the whole miraculous and messy process that day. In those days women, married and unmarried, believed in having their babies instead of getting rid of them.

Though dancing, being chased by the boys, and mysteries of human birth all fascinated me, my greatest interest, when I was eleven, lay in the Church. Though I was a Catholic, I recognized, as I said, that Louise's little Protestant churches had something. I'd watch the grownups praying and would get the same feeling they had of elation, exaltation, of being carried above and beyond oneself.

The beauty that came into the tired faces of the very old men and women excited me. All week long so many of them were confused and inarticulate. But on Sunday, in the church, they had no difficulty expressing themselves both in song and talk. The emotion that had invaded them was so much bigger than they. Some would rock. Some would cry. Some would talk with eloquence and fire, their confusions and doubts dispelled. And, oh, those hymns!

It began to dawn on me that if sordidness left a deep and lasting mark, so could the goodness in life. The big thing in my life was the feeling that I was getting close to God. Not that I could accept all the doctrine preached. My logic, my reasoning powers made me question much of the doctrine.

For example, as a little girl I was told to ask God to forgive my sins. But what sins could a little girl commit?

My search for God and my finding of Him were to begin in one of those Protestant churches where they were having a children's revival. It was there that I came truly to know and to reverence Christ, the Redeemer.

All my girl friends in the neighborhood were going to this children's revival. I went religiously, every day. When the preacher, the Reverend R. J. Williams, called those who wished to repent and be saved, all my gang would go up there to the mourners' bench and kneel down—but not for long. They would pop up quick as hot cakes and as though they had brand-new souls. But we stout hearts in the back knew they hadn't been cleansed of sin but were just trying to attract attention.

"Come up and shake my hand," the Reverend R. J. Williams would say in his booming voice. "Don't you want to be little soldiers of the Lord?"

Two or three times I did go up to shake his hand. Then I'd return to my seat. I wasn't sure I wanted to be saved. "What can I ask God?" I kept thinking. "What have I got to say to Him?"

One night there were only three of us youngsters still left unsaved in the whole congregation. All the rest had gone to the mourners' bench and been redeemed.

"Come!" cried the Reverend Williams, an inspired and fiery preacher. "Get down on your knees and pray to our Lord!"

So I thought, "I will get down on my knees and pray just to see what happens." I prayed, "O Lord! I don't know what to ask of You!"

I did this every night. Every night I was on my knees—and nothing happened. I didn't feel purged of sin or close to the Lord. I didn't feel what some of the others felt so sincerely. It was this way with me right through the last night of the children's revival meeting.

I was the only one left who was still unsaved, and the preacher looked at me. He looked at me and announced he would continue the revival, if necessary, for three more nights—just to save me. I like to think that the Reverend R. J. Williams saw something special and fervent in me, something deep and passionate struggling toward salvation and spiritual expression.

On the last of the three extra nights of the meeting I got down on the mourners' bench, down on my knees once more. And I told myself, "If nothing happens tonight, I'll not come back again."

Nobody had come that night to the meeting, nobody but the very old people who were always there. I was praying hard and hopefully, asking God, "What am I seeking here? What do I want of You? Help me! If nothing happens, I can't come back here any more!"

And then it happened! The peace of heart and of mind, the peace I had been seeking all my life.

I know that never again, so long as I live, can I experience that wonderful reaction I had that night in the little church. Love flooded my heart and I knew I had found God and that now and for always I would have an ally, a friend close by to strengthen me and cheer me on.

I don't know exactly what happened or when I got up. I don't even know whether I talked. But the people who were there that night were astounded. Afterward they told me that I was radiant and like one transfixed. They said that the light in my face electrified the whole church. And I did feel full of light and warmth.

The preacher, the Reverend R. J. Williams, had some compelling force in him that enabled him to contact people. Great actresses and statesmen and other popular idols have that same force, but great preachers most of all. He could soothe you and calm you and also stir you to the depths of your soul with what lay in his eyes, his voice, and his heart.

Somehow, after that, it seemed more quiet in the house. Or perhaps things did not trouble me so much. I was no longer alone and knew now that I could never be alone anywhere, no matter what I did.

I started to go to church every Sunday. Any church to me has always been the House of God, whatever the denomination. I was a Catholic, but I didn't think He would mind whether I went to that church, a Protestant church, a synagogue, or a Hindu temple.

I was not made more grave and solemn by what had happened. I remained the same as before. Everybody smiled and said, "It is wintertime religion that Ethel has. When summertime comes it will wear off."

I smiled back at them. I didn't have to answer. I knew it was not just wintertime religion with me and that my feeling of being watched over and protected would never leave me.

But then one night I went to a little Methodist church's social affair. Among the other girls who were going was Gertrude, the daughter of a very respectable family. Gertrude for some time had been having a romance with a fellow I knew, a love affair on the q.t.

When I arrived in the church vestibule I found quite a group of girls gathered there. They seemed to be up to something. They didn't like me, I guess, and, as it turned out, wanted to make trouble for me. They got me in a corner and told me that Gertrude had said I was going with her boy friend.

Gertrude herself then entered the vestibule. When she saw me she came up and asked me if I was going around with her boy friend.

"I don't want to hear anything more about that," I told her. Actually, I wasn't going with him but couldn't see any reason to discuss it.

Gertrude began to upbraid me. The other girls were nudging one another and laughing. I looked at them, then at her, and used an expression that can mean a great deal or nothing.

"I pay you no mind," I said, "because you're breeding."

Gertrude had long fingernails. Without saying another word she drew back her hand and clawed out long gashes in my face. I tried to fight her, but I couldn't because so many of the other girls held me. When we were pulled apart I went home with my deeply cut, bleeding face. I told the story, and my folks said, "Go to the Lord!"

But I couldn't go to the Lord. I was too angry, too determined on revenge.

The next Sunday was Communion Sunday, held the first of each month in that church. When the minister, who had been told about the quarrel, saw me, he asked me to get up. I did, inwardly asking God to remove the bitterness in me. I knew He wouldn't take me with bitterness. I also knew I couldn't come back into the church with all that hate in my heart. I wasn't going to be a house devil and a church saint.

Despite all the preacher said about forgiveness toward one's enemies, my anger against Gertrude stayed with me. I never did catch her. That, I suppose, was just as well, for, having my family's insane temper, I surely would have killed or crippled her.

It was only years later that I found out what had provoked Gertrude into gashing my face (I retained the scars for a whole year) with her long, cruel fingernails.

When I said she was breeding she was already pregnant and thought I knew it and was telling the world about her shame. She had been doing everything possible to conceal her condition from her "dicty" parents, strapping herself up tight in corsets, and all the rest.

Now you must remember that I, being an illegitimate child, was expected to turn out to be the family prostitute. And I must admit that I gloated over the fact that it was Gertrude, the respectable "dicty" girl, instead, who stumped her toe.

I had wanted to lick her but never got the chance. Her baby was born illegitimate because the fellow she'd been going with wouldn't marry her. So I had my revenge—and was content.

Years later, when I was seventeen, I was performing at Barney Gordon's Bar, at Thirteenth and Kater streets, Philadelphia. The city had Sunday blue laws, and the saloons couldn't open up until five minutes after midnight of the Sabbath Day.

While waiting to get into the saloons lots of people would go to church. One Sunday night Florrie, a sweet church person who was a friend of mine, asked me to go with her and another girl, named Ethel like me, to hear the Reverend R. J. Williams preach. He was holding his meetings then in various big movie theaters. I went to hear him.

During the meeting, as usual, the preacher asked the entire congregation to stand up. Then he told those who were regular members of the congregation to sit down. Next he asked all those who belonged to any church to sit down. Finally he asked all those who were Christians, whether they attended church regularly or not, to sit down.

When that was all over only the other Ethel and I remained standing in that whole place. She would have liked to sit down, but she couldn't as I was holding tightly to her hand, and she couldn't get it away from me. I couldn't sit down because on account of my work of singing risqué songs I didn't feel like a Christian, yet I didn't like to be left there, either, standing all alone.

The Reverend Williams looked at us and said:

"This *is* wonderful. It is wonderful that in this whole vast congregation there are only two people honest enough to admit they aren't Christians."

(Reverend Williams was a shrewd and knowledgeable man, and I think he knew a lot of the people were there only to kill some time until the saloons opened.)

"Come up, ladies!" he said to us. "I want to shake you by the hand."

We two Ethels went up, and he asked us who we were. I told him that I was Ethel Waters and that maybe I had no right being there, seeing that I was singing songs like "Shim-Me-Sha-Wabble" at Gordon's saloon just a few blocks away.

"Ethel Waters?" he said thoughtfully. "The name is familiar."

"It should be to you," I told him, saying I came from Chester and reminding him how he'd once extended a children's revival meeting for three whole nights just to save me.

The Reverend Williams reached down and took my hand again, and he held it as he preached a sermon that tore the hearts out of that whole big congregation and my heart out of me.

"I admire the courage of these two people who remained standing," he said. Holding my hand up, he went on, "This girl refused to lie. She is a child of God, walking the straight and narrow path. Yes, she is the real Christian."

And then the Reverend Williams told that big congregation of how I'd been redeemed and saved in Chester.

Though I'm deeply religious, I still do not go often to any churches, except Catholic ones. The others, to me, have an almost theatrical air. Many of the men and women who go there behave as though the important thing to them is to display their new clothes, to see and be seen. Instead of going to church, I listen on Sunday to all the church programs on the radio.

A church is, to me, a sacred place, and when I hear somebody say, "Oh, there's Ethel Waters!" I feel embarrassed. In church I am not Ethel Waters, the actress, but just another worshiper of God.

Religion is a strong, healthy thing. Any God you worship is good if he brings you love. The Catholic religion gives you a beautiful image to cuddle. I who have always believed in an eye for an eye and a tooth for a tooth try to get God in my corner. His is almost like an inner voice, soothing and calming.

And at home I talk a great deal to Jesus. Often He is my only playmate.

5

Each day Mom seemed to get a little weaker. I was spending a lot of time with her, singing the songs she liked and trying to make her comfortable on her broken-down couch.

But the arguments between Louise and Norman became too much for Mom, and she said she'd go and stay with Aunt Ide. Ide now lived so far out in Chester that you had to go to the end of the trolley-car line, then walk a whole mile.

When Mom left I myself was sick from overeating. In Chester there were no frankfurter stands, Chinese joints, or See Willie's. But there was a Miss Mary's where you could get short'nin' bread.

It was from Miss Mary, who came from the South, that I first learned about pouring molasses or syrup over short'nin' bread. She told me you should only eat it hot. But I'd eat the short'nin' bread hot or cold and drink a lot of water afterward.

But what made me sick this time was eating a lot of fried fish and applesauce, and lemonade to top it off. It was a bad time to be sick. My parents were breaking up their home again. Genevieve was going to live with her father's people. Momweeze was going to work in Atlantic City. I begged her to take me with her, but she wouldn't. Mom, of course, was too ill to take care of me, yet nobody seemed to be worrying about where or how I was going to live.

At some dances I'd met Merritt Purnsley, a little fellow whom everybody called Buddy. He was twenty-three and full-grown, being almost twice my age. There was something about him I disliked and feared, even though he was attractive.

Buddy had attempted some passes, but Genevieve had always been around in her well-paid post as guardian of my virtue. While I was sick Buddy kept coming around to see me, and one night he asked me to marry him. It seemed to me that he wanted to marry me only because he couldn't get me any other way.

I told him I didn't want to marry him. I told Momweeze about his proposal and also that I didn't like him. But when Buddy kept on bothering me to marry him I told him:

"Ask Momweeze. If she says all right, I'll marry you."

I just wanted to get rid of him and counted on my mother to refuse, for she knew very well what I thought of Buddy. But when he asked her about it she double-crossed me by saying:

"Yes, you can marry my Ethel."

I felt betrayed and thought she'd agreed only because marrying me off to Buddy was an easy way of eliminating me as a problem.

I was thirteen. I was in the sixth grade and wouldn't be fourteen for six months. I believe the minimum age for marriage in Pennsylvania then was eighteen, but that didn't stop Buddy Purnsley from getting a license. Large though I was for my age, I didn't look any eighteen. So he just went and got another, older girl to go with him to Darby and got the license in my name.

Buddy found a local minister who would marry us. My wedding gown was a skirt and a blouse. That wedding was awful, and I was heartbroken because Mom couldn't be there. We were just two people standing in one of those smoky little rooms.

Having seen so much of the ugly side of life as a little girl, I dreaded the sex relationship. Yet I knew that sex had to happen to me as to everyone else. My wedding night, however, couldn't have been nastier or more unpleasant.

When Louise left for Atlantic City she gave us the furniture—along with the unpaid installment bills. "It will give you a start," she said. The installments—fifty cents a week for this, seventy-five cents for that—didn't seem much. But they are a lot when you are earning only a few dollars a week. Buddy had a job with the Pennsylvania Steel Casting Company and wasn't overpaid. I didn't know anything about cooking then, and his aunt Martha, who came to live with us, took care of that. She was nice, and so was his mother.

After I was married I continued going to school until June, when I finished the sixth grade. I worked after school hours and when school closed I went out, working by the day.

Buddy kept only older people around me. They thought a husband should be a czar and that the little wife should obey him, no matter how unreasonable he became.

I tried to do this. Being a Catholic, I believed seriously in marriage and I wanted to be a good wife. But Buddy insisted I give up everything I liked—dancing, roller skating, and my friends. He even tried to stop me from talking to the neighbors. He also bewildered me by accusing me of being unfaithful to him.

But what upset me most was Buddy's refusal to take me out to Aunt Ide's. I'd heard that Mom was getting steadily worse. One Sunday I went there with some people who lived out that way.

I found Mom lying on the same kind of broken-down couch she'd had in our house. She looked terribly ill, shrunken. She had cancer, and there was a big hole in her back. Now that I was being buffeted by a husband of my own I had a better understanding of the troubles that had been plaguing her all her life.

Sally Anderson was dying, and I knew it. She asked me to sing "His Eye Is on the Sparrow." As I sang it I wondered if it was the last time she'd ever hear it.

It was. On Friday of that week Vi came in from Ide's house. She said, "The doctor was just out there. I don't think Mom can make it."

I started out right away, but Mom had passed on by the time I got there. She was still lying on the couch, and I picked her up in my arms. With that big hole in her back, she weighed so little—ninety pounds, eighty pounds, nothing. I held Mom tight, Mom who had been all heart and fighting fury. I thought of how hard she'd worked for the little she'd wanted from life and how she never got that little —a clean shack to come back to on her day off, children who didn't disgrace her, the smell and the good taste of respectability. But she'd kept her head up, never quitting or whimpering. I thought, too, of how, after she had acknowledged defeat with her own children, she had turned to me, the unwanted, unloved one, seeing I was so much like her, bold, unvanquished as yet, and strong. . . .

I had the undertaker, Mrs. Parker, bring Mom to my house. She was embalmed and laid to rest there in her coffin. Each morning I would put the crape out for her. Then I would go in, sit down, and talk with her. But the woman in the coffin wasn't like Mom at all. At last there was peace on her face. The forefinger of her right hand had been bent at the first joint and she'd never been able to straighten out the second finger of that hand either. But the two fingers were straight now when she didn't need to use them any more. Yes, I talked to Mom. I tried to explain to her that now at last I understood everything and was for her all the way.

For some time Ching, whom Mom had always loved best of all her children, had been living with a man a few doors away in our alley. Ching had been drinking like a fish.

On the day set for the funeral Momweeze came up from Atlantic City. Vi, too, was there, and Charlie came from Philadelphia. Only Ching, whom Mom loved best and who lived just a few doors away, couldn't make it.

Ching was so drunk she couldn't leave the house. But when they brought the coffin out into the dusty, littered alley Ching was sitting at her window, watching it all. And she was singing in her sweet, low voice "Flee as a Bird," a song she and Mom had always loved.

Momweeze was mad at Ching for getting so drunk she couldn't attend her own mother's funeral. But I thought I understood it. Ching, once so gay and carefree, just couldn't face seeing Mom being buried in the earth.

The next day I went to see Ching. "How was it, Ethel?" she asked. She was quite calm but very much on the defensive. I described Mom's last illness and the funeral, and Ching listened, nodding her head. I think she was regretting never being able to stop drinking too much. If it hadn't been for that she and Mom could have been so much closer.

And three months later Ching, too, was dead from grief over losing Mom.

With Mom and Ching both gone, things got worse for me. I felt I was being slowly suffocated and began to beat my wings a little. I was getting fed up with Buddy's charges that I was unfaithful and his refusal to allow me to see my young friends. Often he berated and beat me.

I couldn't understand it. I was doing everything possible to please him but getting only scorn and abuse. His reason for beating me confused me most of all. He said he did that only because he loved me so much and was jealous.

If I protested, "But, Buddy, I've done nothing to make you jealous!" he would shake his head as though it were impossible to believe. Sometimes I thought, "Perhaps marriage is like this, with the wife expected to give up everything and get nothing in return."

One night I came home and Buddy was waiting for me. He jumped on me and beat me until both his brother and Aunt Martha interfered.

"Don't you dare hit her again," Marth said.

With my face all bruised I told her, "It's all right. I'm going to leave him. If I don't I'll just have to kill him."

Some of the maniacal anger and determination I was capable of must have come through because Buddy was so startled he didn't say anything. As a further challenge I purposely stayed out late the next night, going to see my cousin who lived uptown. When I got home my dinner was on the table and Buddy had no questions to ask. He seemed contrite, and I said nothing more about the beating.

But I'd made up my mind to leave him, though I had to stay there for a while until I'd paid off the bills for Mom's funeral. And it was not long before I discovered why he'd pretended to be jealous of me.

Our court was on Banana Avenue, on one side of Fulton Street. On the opposite side of Fulton Street was a place called Longbottom's Gut, and on his way to work in the steel plant Buddy usually stopped over there. Whenever I'd asked him why, he said, "Got business there."

In the corner of our alley lived an old woman who didn't know who I was. One day as she watched Buddy go off to work she said:

"That's a nice little fellow. Never saw a man so attentive to his girl."

"What girl is that?" I asked.

She described the girl, whom I recognized as an old flame of Buddy's named Pearl. I didn't lose my head, but learning that he was unfaithful, along with everything else, almost killed me.

Buddy had beaten me, humiliated me, and accused me of being unfaithful. On the excuse of loving me madly he'd deprived me of my friends and all pleasure. To find out that all the time he'd been mistreating me he'd been messing around with another girl drove me wild.

Most infuriating of all was the realization that he had fought me and cursed me out all along just because he was two-timing me. Preventing me from talking to my friends was his way of making sure they wouldn't tell me about Pearl. By beating me so much he probably hoped to get me so cowed I'd be afraid to leave when and if I ever did find out about her.

A lot of the old Ethel came out, and once more I didn't come home until very late that night. His mother asked me where I had been.

"How is Pearl?" I asked my little husband.

"What Pearl? Who is Pearl?"

Then for the first time I stood foot to foot with Buddy. I told him that Pearl was a young slut who lived over in the Gut and it was to see her that he stopped on his way to the plant each morning. I worked him over with my entire set of vile words, and my timing and diction were superb. That night I called Buddy everything but "child of God."

I was in such a flaming rage that I frightened him. He even asked Aunt Marth to interfere.

"Don't leave him, Ethel," she said.

"What do you want me to do?" I asked. "Now that I know about Pearl I'd better go, leaving him alive. If I stay Buddy will soon be dead."

When I got into bed he got in with me. But all I had to say was "Don't touch me!" and he didn't. He was acting very chastened and sorry.

But I still didn't quite dare to leave, being, even after all that, frightened of what he might do. When I'd paid off for Mom's funeral I started to work double duty to get five dollars together as quickly as possible. I got out my old straw suitcase and began to gather up my winter underwear. Louise was back in Philadelphia, and I wrote her that I wanted to leave Buddy and live with her. She approved of my leaving him, though she had let me marry him only a few months before.

I had too good sense to antagonize Buddy and didn't tell him I was planning to go away. He never suspicioned that I would leave him because I said nothing more about it. But he sensed that something unusual was going on and tried to be nice to me.

"Give me a chance. I won't fight you any more," he kept saying now that it was too late.

My break came when Buddy decided to go and work out of town for a few weeks. I said I'd visit Louise while he was gone, and he took me to the trolley car.

I was at Louise's five weeks and got many letters and postcards from Buddy. He sent a little money, fifteen or twenty dollars all together.

I started going again to Pop Grey's, but the men there meant nothing to me. All of them looked just like Buddy.

I've always been conscious of having an extra sense. One morning when I woke up I had the feeling that I'd see Buddy that day. I washed all my clothes and hung them out until our clothesline was dancing with my little middy blouses.

And in the afternoon, when I was walking down South Street, I heard my husband call after me. I turned around, looked at him, and decided I didn't like him any better than before.

After asking me why I hadn't answered his letters he said, "You know why I'm here, don't you? I've come to take you back."

I decided to give my marriage another chance. Maybe it would work out better this time, I thought. And I had deep religious scruples against breaking up a marriage. Also, I didn't have much idea of what my rights were, and I was afraid of what Buddy might do to me if I refused to go back with him.

But I was determined, just the same, not to stay with Buddy if I didn't want to. I made him wait outside while I went into the house to tell Genevieve to take my clothes off the line but not to send them to me in Chester unless I wrote asking her to.

When Buddy and I got home we resumed our marital relationship. Though I let it happen, I afterward felt defiled and besmirched. Then it was that I knew I could never be happy with Buddy and would have to leave him for good.

He must have been afraid of that because he refused to go to work for three days and just sat around the house. I worked each day in order to lay away a little money. I was always able to go back to any place where I'd worked before. The people I worked for were always glad to see me come back.

On the fourth day Buddy announced he would go back to work. Meekly he asked me to bring him his lunch, and I agreed to do that.

I packed the few belongings I had left in Chester into paper boxes. When I brought Buddy his lunch at the steel plant he asked me to kiss him. I did, knowing it was good-by. As far as I was concerned, my husband was just a lost ball in the high weeds. I went home to pick up my paper boxes and took the trolley car to Philadelphia.

During the next few weeks I was bombarded with postcards and letters from Buddy telling how brokenhearted he was and saying he'd commit suicide if I didn't come back to him.

I wrote one answer to all these and the messages that came from his family. I wrote, "If you dare set foot on this here soil of Philadelphia I'll have you put in jail for the bad things you did to me."

The marriage had lasted less than a year. Only once during the next year, when I went to South Chester, did I see Buddy. He said, "You're a hard loser!" and asked me to come back to him. I just cursed him down, for he no longer meant a thing. That husband of mine, who had once been so terrifying, had become just another termite to me.

At thirteen I was married, and at fourteen I was separated and on my own. I had a certain amount of battle cry in me.

Having no one but Momweeze to hold onto now that Mom was gone, I worked hard to win her affection. I gave her a servant-like devotion, but I couldn't get close. Her answer to everything I did was "I borned you! I borned you!"

Sometimes I think this big size of mine has prevented me from becoming a human being. Nobody's protective instinct ever seems to be aroused by a huge girl. I was so eager to feel sheltered and have people like me. I was hungry for a kind word. When it didn't come I cried inwardly, but, being myself, I also began to build up my defenses.

Looking back now, I can remember that I was a thin-structured child with a pretty face. But no one then, or ever, could convince me that I had any physical charms.

I started to work in hotels as a substitute for dishwashers, cleaning women, waitresses, or bus boys, whoever happened to have a day off. Such jobs were always available because the work was so rugged. And I was efficient and always worked hard at whatever I was given to do. I guess the feeling of being unwanted and belonging to nobody made me eager to give satisfaction and win the respect of my employers.

My mother had been working as a scullion at the Harrod Apartments in Philadelphia, and when she got sick I replaced her. That was the first place I ever was employed on a steady basis. I looked forward to working with the same crowd of people every day. There were eleven in help at the Harrod Apartments besides me—four bellboys and a substitute, a head cook and second cook, two chambermaids, and two waitresses.

Most of the women were old and decrepit-looking. Some of them had false hair. But without exception they all worked hard to look younger.

At the beginning the bellboys and other male employees considered me new and refreshing material. Paul, the head bellboy, got the shock of his life when his advances were greeted by my usual volcanic profanity. So did the other house Romeos.

If the Harrod house staff had held a popularity contest I guess I would have ended up last. When I substituted for a waitress I gave first-rate service. I scrubbed, mopped, and washed dishes as though I loved the work. I was baffled when my co-workers behaved as though I was trying to show them up.

Once when I got only a dime for serving a meal to a large party the cook said, "I would have thrown the dime in their faces."

"Nobody has to give me a tip if he doesn't want to," I told her.

I couldn't understand the attitude of the other employees toward me. The work I was doing meant my food. I couldn't see any reason to shirk. I was happy to be working in a nice place, run by nice people.

We got the food the customers hadn't eaten. Soon I noticed that when this food was distributed there was never anything good to eat on my tray, no butter or nice vegetables, nothing I liked. I was eating eggs every day. This went on until I blew up and cursed Rebecca, the cook, after she asked me for the steenth time, "Would you like some eggs today?"

Rebecca burst into tears and complained to the housekeeper, Miss Rice. Miss Rice was a kind woman. But she liked her nips and her hair bun was always a little awry.

"I get scraps of food just like the scraps of work I've been doing," I told her. "I've eaten so many eggs I could cackle. I don't want to eat one more motherless egg."

After that I got my fair share. Of course there was another reason for those older women resenting me, besides the fact that I worked with the speed of a girl shot out of a cannon. I was young, my hair was waist-length, and I had those big eyes. But like every other young person, I had no idea that youth was a treasure that inspired envy and hate in vain, older women who found themselves pressing middle age.

I had the most fun at the Harrod Apartments on the days when I substituted for one of the chambermaids. I was allotted a half-hour to make up each room but soon became so efficient I could finish the work in ten minutes.

Then I'd lock the door, stand in front of the full-length mirror, and transform myself into Ethel Waters, the great actress. I played all sorts of roles and also the audience, mugging and acting like mad.

First of all I'd applaud vociferously. When I played the "other woman" in the play I'd pretend she was some girl enemy of mine and hiss her shamelessly. Was she a terrible performer!

When I'd finish portraying all the roles I'd seen played by Negro stock companies I'd imitate the acts I'd seen at the Standard Theatre in Philadelphia, great Negro actors like Drake and Walker; Sandy Burns, the comic; Sam Russell, the Bilow of Bilow and Ashes; Butterbeans and Susie, the Original Stringbeans; and the truly gifted Whitman Sisters. I'd also imitate the performers I'd seen in the beer grottoes and rathskellers around Philadelphia where I sometimes extravagantly drank cream soda at twenty-five cents a bottle.

The vaudeville half of the entertainment started with an announcement by the master of ceremonies: "And now, folks, the famous and spectacular Miss Ethel Waters will sing!" Again there was wild applause from the eager audience, followed by joyful cries of:

"Come on, Miss Waters! Please sing for us, Miss Waters!"

After a slight and dignified pause I'd persuade myself to bow graciously before the mirror. Sometimes I'd be so carried away by my own magnificent performance that I'd forget where I was or what I was doing.

In spite of all this, my big ambition was not then show business. What I dreamed of was becoming the lady's maid and companion of some wealthy woman who was traveling around the world and would take me with her.

But it was about this time that I adopted a manner that caused people to mistake me for a theatrical performer. I was always pleased when they asked, "Are you a show person?" But I'd tell them, "No, I work as a scullion in the Harrod Apartments."

Sometimes I thought it must be my clothes that made them think I was an actress. I was still buying these at the welfare places and rummage sales and was convinced these secondhand outfits showed me off to great advantage. I told myself I didn't give a damn what others thought of my appearance, but I was delighted whenever complimented.

Each year when it got warm large numbers of Philadelphia's working folks went off to jobs in Atlantic City, Asbury Park, and Wildwood, New Jersey. The summer I was fifteen I became a waitress in one of the big white hotels in Wildwood.

Because of my uncanny memory and eagerness to please I was one hell of a good waitress. The cook in the hotel loved me and called me "Baby" because I shared my extra-big tips with her. And whenever a customer handed me a dollar to give the cook, she really got it. I never kept that money like some of the other girls did.

Once, in Wildwood, one of the other waitresses tried to trip me up with a tray. But only that once. I told her, "Any of you bitches who try to mess me better be prepared to sleep here all night. Because I'll knock down the first one who tries it."

I had a good time in Wildwood, particularly on week ends. Each Saturday and Sunday all us hotel workers went to a little saloon where there was a piano. It had a very tinny tone because it had been close to the salt water for so long. I sang and danced there for the cooks, bus boys, cleaning women, and other waitresses.

One day a very light-complected middle-aged man who looked a good deal like Walter White does now walked up to me in the hotel dining room.

"Aren't you Ethel?" he said. "What's your last name?"

"Purnsley," I told him.

When he said he'd heard I was Ethel Waters I explained about my marriage. "My name is Wright," he said, "and I'm married to your grandmother, Lydia Waters. She's hurt, Ethel. She lives here and you've been working here all summer, yet you haven't gone to see her once."

"But I haven't been in contact with her for years, Mr. Wright."

"Do me a favor, Ethel, will you? Go around to see her the next time you have a day off?"

I promised I would, and he wrote out the address on a card.

The house Lydia Waters lived in was a big colonial-type home with tall white pillars in front. I started for the side door, but there was a "Beware of the Dog!" sign there, so I rang the front-door bell. A very impressive woman, who looked white, answered my ring. I apologized for using the front entrance and explained who I was.

"I'm Lydia Waters, your grandmother," she said, and took me in her arms. I felt uncomfortable because I couldn't think of her as anything but a stranger whom Mom had regarded as our enemy.

She brought me into the house and tried to be cordial and affectionate, but I just couldn't let her pet me and fondle me. However, when she asked me to stay with her, I did—for a couple of weeks off and on.

I think my grandmother was drawn to me belatedly because there had recently been another tragedy in her life similar to that brought on by the poisoning of my father.

John Waters had left three sons. Elvi, the eldest of these three, had died under mysterious circumstances the previous summer. A brilliant young pianist, he had competed for first prize—a fellowship in a leading academy—in a music contest. All entries but Elvi and another boy had been eliminated. Then one day Elvi's rival and some other youngsters had invited him out in a fishing boat. They started skylarking and wrestling, finally capsizing the boat. Elvi, the only one in the party who couldn't swim, had drowned.

This second tragedy had been almost too much for Lydia Waters to bear. Just as my father had been her favorite son, Elvi had been the grandchild she loved best. People afterward told me that Elvi had looked enough like me to be my twin. I believe that when she saw how closely I resembled both her loved ones she might have been conscience-stricken and wished to make amends for neglecting me.

But it was too late and no good. Our lives and our manner of living differed so that Lydia Waters and I had absolutely nothing to say to each other. We were destined always to be strangers. It was difficult for me even to call her Grandma, as she wished.

Though she lived long enough to see me enter show business, I never saw her again after that summer in Wildwood. During the last years of her life she sent word to me several times that she was gravely ill, but I never answered her summons.

I had no desire to see her. And in Wildwood I'd noticed signs of jealousy among the relatives who had been around her all their lives. They feared, I think, that I, the little brat who had dropped from nowhere, might wean her away from them and be willed some of her money. I wanted neither their enmity nor her money.

I've always thought that I inherited some of the better qualities of both my grandmothers. From little Sally Anderson, who died in defeat and the grimmest poverty, I got my fighting heart. From Lydia Waters, who died rich but heartbroken and quite possibly tortured by a bad conscience, I think I inherited poise, dignity, and whatever intelligence I have.

No purpose would be served in condemning my white grandmother. People are what they are and are sometimes governed by impulses and forces that are difficult for others to understand. Besides, I learned early in life not to judge others. We outcasts are very happy and content to leave that job to our social superiors.

6

October 31, 1917, was a big day in my life. It was my seventeenth birthday, and I sneaked into the back room of Jack's Rathskeller, where there was a big Halloween party going on. Jack's was on the corner of Juniper and South. No one under twenty-one was supposed to be allowed in Philadelphia saloons. Some of the fellows at the door were the saloon men who had fed me hot meals when I was a hungry little kid. They would have turned me away, but they didn't recognize me because I was wearing a mask. And I was big enough to be twenty-one.

There are some advantages in being so big, even if they usually come in crumb-size packages.

That night many well-known professional entertainers were in Jack's Rathskeller, including Carrie Nugent, the sensational Negro tap dancer who'd hoofed her way around the world and been admired and acclaimed everywhere.

Youngsters representing the wards all over Philadelphia were supposed to compete in entertaining at that party. I was living in the old Seventh Ward. The girl who was supposed to perform for our district never showed up, and somebody at my table yelled:

"Chippie sings! Come on, Chippie, sing for the old Seventh."

I was Chippie.

I had a sweet, bell-like voice. On a clear night you could hear me singing from five blocks away. However, I seldom depended on my voice to win social recognition.

I had developed into a really agile shimmy shaker. I sure knew how to roll and quiver, and my hips would become whirling dervishes. It was these completely mobile hips, not my voice, that won me friends and inspired admiration.

But at that Halloween party at Jack's I sang. In places like that, when there was a party, there was usually a three-man band—piano, guitar, and drums. At least one of the boys could sing and the drummer went in for original and spectacular effects. Some of those boys just out for a good time did all the wonderful things great modern drummers do now.

Joe Jenkins was at the piano in Jack's that night. He was a big, fat kid who could play anything, do anything with the keys. He knew every song, published and unpublished. Joe played just about everywhere, uptown and downtown. The place was jammed whenever he played, and you could count on having to fight your way in and fight your way out.

When you went to any such social event you knew it was all going to start off nice and peaceful and end up in a big free-for-all, with the air full of uppercuts and wild bellowings. During the evening somebody was sure to grab off someone else's chick or step on other people's feet, egos, or emotions.

To us kids it was all part of the good clean fun. As we came in the door we knew that before the party was over the Black Maria would roll up and the cops would rush in to find out what all the noise and hell-raising was about.

And that night at Jack's, Chippie Waters got up and sang the tearful ballad, "When You're a Long, Long Way from Home." The crowd liked my rich, young voice, and I had to give two or three encores.

Among the professionals there were Braxton and Nugent, who had a small vaudeville unit. They said that if I would work on the stage with them they could get me ten dollars a week.

The idea scared me. I considered myself the world's greatest entertainer—but only in a hotel room and behind locked doors where I was safe from criticism.

I told Braxton and Nugent that I was seventeen, too young to be on the stage. I was getting three-fifty a week as a scullion and chambermaid and a dollar and a quarter more for taking home some of the guests' laundry. But that was steady work, something I'd learned to keep a half nelson on whenever possible.

The two vaudevillians talked it over with my mother. They told her they could get me two weeks down in Baltimore if she would only sign a paper swearing I was twenty-one. She signed without any arguments. Momweeze would have signed anything that brought in ten dollars a week. I couldn't see any bright future for myself in show business.

And I refused to go on the stage until she promised to replace me in my cleaning woman's job and to hold it for me until I got back from Baltimore.

I bought the dress for my debut at a rummage store. It was eggshell satin, had buttons down the front, and fastened up around the neck. It was like a Russian dress, and on a scrawny, young crane like me it was a costume.

I wanted to sing a new number that I'd once heard Charles Anderson, a very good female impersonator, do. Braxton and Nugent said it was a restricted song and I'd have to get permission from the copyright owners, Pace and Handy, in Memphis, Tennessee, before I could sing it on the stage.

There was no radio then killing off popular songs in six weeks. Some song publishers permitted only one or two acts to do their restricted numbers. The idea was that these performers would feature the restricted song in their turn wherever they played, and in that way it would slowly become popular all over the country.

The song I wanted to sing was "St. Louis Blues."

Pace and Handy answered my letter by granting me permission. That was how I, a seventeen-year-old novice, became the first woman —and the second person—ever to sing professionally that song which is now a classic and, according to many people, the greatest blues ever written.

Glamorous is not quite the word for the Lincoln Theatre in Baltimore and the other houses I played that first season. Often there were no wings to the tiny stages, no backstage, and no dressing rooms.

Then you had to dress down under the stage, behind a thin partition. On the other side there was another partition behind which the men dressed. If someone was dancing on the stage you got out of there fast. If you didn't, plaster came down on your head.

To get on-stage you came out through the orchestra pit and jumped up a ladder. You tried to get on the stage before the lights went on again. There were no footlights, only lights on the side and one little spotlight covered with colored isinglass.

When this isinglass broke or fell off, you looked like hell. But working from nine in the morning until unconscious, you began to look like hell, anyway, around midnight.

Even if there were wings in these theaters, it wasn't so good. They were made of cardboard and would fall down on your head if you walked by them heavily.

Most of the acts were sad as McKinley's funeral. Almost always the audience gave a peppier performance than the people they'd come to see.

Rugged individualists all, they did whatever they pleased while you were killing yourself on the stage. They ran up and down the aisles, yelling greetings to friends and sometimes having fights. And they brought everything to eat from bananas to yesterday's pork chops.

But they also were the most appreciative audiences in the world if they liked you. They'd scream, stomp, and applaud until the whole building shook. Years later, when I first stepped before a white audience, I thought I was a dead duck because no one tried to tear the house down. They merely clapped their hands. Such restraint is almost a sneer in the colored vaudeville world I came out of.

Braxton and Nugent had another man performer and two girls, the Hill Sisters, working with them. So they made me the third Hill sister.

I was so frightened the first time I walked out on a stage that Nugent had to hold my arm to prevent me from falling flat on my face. Our entrance was a man-and-wife argument, and I sank into a rocking chair soon as I could, happy to get off my feet.

Acting disgusted, Nugent would say, "I'm going off to my other chick."

"Don't leave me, sugar," I'd plead. "Please don't leave me."

After Nugent went off I'd sit there, rocking sadly and slowly.

"When I see how my man treats me," I'd moan, "I get the St. Louis Blues."

Then I would sing "St. Louis Blues," but very softly. It was the first time that kind of Negro audience ever let my kind of low singing get by. And you could have heard a pin drop in that rough, rowdy audience out front.

For years they had been used to Bessie Smith and Ma Rainey. They loved them and all the other shouters. I could always riff and jam and growl, but I never had that loud approach.

That first time, when I finished singing "St. Louis Blues," the money fell like rain on the stage. Nugent had to come on again to get me off or I would have been sitting there yet. But first he picked up the silver for me—the white money, as it sometimes is respectfully called.

I started sending home money at the end of that first week out of my ten dollars and the coins Nugent turned over to me. I've never stopped that and never will want to. Helping my family has always been the biggest satisfaction I've got out of show business.

Even the applause didn't convince me I was all right. After each performance I'd take off my make-up, including my Ford Sterling eyebrows, and rush out to the lobby to hear what the people were saying about me as they came out. They didn't recognize me without my make-up. No photographs had been taken of me for the lobby displays. Instead of that, the management had put out an enormous picture of a big, fat woman. Written under this was:

> Sweet Mama Stringbean, direct from St. Louis
> And singing "St. Louis Blues"

They called me Sweet Mama Stringbean because I was so scrawny and tall. And maybe because there was a very famous male Stringbeans in Negro vaudeville at the time.

So there I'd stand, I who was direct from the mops and pails of the Harrod Apartments and not St. Louis, next to a picture that looked nothing like me, and listen eagerly to the comments.

"Dammit," one man would say, "that old long gal wasn't bad."

"Yep," another would agree, "that bitch sure can sing."

It was all right. These men were no Brooks Atkinsons, but rough-and-ready, fast men with the brass knuckles. They were giving me the most delicate compliments in their vocabulary.

And before each performance I'd get down on my knees and ask God to make the people out front like me. He always did, and when I came off I'd offer Him another little prayer of thanks. I still pray before each show, only I don't get down on my knees. I've found out that God doesn't mind whether you kneel, sit down, or stand up so long as you pray to Him sincerely.

Sweet Mama Stringbean stopped working with Braxton and Nugent the night we concluded our two weeks' engagement in Baltimore. We'd been paid off. The lights had been put out in the theater, and the boys thought I'd left.

But I was still there and I heard them having one hell of an argument. Braxton was complaining with great bitterness that he ought to be given a chance to alternate with Nugent in the work of picking up the coins that were thrown on the stage after I sang "St. Louis Blues."

"I want a crack at palming that money," he told his partner.

Nugent said, "You are too greedy, man, for this bighearted world. Don't we split the twenty-five dollars a week we get for Ethel's act right down the middle, after we pay off her ten? I was first to think of hiring her, so I have honest claim on all the extra money I go South with."

That's when I interrupted the conversation. I walked in, told them what I thought of them, and said I was going home.

But I didn't go back to Philadelphia.

Maggie and Jo Hill said they were quitting the show, too, and invited me to join their act. The girls thought we could get fifty dollars a week in most towns. My third, they pointed out, plus the money thrown on the stage, would mean I'd do all right. So I went off with them on a big tour including the South.

There were no Negro vaudeville circuits then, and the Hills took care of all the business details. Whenever we'd get booked into a city they'd write, enclosing photographs, to theaters in nearby places, asking for dates. Sometimes we could get only thirty-five dollars for the act, so the big trick was to avoid long railway jumps between engagements. None of the theaters paid traveling expenses, although they would advance enough for railroad fare.

For our act the Hill Sisters and I did the same numbers that we'd done in Baltimore. I sang, besides "St. Louis Blues," "I'm Going to Shake That Tree until the Nuts Come Down," "I Wanna Be Somebody's Baby Doll So I Can Get My Lovin' All the Time," and "Come Right In and Stay a While, There Ain't Nobody Here but Me."

Our finish was a number together in kid clothes. In the five-and-dime stores we'd buy lace and sew it on the short dresses we wore in that part of the act. We'd put pink, yellow, and red slips under the dresses. The Hills danced, were kickers, and did the split, and I had nice-looking legs. When singing my numbers I'd wear my hair up in a Merry Widow roll. But for the kid routine I'd let it down, and it looked pretty, hanging down to my waist. The Hills both wore false hair.

White men owned and ran most of the little ramshackle theaters we played. Each night you had to be careful to take home everything, leaving nothing at all in the theater. The management held itself responsible neither for your property nor your life.

Of all those rinky-dink dumps I played, nothing was worse than the Monogram Theatre in Chicago. It was close to the El, and the walls were so thin that you stopped singing—or telling a joke—every time a train passed. Then, when the noise died down, you continued right where you left off.

In the Monogram you dressed away downstairs with the stoker. The ceiling down there was so low I had to bend over to get my stage clothes on. Then you came up to the stage on a ladder that looked like those on the old-time slave ships.

Ever since I worked at the Monogram any old kind of dressing room has looked pretty good to me so long as it had a door that could be closed.

It never occurred to me to grumble about the discomforts connected with playing those little theaters. One of the few advantages of being born poor and hungry is that you expect very little and learn to take everything in your stride. And with plaster falling down on my head as I dressed and undressed, with all the whooping and stomping—and sometimes fighting—that was going on out front, every week seemed like Old Home Week to me.

Momweeze kept writing me for money. I'd send what I could and write back to her to be sure to hold onto that cleaning job at the Harrod Apartments so I could get it again when I returned to Philadelphia. That's how little sense of security I was getting out of my life as Sweet Mama Stringbean.

That tour with the Hill Sisters was a gay adventure, though, exhilarating and interesting. It followed the patchwork pattern of my childhood—melodrama all mixed up with belly laughs. Only now the gay surprises predominated.

America had already entered World War I, but we three girls were only dimly aware of it. We kept pretty much to the tattered and battered sections of the towns we visited, and there we saw no soldiers, no Negro doughboys either in our audiences or on the streets. For all I knew, no Negroes had been drafted. If there were any in the Army, they weren't getting any furloughs, certainly not in the South.

Working from nine in the morning until midnight, sometimes

1 A.M., you would have thought we wouldn't have much time for social life.

But the Hills, who came from a small town, were butterflies and they wanted to live full lives. They were good girls, but gullible to flattery. Going out on parties held enchantment for them. I was different, having already seen enough of night life as a kid on Clifton Street to last me the rest of my days.

The boys who chased Maggie and Jo were always coaxing me to go along and make it a sixsome. But I wouldn't drink anything but soda pop, and I'm afraid I was something of a wet blanket.

I dressed plain, but my partners were always spending more on clothes than they could afford. Every time we hit a new town the Hill Sisters got all wound up and ready to go. Such titivating! The minute we checked into our broken-down rooms they would frantically look over their clothes as they unpacked, run out to buy something new and resplendent, press the clothes, and then promenade down the main drag of the Negro section. They talked of nothing but this big shot here, that big shot there.

Those Hills were always in a dither—and a dream. Though we were working like coolies, eating in dingy Greek restaurants and living in those broken-down rooms, nothing could stop them from thinking of themselves as terrific actresses.

For one thing, in each town the local boys would make a mad dash to get dates. I always liked the ordinary working fellows. The college boys who were learning to be doctors and lawyers gave me a pain.

I could never understand why the Hills should think them so wonderful. They never took us to better eating places than did my uneducated and uncultured admirers. They weren't regular, but just squares who had read a book or two.

But then, all my life I've been prejudiced against wealthy people. No one has ever been able to convince me that Park Avenue folks are as good as my Tenth Avenue friends. There's no hypocrisy in Hell's Kitchen and also much understanding of the shortcomings of others.

Poverty works like a steam roller, crushing a lot of people. But, like the steam roller, it's also a great leveler. In the slums you find out early in life that if you get hungry enough you'll do anything for a meal. Even after you've had the breaks you remember that. Unless you're a complete phony, you never find it possible to think yourself superior to those who haven't had your luck. You can't even despise thieves.

You only can pity them because the jails are so big and strong and always crowded with poor, hungry, desperate men just like them.

The enterprise of those smart-aleck college boys was what burned me up most. I didn't put up any big battle against having dinner with them, though. They were basking in our glamour, weren't they? What greater glory could they expect for taking us to the Greek's place where pork chops cost only fifteen cents?

Even while I was listening to their compliments I would be thinking, "If I meet this John walking with his sister tomorrow morning, he won't even say 'Hello!' to me."

When the college boys took us home they always asked hopefully, "May we come upstairs?" Out of the extra money I was making I always would try to pay for a second room so I could sleep there alone, and I'd go to bed, not caring much for the company. But before long one of the hot-stuff college fellows would stroll in and say even more politely, "May I spend the night?"

That would bring out the old sassy Ethel, and I'd reply, "That depends entirely on how much you have to spend." That answer would stagger them because I knew those tinhorn sports didn't have fifteen cents left in their pockets after buying us a cheap meal.

"But this is a loving match!" the guy would always say.

"It ain't no loving match for Sweet Mama Stringbean, who is strictly a businesswoman," I'd tell him, and set my price at ten, fifteen, or twenty dollars.

"But don't you like me at all?"

"I neither like nor dislike you, buster."

"I never dreamed you were that kind of girl," he'd say as he tottered out, broken in spirit.

Now, I never posed as a saint. But the scars from my months with Buddy hadn't healed. However, I would have slept with a man for nothing if I liked him well enough. I felt that those conceited young doctors- and lawyers-to-be had a yen for us only because they'd seen us on the stage. We were, for the moment, in the public eye, and they could count on us to be here today and gone forever tomorrow.

While we were playing a split week in Pittsburgh, though, I did meet one decent little fellow and got to like him. This boy fell in love with me and became quite serious. He was young and harmless, by which I mean he wasn't all over me like some old octopus.

And when he bought me meals I never felt I was chiseling. We were making so little money that we had to economize somewhere, and he got my company and good will, which was all he wanted.

Now this was the first decent, clean boy I'd ever met. I enjoyed sitting in my room with him just having pleasant and interesting conversation.

My admirer wanted to be a fighter and was a worshiper of the body beautiful. He didn't talk about anything except how he was developing his muscles so he could be a champion in the ring. He was always asking me to feel his biceps and describing his training methods. Like old Bernarr MacFadden, he was hipped on the idea that physical strength and good health are the answer to all of life's little problems.

What he liked best about me, I think, was that I, being an extomboy, would box and spar with him in my room. He taught me to lead with my left, roll with the punches, and to step in and throw the paralyzing counter punch to the bread basket when my opponent missed.

This may sound like a weird romance, but I found these pugilistic sessions fascinating. And the way I was living, I couldn't tell when these instructions in the art of self-defense and slugging might come in handy.

My little lightweight had me meet his family. When we left Pittsburgh he came down to the station to see me off. I knew he was trying to get up courage enough to ask me to marry him, and I did my best to head him off.

But he did ask me. I tried to think of a tactful way to let him down easy. But I was young and hadn't had much experience in letting people down easy, was much better at blasting and blockbusting.

So I said, "I have to answer your flattering proposal with a confession. I guess you've noticed that I don't go out on parties like the other girls. There's a reason for that which also explains why I separated from my husband. My doctors aren't absolutely sure yet, but they think I may have syphilis."

I thought that my little lightweight, so mad about good health, prime condition, and uncontaminated blood streams, would surely be discouraged.

But he wasn't. He had the heart of a champion. He even offered to pay the bills of my baffled doctors. "Even if they decide that you have syphilis," he said, "I will wait for you to be cured, and then I'll marry you."

I could only give him a vague and dreamy smile as I got on the train.

By that time I was getting pretty well known. When we'd come to a town we'd find banners draped across the street, advertising:

"The Hill Sisters, Featuring Sweet Mama Stringbean, Singing 'St. Louis Blues.' "

And I was also starting to find out what professional jealousy was like. My partners, Maggie and Jo Hill, had been in show business for three or four years. They knew I'd been a scullion. Though it mystified me at the time, I understand now why they resented my becoming the star of the act and their having to watch people throw money at me while nobody was tossing so much as an old doughnut at them.

In spite of this, when we were on the road we three Hill Sisters always stuck together. My partners knew that when they went out drinking they could depend on Beany. I drank only cream soda, and if one of them got sick I could get her home all right and see she wasn't robbed or raped.

When we were in Detroit we met a fellow who had a stable—that is, a string of women working on the street for him. One night he talked Maggie Hill into going to a dance with him. I told Maggie that it was dangerous to have a date with this kind of sporting man.

"Suppose you meet one of his women?" I said. "That could mean bad trouble. Sometimes those girls love their pimps and they'll cut up any girl they see with him."

But she wouldn't listen. Jo was going, too, and they coaxed me into going along. When we got to the dance I told Maggie, "I'll sit at a table on the side. Give me your pocketbook. I'll hold it for you."

I had hardly sat down when Jo came rushing up. "Come on, Beany," she said. "Maggie is in a fight." But when I hurried after Jo and into the next room there didn't seem to be such a hell of a fight going on.

As I came through the door Maggie threw a beer bottle straight at me. I never did understand how she didn't see me coming. The beer bottle hit me right in the center of the forehead. A big egg jumped out of my head, and the bottle bounced off and broke into pieces. One of these jagged pieces cut a boy standing nearby so much that he had to have four stitches.

I wanted to go to sleep, but everybody made me walk around and around. They said it was very bad to go to sleep when you had been knocked unconscious.

The next day I had rainbow eyes—black and blue, red and purple. I hadn't wanted to go to that dance and I was sure right. And I don't know yet whether Maggie hit me with that bottle just accidentally.

We went on traveling, though, as partners. I wanted to be a good partner and a good buddy. But after a while even small things began to be resented by the Hills. For instance, having more money than them—I was averaging thirty dollars a week with those gift offerings— I'd pay some kid ten or fifteen cents a day to light the fire in our rooms an hour or so before we came home from the theater. But if I was broke those kids would do it for me for nothing. But they wouldn't do anything for free for Maggie and Jo. My partners didn't like that.

Yet when anything important was happening and the big chips were down, the Hills were always on my side. Another night in Detroit we went out with some fellows who looked to me like sporting men.

One of those pimps put knockout drops in my drink. I took a sip or two and felt dizzy. "Maggie, I feel funny," I said. She took me straight home. If those two girls hadn't got frightened at seeing me look sick they mightn't have rushed me home. The sporting men yelled their heads off about that, but Maggie and Jo got me home and safely in bed. If they hadn't been buddies that night, I know the most terrible thing that can happen to a woman would have happened to me.

That is the gang-up. Men like those put you to sleep with their drops. Then one man after another goes in and takes you. Then these men go all over town next day and boast of what they've done to you.

Yes, I think I know by now all the bad things that can happen to a woman. And the gang-up is the worst.

When we got to Cincinnati we had quite a layoff. So we did what lots of Negro acts do when hard-pressed for eating money: we got jobs with a carnival. It was Bob White's Greater Shows which we joined in Lexington, Kentucky. The colored people in Lexington wouldn't let carnival show girls into their homes, so we couldn't get a room.

We ended up sleeping in the carnival's stable. The Hill Sisters, who never stopped thinking of themselves as terrific actresses, didn't care for this arrangement. They considered it quite a comedown to have to sleep in a stable. But we put down straw, spread canvas over it, and went to sleep there.

I didn't mind. For once, there were no bedbugs to disturb my dreams. The horseflies also co-operated beautifully by sticking close to the horses.

I pointed out to Maggie and Jo that Jesus Christ himself had been born in a stable without getting any inferiority complex over it. I said that it wasn't as though we were forced to share sleeping quarters with broken-down nags or vulgar beer-wagon horses. Only blue-ribbon winners, prize horses that many a highborn horseflesh fancier would have been proud to sleep with, were our companions. But nothing would comfort them.

Baby Jim, the show's fat man, had to sleep in the stable, too, but for a different reason. He weighed between four and five hundred pounds. Like all carnival fat men, he was supposed to be the fattest in the world. In all Lexington there was no house with a door big enough for Baby Jim to get through, and no bed strong enough to hold his weight.

Again we worked from 9 A.M. to 1 A.M. The Hill Sisters and I got eighteen dollars a week each, sleeping space in the stable, and meals. The food was so bad, though, that we often couldn't eat it. Being tried-and-true performers, we furnished hot competition for the cootch dancers, headed by Zalla, the top attraction in the Plantation section of the carnival. Bob White was a good spieler, and we Hills were packing them in at every show. Going on the bally in front of our tent before each performance, we moved fast. But we didn't shimmy for the bally; we saved that for inside the tent. We shimmied only for the special delight of the men who paid their dimes to see us.

When we moved on to Lima, Ohio, the next stop, we traveled in an open freight car. This, too, was on account of Baby Jim, who couldn't walk much or get up the steps of a passenger car. None of the Samsons and Mighty Ajaxes in that carnival could lift him. So Bob White said it would be nice if we girls rode in the open freight car with Baby Jim so he wouldn't get lonesome.

The warm weather had come, and it affected Baby Jim terribly. He had rolls and rolls of fat around his neck and I would sponge the perspiration off these rolls for him, and he developed a great paternal affection for me.

This gave me some uncomfortable moments. Apparently I was all things to all freaks that year, because the Human Skeleton in the show fell head over heels in love with me.

He was too shy to talk much to me, but that poor bag of bones kept sending me mash notes and little presents. Freaks are very sensitive and have bad tempers. They will cut you to pieces if you offend them. I was afraid the skeleton might misinterpret my friendship with Baby Jim, the fat man, and go berserk in his jealous rage. But he was, as it turned out, a very humble Human Skeleton, and nothing like that happened.

I liked being in the carnival. The roustabouts and the concession-aires were the kind of people I'd grown up with, rough, tough, full of larceny toward strangers, but sentimental, and loyal to their friends and co-workers.

The carnival work was colorful and a new experience. But I didn't like it when it rained. It was bad underfoot in the tents then because no planks were put down. We had been with the carnival for six weeks the day there was a chilly rain, and I refused to go out in the storm and do the bally.

"There's no use to open today," I told Bob White. But he was a human torpedo when it came to going after a buck, and he wanted us to go out.

"All we'll be able to coax into the tent today will be raindrops," I said. "I won't go out there without a coat."

The Hill Sisters backed me up. They were always good at that, though they were too scared ever to take an independent stand themselves. I was always the one who had to take the stand.

"Oh, we got coats for you," said Bob White, and he had the boys bring us these coats. They were red, had epaulets, gold braid, and tails in the back.

"You want us to bally in those?" I said. "Not me. I'm not gonna look like any damn monkey in a red coat."

So we didn't go out for two ballys. Then the rain stopped. At the end of the week Bob White wouldn't pay me in full. He claimed business was beginning to taper off. But I had made some rugged friends and I called on them for help. They were the keepers of the bears, and all they had to do was show their muscles and Bob White paid me off in full.

We quit the carnival on that sour note and went back to vaudeville and into the South. Everywhere we went there were great gobs of love and clandestining.

There is a type of white Southerner who respects certain Negro individuals. One of these that I met on the tour was a Mr. Charles Somers, who owned the theater we played in Richmond, Virginia. He saw that I had none of the humility of most Negro people living in the South, and respected me for it. When he saw that I drew business he offered us several weeks at three little theaters he had in North Carolina.

One of these was in the Hills' home town. While we were playing there we stayed at their aunt's house. This was the first time I ran into real Southern living. It was a warm and comfortable place, but they were always eating grits. They ate a lot of rice, also, in that house and grew their own greens and raised chickens and hogs. They ate their big meal at noon and kept eating all of the time.

I found this a very happy state of affairs. But the large quantities of food I ate and the round-the-clock system of eating caused me to become bloated and stuffed.

One day I got so sick I had to stay in bed all day. In the early evening a relative of the Hills toted—that's the word they use down there, toted—me to the theater in his little old car.

I fainted in my dressing quarters. When I came to I was lying on two chairs and an ironing board. The manager came back and said, "Ethel, I don't know what to do. I went on the stage and told the people out there that you were sick, but they said they would wait until you got better. They want to hear you sing so much they refuse to take their money back."

This was my introduction to the show-must-go-on tradition. But what performer could be indifferent to admirers willing to sit on hard seats all night just for the chance to see her?

I couldn't stand up. So they kept the curtain down and carried me out on the stage. They sat me down in a chair, and I sang "St. Louis Blues" and two other songs. I was dizzy and almost fainted again before I got through. But I was all right the next day.

Because we were flush when we got to Charleston, we bought three white poodles—Shine, Bernie, and Snowy—for ten dollars. My dog was Snowy, and all three of them played star roles in a little domestic incident when we reached Savannah, Georgia, another jumping town.

For some time Maggie Hill had been restless. An actor named Jules

McGarr had been pestering her to join up with him in a man-and-woman act. Maggie said she'd quit our turn after Savannah. Her sister Jo was heartbroken over this. But in Savannah she acquired a boy friend, Happy, who was also in show business, and Happy broke Jo's blues about Maggie leaving us.

The Savannah theater where we worked was run by a Mrs. Styles, who had a flashy dresser of a son, Willie. This Willie Styles fell for me and showed us a big time. But I was too smart to fall for Willie.

I had already noticed that it can be very expensive indeed for a girl to romance with anyone who has any connection with the management of a theater. I kept thinking that if it was Willie Styles who was to pay us off at the end of the week, the result might be calamitous. I was never an actress who cared to be paid off with hugs, kisses, and excuses.

I didn't hit Willie with any ax, but I kept our relationship on a simple hail-fellow-well-met basis. One night after Jo and I got into bed—Maggie was off somewhere with Jules McGarr—and put out the light, the dogs started growling and scurrying under the bed. I told them to stop barking, but they paid me no mind.

The rumpus under the bed kept up so long that finally I lit the lamp and had a look. And there under the bed, lying on the floor, was the dandified Willie Styles.

Before we came home he had sneaked into our room. He wanted to see if I was entertaining any of his rivals that night. But he forgot about the dogs. Though Willie was one of the best-dressed fashion plates in all Savannah, I never saw anyone look more disgruntled, disheveled, and disgusted than he did that evening. And the dogs who had been licking his face and nibbling at his clothes made noisy objections to his leaving.

When we finally opened the door so Willie could leave, we found Jo's boy friend, Happy, out there, listening at the keyhole. He had cooked it up with Willie to rush in and help beat the daylights out of the competition.

Our last date as a trio being in Savannah, Jo had to write out of there, asking engagements for the Two Hill Sisters. All the wires that came back said the same thing:

"If the tall, skinny one is no longer with act, we don't want you."

But despite such recognition, the applause and stomping and money thrown to me on the stage, the brave banners announcing "Coming!

Sweet Mama Stringbean in Person!" I still had only one ambition. That was to become the personal maid of some lady who would take me with her around the world.

For me, nothing can beat the smell of dew and flowers and the odor that comes out of the earth when the sun goes down.

I had not found many sweet smells in show business—only squalor and contentiousness and professional jealousy. I still had no feeling of having roots, of being on a team and belonging to a group. I was still alone and an outcast, even though I was starting to get top billing.

Sweet Mama Stringbean was having adventures she'd never forget, but what she wanted more than anything in the world was what she'd never yet had—in show business or out of it—clean surroundings, a decent, quiet place to sleep, some sense of order, and good meals at regular times of the day. These I thought I surely would find as a lady's maid traveling around the world with some kind and generous boss.

7

Two vaudeville theaters squatted side by side on Decatur Street in the blowzy, noisy heart of Atlanta's Negro section. As a two-girl team, Jo Hill and I were booked into the showhouse at No. 81 Decatur. This was run by Charles P. Bailey, a Georgia cracker and a sort of self-appointed czar. You did what Mr. Bailey said—if you wanted to work for him. He even made all the performers on his bill live at Lonnie Reed's boardinghouse.

One nice thing about little theaters like Mr. Bailey's was that they put on melodramatic afterpieces. Sometimes when you finished your two weeks of vaudeville there you'd be kept on to appear in these olio shows.

Bailey's theater always drew big crowds. A Jewish fellow who ran the place right next door to it, at 91 Decatur Street, had to bring in big-name players to attract business.

One of these big names he booked while I was there was Stringbeans, one of the highest-paid acts in the Negro theatrical world at that time. Mr. Bailey, too, booked important names, turns like Speedy Smith, Buddy Austin, Joe Bright, and Billy Higgins, who later wrote "There'll Be Some Changes Made." Eddie Heywood's father played the piano at No. 81, and Ben Bow was a partner in the management of the stock company.

So the original Stringbeans was playing at 91 Decatur Street while I, Sweet Mama Stringbean, the feminine version of that long, thin green vegetable, was working just next door.

Stringbeans, whose real name was Butler May, was a fine man and a good buddy. He never resented my taking over his professional name. He and his wife, Sweetie May, became good friends of mine. His wife worked with him on the stage, and their act was billed as Stringbeans and Sweetie. Stringbeans accentuated his thinness by wearing very tight clothes. When he walked out on the stage he wore a thick chain across his vest with a padlock on it. The chain was just slack enough for the padlock to hang in front of his pants fly. This always got a guffaw from his admirers out front.

I stopped working for Mr. Charles P. Bailey for a grotesque and comical reason, with love being the cause of my dismissal. It seems to me, sometimes, that having a sense of humor always interferes with enjoying a love life on any large and satiating scale.

Anyway, one of the actors in Mr. Bailey's stock company fell for me. His wife, he, and I were all working at the time in an afterpiece. There were no rehearsals for these, and you gave your own cues. I liked being in these olios because you could die sitting down, standing up, or any other way you found convenient. If you forgot your lines you just made up other lines as you went along. The whole thing was so informal it bordered sometimes on chaos.

In this particular afterpiece the action called for my admirer's wife to stab me in the back. One night a pal buzzed me that she was going to use a real knife on me instead of the paper one supplied by the management.

Where I come from it ain't ethical to blow the whistle even on people who are planning to stab you. The situation required fast strategy, but the only out I could think of was to report sick to Mr. Bailey, hoping to be excused from the slicing party.

Mr. Bailey glanced at me and said I never looked healthier, and fired me. Jo Hill and I lost no time in going to work for his opposition next door.

My girlish reticence continued to attract the wolves, and Speedy Smith was one of these. Men like Speedy always behaved as though I was using my standoffish attitude as a come-on. I could never convince any of them that all I asked was a little time and freedom to make my own selection.

Now Speedy was short and stout and I, being a long, lean, and lithesome stringbean, was not at all interested in his suggestion that we have a Mutt and Jeff type of romance. One night the determined Speedy risked life and limb by climbing up the rain pipe that led past my bedroom. The rain pipe broke and he bounced on the sidewalk, narrowly missing an ash can.

Bessie Smith was booked into 91 Decatur Street while I was working there. Bessie was a heavy-set, dark woman and very nice-looking.
Along with Ma Rainey, she was undisputed tops as a blues singer.
When she came to Atlanta she'd heard a good deal about my low,
sweet, and then new way of singing blues.

Bessie's shouting brought worship wherever she worked. She was
getting fifty to seventy-five dollars a week, big money for our kind of
vaudeville. The money thrown to her brought this to a couple of hundred dollars a week. Bessie, like an opera singer, carried her own claque
with her. These plants in the audience were paid to throw up coins
and bills to get the appreciation money going without delay the moment she finished her first number. And if Bessie ordered it, her followers would put the finger on you and run you right off the stage
and out of sight, maybe forever.

Bessie was in a pretty good position to dictate to the managers. She
had me put on my act for her and said I was a long goody. But she
also told the men who ran No. 91 that she didn't want anyone else
on the bill to sing the blues.

I agreed to this. I could depend a lot on my shaking, though I never
shimmied vulgarly and only to express myself. And when I went on
I sang "I Want to Be Somebody's Baby Doll so I Can Get My Lovin'
All the Time."

But before I could finish this number the people out front started
howling, "Blues! Blues! Come on, Stringbean, we want your blues!"

The two-man orchestra struck up Bessie's music and kept it up
through three refrains while the audience, feeling cheated, kept yelling, "We want Stringbeans and her blues!"

Before the second show the manager went to Bessie's dressing room
and told her he was going to revoke the order forbidding me to sing
any blues. He said he couldn't have another such rumpus. There was
quite a stormy discussion about this, and you could hear Bessie yelling
things about "these Northern bitches." Now nobody could have taken
the place of Bessie Smith. People everywhere loved her shouting with
all their hearts and were loyal to her. But they wanted me too.

There had been such a tumult at that first show that Bessie agreed
that after I took two or three bows for my first song I should, if the
crowd still insisted, sing "St. Louis Blues."

And each audience did insist. I remained courteous and deferential
to her, always addressing her as "Miss Bessie." I was as crazy about

her shouting as everyone else, even though hers was not my style, but I didn't enjoy the conflict. It was just more of the contentiousness I'd known all my life. Besides, I sensed this was the beginning of the uncrowning of her, the great and original Bessie Smith. I've never enjoyed seeing a champ go down, and Bessie was all champ.

When I closed my engagement in that theater Miss Bessie called me to her. "Come here, long goody," she said. "You ain't so bad. It's only that I never dreamed that anyone would be able to do this to me in my own territory and with my own people. And you know damn well that you can't sing worth a——"

Bessie was an earthy, robust woman, and after that we always understood each other. I liked her and I hope she came to like me.

I'd encountered Jim Crow all over the South and in many Northern towns as well. But it was in Atlanta that I learned how racial discrimination can hedge in a colored person and make him feel boxed up. There was a strict curfew law for Negroes in Atlanta which said we all had to be off the streets by midnight. Being a tall, high-spirited kid from the North, accustomed to keeping any hours I chose, I didn't like this.

The white people I encountered in the South never overlooked a chance to put me in my place, as it is called. They could tell I was from the North by my accent and possibly my manner, which has never been that of a downtrodden untouchable.

If I went to buy something in an Atlanta store, the white clerk would give me one look and say:

"I see you're one of those fresh Yankee niggers."

What disturbed me much more than this was the usual reaction of the Southern colored girl with me. "Don't answer," she'd whisper nervously. "Don't say *anything*."

Now when I was called a nigger in Philadelphia it never meant a thing. But I was beginning to find out it did mean something in the South. Young as I was, I felt the acceptance of inferiority by the Southern Negro was a big, important factor. I regarded the whites, showering their scorn and contempt on other people because of their color, as odd and possibly feeble-minded and the tip-off that they were scared to death of us.

But that three fourths of the Southern Negroes should complacently accept all that contempt upset me. I was also shocked to find out that

Southern Negroes were prejudiced against those of their own people like me who lived in the North.

I keep learning more about racial prejudice all the time. My biggest surprise of all has been the reaction of white people who wear their tolerance like a plume when I tell them I've never minded even slightly being a Negro.

They are stunned. It's difficult to convince them that I mean that and am not just keeping a stiff upper lip and being brave and gallant.

Keeping a stiff upper lip, hell!

I have the soundest of reasons for being proud of my people. We Negroes have always had such a tough time that our very survival in this white world with the dice always loaded against us is the greatest possible testimonial to our strength, our courage, and our immunity to adversity.

We are close to this earth and to God. Shut up in ghettos, sneered at, beaten, enslaved, we always have answered our oppressors with brave singing, dancing, and laughing. Our greatest eloquence, the pith of the joy and sorrow in our unbreakable hearts, comes when we lift up our faces and talk to God, person to person. Ours is the truest dignity of man, the dignity of the undefeated.

I write all this to explain why I am not bitter and angry at white people. I say in all sincerity that I am sorry for them. What could be more pitiful than to live in such nightmarish terror of another race that you have to lynch them, push them off sidewalks, and never be able to relax your venomous hatred for one moment? As I see it, it is these people, the Ku-Kluxers, the White Supremacists, and the other fire-spitting neurotics who are in the deep trouble.

Dictys and the others among my own people who despise Negroes who are poor and ignorant and condemned to live like animals arouse my fury as no white people ever can. We Negroes have lived through so much together—centuries of slavery, terror, segregation, and unending concentrated abuse—that I'll never understand how some of us who have one way or another been able to lift ourselves a little above the mass of colored people can be so insanely brutal as to try to knock the hell out of our own blood brothers and sisters.

Incidentally, during my first tour of the South I noticed that we of the stage were considered not much better than cattle by respectable Negroes. We were not, remember, top-bracket show folks, but in the flotsam-and-jetsam category.

Traveling in the Jim Crow railway cars, we could feel this Southern resentment all around us. Getting out of a place like Richmond on a Sunday, for instance, was none too pleasant. The train stopped at a hundred places, and people would get on carrying pots, pans, their bedding, and even live chickens.

These travelers were going only a few miles away, but they would get a bigger send-off than folks starting out for Madagascar. Their families and their many friends would come down to the station to see them off, bringing their tears, their sighs, and their best wishes for a happy and safe journey.

Our heavy-laden fellow travelers would stumble on the train, dump their stuff on you, then lean past you for one last heartbreaking handshake and kiss through the window to the dear ones they were leaving behind. Their emaciated but belligerent chickens would peck at you.

The train conductors knew all of them. It was "How's Joe, Jim?" and "How's poor Mary's back?" all over the place. Most of those squares dipped snuff. They chewed tobacco and they'd spit it past you as the train started off like some lazy mule.

Huge families would take Sunday excursions on those trains to see Aunt Dinah or dear old Uncle Jed. We'd be asked questions, but to me Southern hospitality ain't nothing but curiosity. That "Good morning" stuff doesn't mean a thing. Those Southern Negroes, knowing I was from the North, would do everything to pressure me out of my seat, spitting and poking, elbowing and knocking my hat off.

When Jo Hill and I played Birmingham we stayed at the house of Miss Rose, a goodhearted woman who ran a blind pig. A pitcher stood on each of the tables in Miss Rose's place. She filled these from a demijohn, keeping the rest of her corn whisky buried.

Southern cops don't bother to knock at a Negro's home. They just kick the door down and walk in. But Miss Rose, the moment she heard the Law outside, could make that big demijohn disappear under her dress like magic. She was a thin woman, but the coppers never suspicioned she was hiding the whisky under her clothes.

While in Birmingham I met some of the great Negro performers I'd watched at the Standard Theatre back in Philadelphia: Ma Rainey herself, Legge McGinty, Alice Ramsey, and the ventriloquist, Johnny Woods.

I also met Maud Mills, the sister of the immortal Florence. Maud, Florence, and a girl named Kinky, who was no relation of theirs, were doing an act under the billing of the Three Mills Sisters. When we were the Three Hill Sisters people were always confusing the two acts. But I didn't meet Florence Mills until years later.

My big thrill in Birmingham was having a chance to talk with the Whitman Sisters, very light-skinned women who developed some of the best of our Negro performers. Like Gus Edwards, the Whitmans helped many talented youngsters make their start. Some of their protégés are still around.

We opened the act I was doing with Jo Hill with a duet, followed by Jo's song and specialty dance. Then I'd sing my blues and we'd close, wearing our short dresses for the kid routine.

One night I came out of the theater in Birmingham to find the whole street in wild commotion. A copper had shot a young Negro in the stomach. I got close enough to the boy to see the two burned holes in his stomach. He was lying there writhing.

All the way home to Miss Rose's I kept thinking of how the boy had begged for water, while the people around him kept saying drinking water would endanger his life.

Miss Rose was shaking her head sadly when I came in. She told me that Tuney Murray, a chauffeur whom I had met at her place, had been killed that day in a car accident. Tuney had been driving one of those cars you hire for three dollars an hour. Often, in various towns, we performers chipped in to take an hour's ride to see the sights. If we were flush we'd get up six dollars and buy a long two-hour ride.

The next day Miss Rose asked me to go with her to see Tuney's body in the funeral parlor. While I was there I saw the coffin of the boy who had been shot on the street. He'd died during the night. The two tragedies deeply depressed me. I decided not to go on any more pleasure trips in rented motorcars.

After we played two weeks in Birmingham the manager offered us four more weeks of bookings, two each in nearby Anniston and Ensley, a suburb. That meant six weeks of consecutive work just around Birmingham, almost a record run of uninterrupted work for our act.

In Anniston, along with the two other acts on the bill, we'd go each night, after the final curtain, to an eating and drinking place where the owner would let us run up tabs because we were performers. There, as in other towns, the men who had seen me on the stage would vie to wine and dine me.

I had learned to keep an eye on those tabs. Somehow, after being so warmly toasted and sandwiched, I would discover that I had been charged for all that free handed wining and dining by my public.

There was one kid chauffeur who was so flattened by my s.a. that he came around three nights in a row to invite me out for a drive in his white boss's car. The boss, he said, had given him permission to take me out for a spin. I refused each night.

On each of these three nights the constable in Anniston, a white man, had overheard these conversations when he came around to make sure we all were obeying the curfew law. Now this constable, not knowing I feared cars because of what happened to Tuney Murray, praised me as a fine, virtuous girl for resisting temptation that way.

But my fellow performers were less appreciative of my high-mindedness. The chauffeur, who was a small jockey type, had told them all they could come along if I'd go with him in the car. Everybody on that bill in Anniston was getting quite salty and sassy with me and saying I was selfishly robbing them of free automobile rides in a shiny new Buick.

After the last Saturday night show an anguished roar went up when I announced I intended to go to Birmingham and spend Sunday with a man there whom I had quite a crush on. Having nothing else to do, the chauffeur and the gang all came down to the station with me, hoping I'd change my mind about taking a ride at the last minute.

The Birmingham train was very late. Immediately all the actors began whipping up arguments why I should take a refreshing little ride in the Buick touring car. They said they were even willing to sacrifice their own morning and come along just to make sure my jockey-type boy friend got me back to the station in time to take the train.

I had a big sixth-sense hunch about going on that ride. Though I let them talk me into going, I still felt uneasy as I climbed into the front seat next to the chauffeur. The car was a seven-seater, and the two other girls and three men got into the rear.

A little way out of town we came to a bend. As we turned this, we saw directly ahead a two-horse buggy that was straddling the road. Our driver swerved to avoid hitting the horses. The car went over the shoulder of the road and turned over on its side with an earsplitting crash.

The driver and four of the people in the back were thrown clear of the car. But one girl in the back and I were tightly pinned under the wreckage. The jagged, splintered glass from the smashed windshield fell all over me. Boiling-hot water from the cracked radiator began to drip on my breast and stomach.

I could hear the girl in the back screaming. I didn't cry out in my pain. I was too busy praying. "O Lord, please forgive me!" I prayed. "Please help me! Don't let me die here, please, God, *please!*"

All of us knew only too well what happened to Negroes who went joy riding in white men's cars and wrecked them. Four of our companions were so terrified that they ran away without helping to free us. Among them was the little chauffeur who'd been dying of love for me right up to that moment.

But one of the men had the courage and humanity to stay there and take his chances with the Law. But he couldn't budge either my body or that of the girl in the back, who had fainted. I kept on praying.

After a long time two white men approached. They looked at the wreck and at us. One of them said indignantly:

"What have you niggers got here? So you've been riding around in white folks' cars, have you? I guess this will teach you a lesson." They started to walk away, but our friend apologetically stopped them.

"But don't you see?" he asked. "There are two girls pinned under that there wreck."

"Two what?" said the white man. "You mean two nigger bitches, don't you?"

"Yes, sir. But if they don't get help soon, they may die."

"Good!" laughed the white man. "The more dead niggers there are, the better I like it."

I was in agony and I had listened patiently. But now I spoke up, saying, "I'm suffering. I am a human being, and so are you. You know that if two colored men came along and found two white women pinned under a car they'd help them. How can you be so inhuman?"

I kept talking. And God must have touched their hard hearts. In the end they and our companion pulled us out of the wreckage. By that time I was in such agony as I'd never known. My right leg had been cut almost to the bone, and the broken glass ground into my wound as I was dragged out. The tendons and muscles of that leg had also been cut, and the hot water had scalded my breast and stomach.

They pulled me out first because the other girl had fainted again. It turned out later that she had been more frightened than hurt.

The two white men went off, and our friend ran in a panic from one farmhouse to another, trying to locate a phone from which to call an ambulance. I tore strips from my dress and bound up my wounds as best I could.

When that ambulance arrived the intern found me sitting on a rock. I was singing. I was in a state of shock and not conscious of any pain. With the other girl I was taken to a hospital in Anniston.

When a white doctor untied the rags binding my right leg it fell down on the floor like some dead, useless thing. He told me a tendon had also snapped in my left leg.

Putting a rubber hose on my right leg, he let boiling water run into the wound, over the raw flesh, cut muscles, and tendons. My leg had been ripped open from my knee all the way to my hip. When I screamed he told me:

"You needn't holler, gal. This is what all you niggers should get when you wreck white people's cars."

Before sewing up my leg he gave me as much ether as he thought safe. But I remained conscious and could watch him as he sewed up that great wound with dozens and dozens of crisscross stitches. When he finished he told an attendant:

"Take this girl over to the nigger quarters."

The attendant got angry when I wanted to take it easy. He forced me to walk over the gravel, tar, and pebbles to the Negro building in the rear. When we got there it was still very early in the morning, and the night nurse—only Negro doctors and nurses were assigned there—had gone to bed. I was told she couldn't be called.

Left alone and stretched out on two hard chairs, it was hours before the day nurse came on. She said there was no bed available and I'd have to remain there until one was empty. I said I was terribly thirsty and asked her for ice water.

She brought the pitcher, set it down at my side, and went away. As I was about to drink the ice water I suddenly recalled hearing somewhere that drinking ice water after taking ether was dangerous. So I kept my parched lips wet by licking off the moisture that formed on the outside of the pitcher.

The day nurse paid no more attention to me. For hours I lay there on the two chairs and in my bloody rags, crying and sobbing with pain and fear. No one washed me. No doctor visited me until the afternoon, almost twelve hours after the accident.

And even after a bed was found for me I just lay there, caked in dirt and the clotted blood. Then Jo Hill came out with fresh clothes, a nightgown, a comb, and soap. I'd asked Ted for those things, only to be told the hospital didn't furnish them to colored patients.

I was in a bad fix and I knew it. I couldn't eat the grits and buttermilk, the only food they served us in that crowded ward, and was given nothing else to eat. The nurses just shrugged and took my untouched tray away after each meal.

My bandages were not changed for days at a time. The Negro nurses ignored me. I was a Yankee and, because of the accident, they looked upon me as one who'd come down and made life a little more difficult for all Southern Negroes by riding in a white man's car and wrecking it.

The third day I was in that hospital my right leg began to give off a disgusting odor. But gangrene, losing my leg, was only one of the possibilities I had to worry about in that house of mercy. Only a thin partition separated us from the men's ward. Some of the patients there were mental cases who might go berserk at any time and attack us.

On being admitted to the hospital I'd had thirty-five dollars in cash and a few pieces of jewelry. Both were gone in a few days. The hospital charged Negro patients such high rates that if you were there for any length of time you got deep into its debt. There were dozens of other colored people who had been working at menial duties around the hospital for months, trying to pay off the big bills they'd run up while sick there. I didn't want anything like that to happen to me.

Yes, I was in a bad fix. But once again God, to whom I kept praying day and night, came in on my side. God and a few blessed human beings, both white and colored. That's the part I like to remember about this blood-chilling experience of mine in a hospital in the Deep South.

First of all, there was a little white nurse in the hospital who heard of my case and was touched. Every chance she got she'd come back to the Negro section of the institution where she wasn't supposed to be —to comfort me.

If I'd been that girl's own sister she couldn't have worried more about the danger of losing my right leg. "You have to get out of here, Ethel," she'd say, her sweet young face full of compassion. "We have to get you out."

It was she who told me that that hospital was nothing more than a debtors' prison for colored people like me. And she told me how I might escape. I had to find someone who'd sign a paper asserting he was a relative and could provide for me so I would not become a public charge. Otherwise I could not be released from the hospital until cured or killed, she said.

Fortunately, finding such a person was not difficult. On being told of the situation Miss Rose immediately perjured herself by signing such a paper. She brought the document down, duly attested and witnessed, and I was taken to her house on the following Sunday. And she paid off the twenty dollars the hospital claimed I owed.

The hospital authorities just laughed at Miss Rose when she asked for an ambulance to take me to the train. I was carried to the station on a board and put in a Jim Crow car. I rode to Birmingham with my crippled leg straight out and resting on the seat opposite ours. As we rode I asked Miss Rose about my little dog Snowy.

"I have bad news for you, Ethel," she said. "Snowy died this morning—of starvation. She refused to eat anything from the day you were taken to the hospital."

Nothing could have saddened me more. I'd been looking forward to cuddling Snowy and having her lick my face.

Hundreds of Negroes who had heard of my accident were at the station in Birmingham to greet me. Miss Rose had a car waiting to take me to her house, but I said I was frightened of cars. I consented to get in only after the driver promised to drive carefully and slowly all the way.

I cried over Snowy when they put me in bed. Miss Rose tried to cheer me up by telling me some heart-warming news. Many of her customers who knew of the accident had got in the habit of leaving an extra quarter or half dollar with her to help pay my medical expenses.

Some of these people had seen me on the stage. But others had just met me around the house. They were poor, could ill afford charity to others in trouble, but that hadn't mattered. A stranger was in trouble; a Negro like themselves was in trouble and pain. So they had to help, had to give all they could from the little they had.

A Negro surgeon came to see me. He looked at the brown blood on my leg, sniffed at the odor coming from it, and shook his head when he inspected my wound.

"I shouldn't treat you here," he told me. "I should get you into another hospital. Then you could sue the hospital where you were disgracefully neglected. It breaks my heart to think that you were all but ignored there—just because you're colored and from the North. No, I shouldn't really treat you, but maybe I can save your leg if you'll help me."

"I don't want to sue anyone," I told him. "All I care about is saving my leg."

"This is going to hurt cruelly and terribly," he warned me. "I can't give you any anesthetic whatever, not after all that ether you had. I will have to probe—with no drug at all to lessen your pain."

"The pain won't matter," I told him, "so long as I don't have to go through the rest of my life a cripple."

The doctor told Miss Rose to go out and bring in the four strongest women in the neighborhood. "They'll have to be strong," he said, "to hold this poor girl when I start probing and cutting."

All four women were needed when he started to probe and gouge out of my leg the decayed and dying flesh. He was horrified to discover the oil, dirt, and gravel that had been ground into the wound as I lay pinned under the car. These had never been cleaned out of the big hole in my leg.

I screamed and struggled and fought as he cut, gouged, and probed with his long, cruelly sharp instruments. Before the week was over all of the four women quit. They said they couldn't endure watching my agony or listening to my wild screams. Miss Rose had to hold me down all alone. Each day my doctor became one mass of perspiration as he worked over me.

And when the day came that he saw healthy blood spurt for the first time from my leg, it was like a celebration. After that the pain seemed nothing. "We have to keep this red blood flowing," the doctor said as he sewed together the mangled flesh tissues, the ripped muscles and broken tendons. "If we can do that, you'll walk again."

It was a full month after the accident before I could get up from bed. The doctor said I could try to walk about with a cane. But when I put my other foot down it flopped to the floor like a dead flounder.

"O Lord!" I prayed. "Am I going to be crippled in this left leg now, after all I've been through?"

My doctor confirmed what I'd been told at the hospital: the tendon in the left leg had been snapped. One day when I was all alone I got an idea. Hobbling painfully over to the closet, I got out a pair of new shoes. The shoes had high heels and short vamps, that being the fashion just then. It was trouble to bend over and put the shoe on my left foot and lace it up tight. I hesitated before I dared try to move my toes with the shoe on. While I waited I offered up a fervent prayer.

And then I tried it. My foot moved! I could move my toes! I screamed and laughed and sang hysterically. When my doctor came he was completely mystified. He took the shoe off, and my left foot flopped down again. After that I insisted on keeping the shoe on even while I slept. And I became confident that I'd walk again.

My admirer, the jockey-type chauffeur, had been picked up, arrested, and tried. His white employer testified he'd never given the boy permission to use his car to go joy riding. The chauffeur was sentenced to several years on a chain gang.

The Anniston authorities then tried to get me as his accomplice. But the white constable there stopped the prosecutor from having me arrested. The constable told of hearing me refuse three nights in a row to go riding with the chauffeur in the Buick.

"She's a good girl," he said. "Never did know of another nigger girl to refuse to go joy riding in a big shiny new car."

I was cleared of suspicion through his help.

Now I'd been suffering hellish torture because people were cruel and mean to me. But I'd started learning about that side of humanity almost on the day I was born.

What I'd also discovered while I had my back to the wall was that human kindness was depthless, immeasurable, and broke across all color lines and geographical boundaries.

After all, ten times more people, colored and white, had tried to help me than had callously permitted me to suffer. There was that little white nurse; Miss Rose, who made her living illegally, selling corn whisky; her openhanded, openhearted, tough customers; the Negro doctor who, without thought of fee, had labored like a slave to save my leg, and finally the white constable in Anniston.

The whole experience convinced me that basically there is no difference between whites and blacks, browns and yellows. I decided to think no more of people as Northerners and Southerners.

All the rest of my life since, I've never been able to recognize and appraise people, love and hate them, because of their skin color or the part of the world they came from. I would have to be guided, henceforth, only by the good or evil that was in them.

I also knew there must be millions of men and women everywhere, people of every conceivable color and creed and religion, who were like those who had helped me. Men and women who never betray or cheat you.

This I knew with all the burning conviction I had about there being a living God who was good and all-powerful and was loving me, watching over me, and forgiving my trespasses.

This being true, the evil ones could never count, would never be able to hurt me so much again.

8

I was just starting to limp around my room a little when the man who ran the three little theaters—in Birmingham, Anniston, and Ensley—came to see me. He said he could give me three or four weeks' work.

"But I can't even walk across a stage," I told him.

"My people won't mind if you can't walk," he said. "What they want is your blues."

I'd just learned that Jo Hill, apparently believing that I'd never be able to work again, had found herself another partner. They'd tried to get bookings out of town, but the owners had again wired back, "If long, tall girl who sings is no longer with act we don't want it." What hurt me was that Jo had said nothing to me about going out with somebody else as the Hill Sisters. But I continued to work with her.

In the three Birmingham theaters I went on three or four times a night, closing the show. The backstage fellows would carry me out and prop me against a wall. When I'd finished singing they had to help me off.

If I moved even a little when out on the stage, there would be a pool of blood around my feet. But my doctor had said I should not try to stop the blood because my leg would become strong and healthy again only if I let it flow freely.

Out-of-town managers began asking for our act while we were still working around Birmingham. I began to think that maybe I could sing my way home.

I went to see my Negro doctor and told him I would have to leave. He said I only owed him between fifty and sixty dollars, and I promised to pay up as soon as I could. I explained that I wouldn't be able to pay for medical attention while traveling.

"Couldn't I dress my leg by myself?" I asked.

He told me to buy bluestone, bichloride of mercury, iodoform, and Castile soap. He instructed me to wash out the wound with the bichloride of mercury and the soap two or three times a day, then bandage it with gauze soaked in iodoform.

"You'll have to tear off the scabs as they form," he said. "But when the blue skin begins to appear, leave it. That blue skin will be the sign that your leg is getting better."

He had me dress and bandage my leg twice in front of him to make sure I would do it right. So I was loaded down with medicines and gauze when I headed home.

Our first stop was at Petersburg, Virginia. There and in the other towns we played we found out there had been much word-of-mouth publicity about my accident, and big crowds came out to see me. The whole trip North took about six weeks, and the audiences were so generous with their gift offerings that by the time I got home I'd been able to pay off all but ten dollars of the doctor's bill.

Some of the theaters we played were airdomes. When it rained the managers of those open-air places behaved just like the owners of the Polo Grounds in New York, who hate to call off any game when there is a good crowd until at least four and a half innings have been played. There had to be an avalanche before the managers would give the money back to their half-drowned customers. So Sweet Mama String-bean often had to sing in the rain.

The week I played Washington, D.C., I was invited to sing at the two special Sunday shows put on each week at the Howard Theatre, the best colored theater there. This house was built and run by the Howard brothers, Negroes, and they booked only the top stock companies and vaudeville acts.

As in Boston, actors were not allowed to dance on the stage on the Sabbath and couldn't wear anything but their street clothes while performing. The Howards ran their regular shows twice a day six days a week. For their special Sunday shows they tried to get the best Negro acts who happened to be in Washington.

Many Negro acts considered it a great honor to be asked to play the Sunday shows at the Howard. But others wouldn't work there because of a peculiar box-office rule of the management. For two evening performances and one matinee during the week they would sell tickets only to very light-colored Negroes. At those three performances you could see no black spots at all out front except when the lights were turned down.

I thought this snobbish house policy—color discrimination against some of our own people by the dictys—ridiculous and laughable. But I played the Howard that Sunday anyway, being eager to send my Birmingham doctor every dollar I could. Jo hadn't been invited to perform, so I went on alone. I sang "St. Louis Blues" and had to do one encore.

I'd been away from home the whole season, almost a full year. My return to Philadelphia turned into something of a triumph when we were booked for two weeks at the Standard Theatre, where I'd watched shows from the peanut gallery. It was still the city's leading Negro showhouse, and the engagement meant I was recognized in my home town as an established professional performer.

After we closed at the Standard we broke up our act. Jo went back into night-club work. I took a job bussing dishes at Horn and Hardart's Automat. I got seventy-five cents a day with one hot meal thrown in.

I didn't look upon this as any comedown. In fact, that summer I turned down plenty of offers to sing at Atlantic City and the other New Jersey beach resorts. I've never been able to feel that there is anything undignified about making your living by the sweat of your brow.

And I was happy to be home with my family. I felt I'd already circled the globe and wanted no more traveling. Momweeze had taken a little house on Fawn Street in Philadelphia, and I moved in there with her, Genevieve, and Vi. I found it easier to take care of my leg while living in one place.

But the thing I liked best was that Genevieve had had a cute baby girl whom she'd named Ethel, after me. Apparently my half sister bore me no grudge for all the times I'd stuck my big toe in her face when we were kids.

I had a wonderful time playing with little Ethel, washing her and feeding her. The child looked very much like me, and when I'd show her off to my friends they'd say:

"Why, Ethel, no one told me that you had a baby."

"But it's Genevieve's child," I'd tell them.

Then they'd get wise and knowing looks on their faces. One woman said:

"Well, that's as good a story as any I could tell."

I didn't try very hard to convince them because I knew they'd just go on thinking what they pleased. Anyway, nothing in the world could have made me prouder and happier than having a baby of my own. I would have sung out *that* news from the housetops.

I hadn't been hustling dishes at the automat very long when Toots Moore, a drummer who was working in Barney Gordon's big saloon, came to see me.

"There's a fill-in job open at Barney's," he said. "He needs a singer to work Friday and Saturday nights. He pays two bucks a night, and the tips are good there. Why don't you take it, Ethel?"

"I can't dance on account of my leg," I told him. "And I never drink with the customers."

But Toots insisted on my going to see Barney Gordon. His saloon was on the corner of Kater and Thirteenth streets. Barney Gordon was a good-natured Jewish man with only one fault; he loved to make long-winded political speeches after he'd had a few balls. If nobody interrupted his long speeches Barney stayed amiable and happy. That's all he asked of life.

Barney hired me, and after I'd sung two nights at his place he offered me a steady job at fifteen dollars a week. I sang there six nights a week and on Thursday afternoons. Servant girls and house-workers had that afternoon off, and they'd come to Barney Gordon's to drink and relax. We called them "the Thursday girls."

But before I took the full-time job at Barney's I asked the manager of Horn and Hardart's if I could come back and work for him again when I finished my job in the saloon.

"Any time at all, Ethel," he said. "You're a hard and willing worker."

I got vast satisfaction out of that. I was a hard and willing worker, and, as I've said, it always pleased me when my bosses noticed it.

Barney Gordon's saloon was on the ground floor. We entertained, though, in a big room upstairs where the customers sat at tables. There was only a two-piece band. Toots Moore, the drummer, and a piano player who could play only in two keys.

For a short while I lost my voice trying to sing in his two keys. Barney kept me on while my vocal cords were making their speedy recovery because I could shimmy so good. "Shim-Me-Sha-Wabble," the big shimmy song, had just come out. When the boys played that

I'd put my hands on my hips and work my body fast, without moving my feet. There was never anything vulgar about my fast and furious wrigglings. Even in towns where other girl performers were stopped from shimmying by the local bluenoses, no one objected to my doing it.

However, it was my blues that drew big trade, and soon Barney hung out banners reading, "Our Ethel Is Back!" to draw in all my old friends.

Barney Gordon's was no temple of culture and refinement. But there, as in the tough spots up in Harlem where I worked later, I had little trouble with drunk or rowdy customers.

One good reason for this was that I had several paternal-minded sporting men watching out for me. Some pages back, when I wrote that big girls like me seldom arouse men's protective instincts, I guess I was forgetting these self-appointed underworld guardians of mine.

At Barney Gordon's there were the Brown brothers, Willie and Louis. The two Browns were bartenders and had fed me in their back rooms when I was a hungry little schoolgirl. Another protector of mine at Gordon's was Jack Blackburn, the old-time lightweight who afterward trained Joe Louis for his championship fights. The Browns and Jack Blackburn would have slapped me from Independence Square to West Philadelphia if they saw me doing anything they thought would hurt me. Of course, being sporting men, their ideas about this were on the unorthodox side.

When I celebrated my eighteenth birthday at Barney Gordon's, Louis Brown came in and pried a diamond chip out of his locket and handed it to me with three one-dollar gold pieces.

"Keep this little stone, Ethel," he said, "until you get some money. Then trade it in for a bigger diamond. Keep doing that. You'll find it's a good way to save."

"What's the gold pieces for?" I asked.

Louis laughed and said, "That yellow stuff ain't bad to have laying around handy, either."

By that time I had acquired a boy friend. He was West Indian Johnny, a big-time gambler, whose real last name was Sinclair. Johnny was tall, dark, and handsome. He spoke five languages and was very kind and easygoing with me. I'd met him years before at Pop Grey's dancing place on South Street, and he knew my whole family.

When news of our association got around Barney Gordon's the word went out: "Hands off Ethel! She's West Indian Johnny's pet!"

I never could take any boy friends home to Fawn Street because I never knew what strife and hell-raising we might run into there. But it was different with Johnny. He understood about such things, and he and Momweeze liked each other. He always told her, "Louise, don't let nothing worry you. If something is bothering you, just tell West Indian Johnny and he take care of it for you."

Though he was a five-language linguist, that's the way West Indian Johnny spoke English. He was twice my age and seemed an old man to me. But I was very fond of him.

I was getting such good tips at Gordon's that I was able to support my whole family. I was happy to assume that responsibility and to know that Genevieve's baby was getting everything she needed.

Our little place on Fawn Street swarmed with animal life. Momweeze had adopted whole tribes of stray dogs and cats. Her favorite was a cat she called Tim. He outraged her one day by having kittens. For days my mother went about the house muttering that she'd never trust another cat.

Between the baby and the animals I had a hard time getting any sleep. And on the corner there was a tiny store-front church that jumped with more noise than half a dozen night clubs. The parishioners were hard drinkers as well as hard prayers. Between sessions of rocking and praying they'd sneak out for a few fast nips, then dash back into the church again to holler to the Lord louder and better than before.

Momweeze, too, had gone back to her old rip-roaring religion. When the urge to pray moved her she'd make everyone in the house get down on his knees and pray with her. Her praying bouts sometimes lasted more than an hour. We prayed so much in that house that even Ethel, the little baby, seemed to know the rituals.

My mother was very eager to set herself up as a savior and redeemer. She decided to make a start in this work by curing Vi of her drinking habits.

Vi was still drinking too much. She'd go into saloons, drink all she wanted, and then laugh at the bartender when he asked her to pay up.

"I was just robbed and have no money," she'd tell him. "What are you going to do about it?"

The bartender would send for me. I'd pay for Vi's drinks and lead her back to Fawn Street. One day when Vi came home a little stiffer than usual, Momweeze announced:

"This is the day I will pray the liquor out of Vi. When I get finished she'll never touch another drop."

That afternoon my mother kept Vi and the rest of us on our knees so long our legs fell asleep. Finally Vi yelled out:

"For God's sake, Louise, throw in that Amen!"

"Amen! *Amen!* AMEN!" said Louise. "And I thank You, O Lord, for making Vi see the light. She will drink no more. Amen!"

As we scrambled to our feet Vi explained that she wasn't going to stop drinking at all. "I just couldn't stand kneeling there one second longer," she explained. "You put me in the cat's corner. But thanks for that Amen, Louise!"

My uncle Charlie was still coming around, but only when he wanted a dollar from Louise or Vi. He'd work when he could, but then we'd never see him. He visited us when he was broke and his girl friend had put him out of the house.

If Charlie couldn't beg or snitch a dollar he'd leave, complaining about his family's cruel selfishness. And in a few days we'd get a penny postcard reading:

My darling Sister,
     You are nothing but a dirty old bitch not to give me a dollar.
                    Your loving brother,
                         Charles Anderson.

When this kept on happening Louise decided that Charlie had better be sent to the Philadelphia General Hospital to have his wits appraised. But none of us wanted to take him there.

"Nobody will have to," my mother said.

The next time Charlie came to the house she gave him a letter to the hospital people—and a dollar. The letter, which she had not sealed, said she was afraid her brother Charlie was going crazy and to please keep him there. Charlie went off to the hospital, promising faithfully to deliver the letter.

"He'll do it without reading it," Momweeze insisted. "Give Charlie a dollar and he loses interest in anything else."

She was right. Charlie did deliver the letter without reading it. They kept him under observation in one of their loony bins for fifteen days. Then he was released and came back to Fawn Street. He had a letter from the hospital people. This, too, was not sealed, but Charlie hadn't read that one either.

"I know what's in it," he said. "The doctors told me that it said I am harmless and it is all right for me to go anywhere I want."

Charlie hadn't minded at all his fifteen days in the observation ward. He said it had been quite pleasant there and the food had been good.

"Feller doesn't have to worry about nothin' there," he explained, and added proudly, "Those doctors were fascinated by me."

The big menace of my teen age came into my life in Barney Gordon's saloon. I'll call him Rocky, because he's still around. For almost a month he came there three or four times a week to hear me sing. I never saw him because he sat in another room, out of sight. But each time he sent a dollar to me by a waiter with a request that I sing his favorite song, "I Lost You so Why Should I Care?"

I had got pretty curious about this man who stayed in the back room while I sang his favorite ballad. And one night he sent the waiter to ask if I'd have a drink with him.

"Tell him I don't drink nothing but milk," I told the waiter, "and that the customers get disgusted and say they won't buy me any damned milk."

Word came back that this customer would be very happy to buy me milk if I'd sit with him. I went to the other room. To my surprise the man who always wanted to hear "I Lost You so Why Should I Care?" turned out to be just my age. He was very good-looking and immaculately dressed.

"Why do you sit back here," I asked him, "where you can't watch me as I sing your song?"

A dreamy look came into his eyes. "I like to visualize you as I listen to you sing. It relaxes me."

Each time he came in after that I'd sit with him awhile drinking my milk. One night he asked me to go for a ride with him in his car. I probably wouldn't have gone if I hadn't been annoyed with West Indian Johnny. He was away.

I was used to Johnny going away for three or four days at a time to sit in big-stake, round-the-clock poker games. But this time I'd heard that a woman gambler had come down from New York to tangle with the best local cardplayers—and had decided to go shooting for my Johnny. Shooting, in underworld talk, sometimes means going after somebody's affections. Resenting that, I went for the ride with Rocky.

A few days later West Indian Johnny came to see me. "I hear that boy you went riding with is no good," he said. "I don't want you seen around with him."

"You're not my boss, Johnny," I told him.

"Then I no see you again," said West Indian Johnny. "But I go find out about this boy and let you know."

"Don't bother."

Rocky didn't come around to see me for a whole week after that, and I kept thinking about him. During our car ride he hadn't made a pass at me, which made him almost unique in my experience with men.

One evening, on reporting to work, I was handed a five-dollar bill with a message to call up Rocky. I phoned the number, and the woman who answered said Rocky wanted me to bring him some oranges and sandwiches when I finished work, and gave me the address.

When I arrived at the house with the food I found Rocky lying in bed. He was wearing very flossy-looking pajamas. He said he hadn't been around to see me because he had been sick.

I'd expected that I might have to fight my way out of the place, but again he made no grab for me. Instead he talked to me like some poet, and I'd never heard anyone talk like that before.

He said I was beautiful and used expressions like "your hair is lovely as black moonlight." Stuff like that. I was intrigued. This was something entirely new to me. And I enjoyed sitting there and not being clawed at and mauled, just listening to his high-class sweet talk.

Rocky mentioned marriage that night, but I said that was impossible because I was married to somebody else. And he just went on talking in language that rippled and sang and danced. I got more and more mystified—and fascinated.

If I'd known more about junkers I would have suspicioned he was one. I later learned that all junkers talk in terms of beauty and unreality when they've been "smoking."

And for weeks after that Rocky continued to be a perfect gentleman, behaving as though I were some fragile and lovely flower. By the time I discovered he was a knight on a white horse only when high, and a sniveling, treacherous human wreck the rest of the time, I was hooked, a girl well sunk.

Meanwhile, West Indian Johnny had been investigating Rocky. One night at Gordon's he got us both to a table. "Ethel is a nice girl," he told Rocky. "I know her long time. I want you leave her alone. I hear you smoke hop. I hear you steal."

"I don't steal," said Rocky.

"Hop?"

"I don't smoke no more. I was sick and my doctor started me on a habit. But I'm off hop now."

I could see that West Indian Johnny didn't believe one word of this. But the more he put the knock in against Rocky, the more stubborn I became. As Johnny got up from the table he gave Rocky a final warning:

"If Ethel want to be your girl, all right. But you better be good to her. If I hear you mistreat her I'll run you out of town. But first I will beat you up, and good."

Not being able to get enough sleep during the daytime, I'd rented a room in another house. I was sleeping there one cold winter night when the rubber tube that connected the gas stove and the wall fixture began to leak. It gave off such a loud hissing sound that I thought a snake was in my room. Smelling the escaping gas and still only half awake, I stumbled to the window and opened it. Then, overcome by the fumes, I fell to the floor beside the open window. I slept there for the rest of the night. It was snowing outside, and in the morning when I awoke my chest was covered with a blanket of snow.

I told my friends at Barney Gordon's about this. Underworld people have highly romantic minds. The story went around that I'd tried to commit suicide because I'd lost the love of West Indian Johnny, the big-time gambler.

My Rocky's wooing methods had been so insidious that no one could disillusion me about him. I was at a movie one day when Kid Asher, a city detective, slipped into the next seat. I'd known him since I was little and always called him Uncle Kid.

"Ethel, why don't you stay away from that Rocky?" he asked. "I sent word to you about what sort of man he is through West Indian Johnny. Didn't Johnny tell you about him?"

I didn't reply.

"I just took Rocky downtown," whispered Uncle Kid Asher.

Downtown meant only one thing, of course: police headquarters.

Within an hour I had arranged with Barney Gordon's brother, a bail bondsman, to get my pickpocket lover out of the jug. I'd been raised to twenty dollars a week and was getting plenty of tips. But after that day I had to bail out Rocky so often I found myself working for nothing.

And before long I discovered that West Indian Johnny had made no mistake when he openly accused Rocky of being a junker as well as a thief.

Being a child of the underworld, the Jekyll-and-Hyde character of my boy friend fascinated me more than it shocked me. When high, nobody could be more pleasant, courtly, and attentive than Rocky. But off the stuff, he was cross and irritable.

But like most girls who are caught on the well-baited hook called love, I found it impossible to walk out. There was another reason why I stayed with him as long as I did. Watching him intrigued me, held the same excitement and suspense most people find in murder stories and blood-and-thunder stage melodramas. I couldn't wait to find out what was going to happen next. And I was *living* my melodrama, not just losing myself in other people's make-believe.

Rocky turned out to be a three-letter man as a junker. He took C, H, and M. In dopehead language C means cocaine, H heroin, and M morphine.

We quickly reached the love-spatting stage. Before Rocky admitted to me that he had a habit, I used to do one thing that drove him wild. Often I'd find in his bureau drawers a spoon with the bottom burned, a needle, tape, and a medicine dropper. Thinking they were just rubbish, I threw them out.

Later Rocky told me he made his own bang-needle gun out of those things. He'd tape the needle to the medicine dropper and heat up the dream powder in the spoon. After using it he'd take it apart. If a hypodermic needle was found in your room you could be arrested for possession. But the cops couldn't arrest you for having a needle, a medicine dropper, and a burned spoon in your place—even if they knew what they were used for.

Rocky was a knifeman and always carried a shiv. But that never alarmed me. Except when on heroin, which puffs up a junker's courage, a hophead is too weak and cowardly to be dangerous.

Whenever we got into our frequent fights Rocky would call me a bitch and I'd go down my long list of invectives and vile epithets.

But I quickly found that he didn't mind, except when I called him a rat and a thief. Naturally, I stopped wasting my breath on mere cuss words and concentrated on those two.

One time, late at night, when I called Rocky "a thievin' rat," he couldn't take it. He got out his knife, and I ran like a rabbit. Waving the shiv, he chased me up the street. I headed for my mother's house on Fawn Street.

I had told Rocky I couldn't run on account of my bad leg. But I was so scared that night that I raced right past Momweeze's house. I kept going until I saw two cops across the trolley tracks and tore over to them.

Looking back, I saw that Rocky had stopped on the other side of the street. "Arrest that man," I said. "He just chased me with a knife."

"We can't pinch him," the cops said, "unless he comes over on this side of the street. Those trolley tracks divide our precinct from the next one."

"I'll get the rat over here," I told them. "Will you arrest him then?"

"Sure," laughed the cops.

I went to the edge of the tracks and called Rocky every bad name I could think of. In a rage he dashed at me, and I hastily retreated to the safety of the cops' territory. But Rocky stopped short on his side of the tracks. Then he went back to the pavement on the opposite side.

I returned to the tracks and showered him with fresh abuse. Once more he lunged at me and I ran back. I guess he knew the cops wouldn't arrest him so long as he didn't set foot in their precinct.

I was beginning to enjoy myself and gave him the back of my tongue again and again, retreating when he blew up. I'd advance to the tracks on getting back my breath and seeing him safely on the other sidewalk once more.

The cops were laughing. But finally one of them said, "Ethel, how long do you intend to keep this up?"

"What's the matter?" I asked. "Ain't I putting on a good show?"

"Yes, but we're about to go off duty. Why don't you let us take you to the station house? He won't dare follow you there."

"But I gotta go home sometime, and then he'll cut me good."

I didn't want to go to their police station. In my whole life I'd never heard of a girl getting rich, famous, or happy by going to any station house with cops. So I talked them into waiting there with me until their relief man came on the beat. He took me to Fawn Street.

All that running had made me hungry, and I coaxed Momweeze into going out with me to a Chinese joint. We saw Rocky lurking outside. We had hardly sat down in the chop suey place when he came in.

Momweeze was wearing my hat and coat. Her back was turned to him. Thinking Momweeze was me (I was on the inside seat where he couldn't see me), he cussed her out. With a yelp of rage she jumped up and started to hit him and shake him like a puppy. He was so amazed that he didn't try to defend himself.

I sat there laughing so loud that the windows rattled. I was wallowing in joy over Rocky's mistake. Finally Rocky jerked himself free and slunk out. I congratulated my mother and said that, seeing she could fight so good, she could be my official bodyguard and take me to and from Barney Gordon's every night.

She'd take me there, leave, and come back at closing time. Rocky came in one night. "I just want to ask you one question," he said. "What in hell did you mean by telling me you couldn't run because your leg was in such bad shape?"

That made me laugh, and a short while later I went back with him again. I was really hooked and I've never been a promiscuous woman. Having one man at a time has always been enough for me. Sometimes it's been too much. Almost every love affair I've had lasted four or five years, and so long as that love was alive I never looked at another fellow.

My attitude toward the various men I've loved has always been the same. If my man told me he had other women, I didn't mind. But if he had other women and didn't tell me, I felt deceived and double-crossed and got into a fury. With me it was never the act of infidelity that mattered so much as the cheating and lying part of it.

I stayed with Rocky even after I learned he was messing around with other women. As I've mentioned, I was held because I never knew what I'd find him doing when I came home. Sometimes, when he was high, Rocky would be down on his knees, scrubbing the floor and being the spirit of Old Dutch Cleanser. He'd tidy up the whole place like some finicky woman.

On such nights he would be very secretive. He'd refuse to speak to me above a whisper, and in a few moments he'd have me whispering, too, as though we were surrounded by assassins.

At other times when he was high he'd stand up behind the window all night, watching people on the street who weren't there. He'd hear noises in the walls and out in the hall that I couldn't hear because they existed only in his hopped-up head.

Rocky hadn't yet admitted to me that he was a junker. Whenever he was high he'd explain that he'd just been to his doctor or had taken some medicine.

One time he stayed away for three whole days and nights and I became very worried about him. When he showed up he had a broken jaw. He'd been caught, he said, "lifting a hide" from a man's pocket and the man had socked him, breaking his jaw with that one blow.

Rocky said he'd been to the hospital to have the jaw wired. Though he gave all these details freely, he became nasty and evasive when I asked him why he hadn't come home for three whole days and hadn't even sent any word to me.

However, I have eyes like a cat. When Rocky took off his shirt I saw that he had a big red love cherry on his shoulder. Then I knew he'd been with his other girl.

Having been so worried about him for three days, I started cussing him out. Rocky pulled his knife, held it at my throat, and started hitting me with his free hand.

"How can I fight you fair when you got that knife in your hand?" I asked. "At least give me a chance to defend myself."

When he didn't put the knife down I told him, "I'll yell for the Law if you don't take that shiv away from my throat. I'm going home to my mother."

"All right," he said. "Get the hell out of here and stay out."

Rocky walked out to the hall with me, the knife still in his hand. Actually, hopheads are such cowards that I wasn't too afraid that he'd cut me up. But I wasn't going to be fool enough to walk downstairs ahead of him and give him the chance to kick me down to the next landing.

The idea that I would kick *him* downstairs if he went first must have occurred to Rocky because he wouldn't go down first either. So we walked down together, with him holding the knife at my side. On coming out on the street he saw two cops on the corner and put the shiv, still open, in his pocket. It was Election Day, and the cops had been assigned to watch a polling place.

I smiled on seeing them and made a little speech to Rocky. "Now, Rocky," I said in a sweet, almost motherly voice, "I didn't do nothing wrong. You hit me and called me all kinds of names. Just because you were with that other girl."

Then I looked down the street to make sure the cops weren't going off for a cup of coffee or a bite of lunch. They were still there, so I hauled off. Aiming carefully, I hit Rocky with all my might—on the jaw. I threw him one of those terrific short jabs my Pittsburgh light-weight had showed me. Rocky's jaw fell down like a little gate, and stayed down.

The two cops watched me walk off jauntily. I suppose they knew Rocky was a pickpocket and thought socking him was a brilliant idea. I went to Fawn Street and got Momweeze to come back with me to Rocky's room. I told her to sit down so she could watch me in comfort as I ripped to shreds my boy friend's new shirts, lovely ties, and flossy pajamas. I dropped everything in the center of the floor and then went to work on an expensive hat Rocky had just bought. I punched the crown out and tore out the lining.

I was doing an Indian war dance, complete with victorious battle cries, when Rocky walked into the room, his jaw still hanging down like the jaw of some skeleton in a museum. He couldn't speak, but he managed to groan. Then he turned and left. I found out later that he went straight back to the hospital to have his jaw rewired for sound.

Within a few nights Rocky was hanging around outside of Barney Gordon's, complaining to everyone about how I socked him. When he found courage to come in he pointed to his face, crying, "Look what you done! Look at my mouth! It still hurts."

Once again I went back with him, and our lives for a couple of weeks were all sweet talk and patty-cake. But the love and passion I'd once felt for Rocky were gone, and there was only compassion left.

I was still held not only by pity but by that grim fascination. It was both bizarre and heartbreaking to watch that boy, who was no older than I, in the throes and chaos of his dreadful bondage. It was like catching a glimpse of some remote and mad world crowded with nightmare and ecstasy, supreme moments of joy and release followed by indescribable misery. Nothing destroys mind and all character so quickly as dope, and Rocky, who loved me as much, I think, as a junker can love another person, was willing to destroy me when his wild craving for drugs overwhelmed him.

One Sunday he suggested we go for a trolley-car ride. "I got an important mission uptown," he said.

"Why do you want me to come along?" I asked.

"You are always saying we never go anywhere. Come on, Ethel. Afterward I'll take you to a restaurant. We'll have a fine time."

We got off the trolley car in a dreary section of Philadelphia. I asked him what sort of mission he could have in that neighborhood.

Rocky didn't answer. Instead he led me slowly up the street. Suddenly a scrawny man appeared out of nowhere and asked Rocky for a light. While Rocky was giving it to him the man shoved something into my boy friend's fist. Then he disappeared as mysteriously as he'd come.

As he went away someone knocked on the window of a store across the street. I looked over and saw it was a cop. He came out of the store on the run, yelling, "Don't move!"

Rocky pushed into my hand the stuff the other man had given him. Bewildered and not understanding what was going on, I froze up. The cop came over and frisked Rocky.

"Did you see that fellow who was just here give this man anything?" the cop asked.

I shook my head automatically. My fist had closed, and if that cop had looked down and made me open my hand he would have found what he was looking for. But in simple clothes and with my hair down I looked so young that the policeman didn't think of searching me.

"What is a kid like you doing in this tough neighborhood?" he asked. "And particularly with a guy like this? You have no business being around here, girl."

That was all, and he let us go. When we got on the trolley car to go home, I opened my hand. "What's this all about?" I asked Rocky. "What happened?"

"Put that stuff in your pocketbook," he whispered in a panic.

When he got me home he took the stuff—two little paper-wrapped sticks about the size of penny slabs of chewing gum. He explained they were two decks of dope, one of cocaine, one of heroin.

"But why did you slip them to me when you saw that cop coming across the street?" I asked.

"What else could I do, Ethel?" he said. "If that cop had found those two decks of junk on me I would have been given two years for possession."

"And if he'd found them on me?"

"Oh, you'd probably have drawn a suspended sentence—as a first offender. Why, the toughest judge in town wouldn't give you more than a year and a day."

After that almost tragic incident Rocky didn't talk any more about having been to the doctor or having just taken "some medicine." He prepared dope and joy-banged himself right in front of me. And he came to depend on me utterly—when he had to.

The fear of going to jail haunted Rocky. When flush he kept a couple of hundred dollars around the house so I'd be able to bail him out whenever he was arrested. But it wasn't the iron bars that terrified him nearly so much as being in a place where he couldn't get junk. That always threw him into a state of wild fright.

The belief that dope fiends try to inveigle other people into going on a habit with them is nonsense. Junk is far too costly to share with anyone else. Rocky never suggested I try it.

Junk is expensive enough even when not adulterated. If Rocky bought some and it proved to be thinned out with other powder, he'd storm and rant against the peddler like a maniac.

Having taken me into his full confidence, Rocky came to need me more and more. Sometimes, after sleeping off his habit, I'd find him dripping with perspiration and too weak even to pull the bed sheet up over himself.

He taught me how to give him a shot. If he'd taken an overdose of cocaine I'd have to bang him with heroin to counteract it. Once he was too feeble to leave the house and sent me out for a deck of junk.

Few peddlers use drugs themselves, but this pusher was also an addict. I found him in such a state of collapse that I had to give him a bang before he could pull himself together and locate the junk in the place where he'd hidden it.

While living with Rocky I had a second narrow escape from the Law. I had gone out for a newspaper and noticed some sort of disturbance up the street. As I stood there at the newsstand a man I knew only as Benny came dashing past me. He thrust a pair of gloves into my hands. "I'll be back in a minute," he said. "Hold these while I go around the corner."

A moment later the coppers caught up with him and took him

away. I went home with the gloves. I told Rocky of the incident, and we opened the gloves. Stuffed inside were a hundred decks of dope.

Rocky was jubilant until I flushed all of this dream powder down the toilet. We almost had a bloody battle over that. But by then Rocky was no more than a microbe to me. Soon afterward he was drafted into the Army and was sent to a camp in Chillicothe, Ohio.

In all the spots we entertainers were singing war songs like "America, I Love You," "Liberty Bell," "Good-bye Broadway, Hello France," and the greatest of them all, "Over There."

However, I remained fairly indifferent toward that great war. My life was full and interesting. I imagine that the attitude of most Philadelphia Negroes toward World War I might have been summed up by the Boardola Brothers, two boys who played music on washboards.

A song they sang went:

> *"I don't think I want to go.*
> *The white folks makes the law*
> *Let white folks fight the war."*

They were wildly applauded when they appeared at the Standard Theatre. But one night the Army came right out on the stage and took them away. They, too, had been drafted.

The war made business drop off sharply at places like Gordon's. I was laid off except for a couple of nights a week and went back to working part time at Horn and Hardart's.

But soon I got a wire from Joe Bright, the Negro actor-producer, who'd been on bills with me in the South. Joe was putting on stock shows at the Lincoln Theatre in Harlem, and his wire offered me a week's work there. The wire said that, besides singing the blues between acts, I'd have a few lines to speak in the olio show.

I took the engagement.

But I still could not foresee a permanent career in show business for myself. When I started out with Braxton and Nugent I had got my mother to take my place as a chambermaid. Now, before starting out for my New York debut, I asked another girl if she'd replace me at the Automat until I came home.

I was making sure I'd have that bus-girl job to come back to when I finished that first one-week date up in Harlem.

9

That was a big trip for me.

New York is only ninety-seven miles from Philadelphia but was the Big Time as no other American city has ever been. The greatest acts in colored show business had long made Harlem their home and favorite stamping ground. When other performers had spoken to me about Harlem their eyes had filled with excitement and a dreamy wonder. I didn't know whether I could make good in such a place.

I'd been warned about the pitfalls a young girl faced in New York but gave them no mind. With my Clifton Street background, I was able to laugh at those stories about women being forced into prostitution. And the yarns of how you were drugged in Chinatown and woke up to find yourself a love slave in an opium den sounded like fairy tales to me.

On reaching New York I went straight to Harlem and stayed there. The Woolworth Building, the Statue of Liberty, and all the other seven hundred wonders of the city were downtown, in white man's territory, which I had no interest in exploring.

What impressed me most about New York, oddly enough, were its huge apartment houses. I'd never seen homes more than three stories high. That dozens of families who didn't know one another could live together under a common roof struck me as fantastic. It took me a long time to get used to that idea.

In those days Harlem was anything but an exclusively Negro section. The black belt ran only from 130th to about 140th Street, between Fifth and Seventh avenues. Thousands of the people who had come up from the South to work in local munition plants during the war had been crowded in with the folks already living in that narrow slice of Uptown New York. The district was swarming with life—men, women, and children of every shade of color.

Mr. Jim Crow, antagonistic and over-quick to take offense, lurked all around us. There were other Negroes living downtown, in the San Juan Hill district, and that was the scene of frequent street wars and bloody race riots between blacks and whites.

One Hundred and Twenty-fifth Street was still a white boulevard, and we weren't welcome there. Colored people could buy seats only in the peanut gallery in B. F. Keith's Alhambra Theatre, and none at all in the other white showhouses. My people were even barred from the burlesque house on 125th Street, which marks high tide, I think, in white snobbishness.

The most popular hangout for Negro sporting men and big shots was Baron Wilkins' famous night club, which also drew white trade from downtown. But the ordinary working colored people weren't wanted there and knew better than to try to get in.

The Baron's brother, Leroy Wilkins, ran another club at 135th Street and Fifth Avenue, and the sports with middle-class bankrolls went there and to Harry Pyle's place, three blocks farther north on Fifth. The sophisticates, bowed down as always with culture and ennui, congregated nightly at Connors' Club on 135th Street, between Lenox and Fifth avenues.

For entertainers, the last stop on the way down in show business was Edmond's Cellar at 132nd Street and Fifth. After you had worked there, there was no place to go except into domestic service. Edmond's drew the sporting men, the hookers, and other assorted underworld characters. Banks' Club, on 133rd between Lenox and Fifth, was in the same low-down category.

I was given a good reception at the Lincoln Theatre and was held over for the second week. What pleased me most was that so many entertainers who had caught my act at Barney Gordon's dropped in to see me.

Alice Ramsey, a dancer whom I'd met in the South, came backstage. Alice said she was working at Edmond's and sharing a flat with Lola Lee, another of his entertainers. I accepted her invitation to move in with them.

"Why go back to Philadelphia when you're through here?" she asked me. "I want you to come down one night and meet my boss, Edmond."

I promised I'd do that when I'd concluded my engagement at the Lincoln. While working I never cared to go to night clubs. I always worried about the heavy cigarette smoke hurting my throat. When I did go down to Edmond's, Alice, after introducing me to Edmond (Mule) Johnson, suggested that I go out on the floor and do my "Shim-Me-Sha-Wabble" number.

"Will you give Ethel a job?" she asked him after he'd watched me work.

He shrugged and grumbled, "All I've seen her do so far is shake her behind. But if she wants to put her money in the kitty she can work here."

Edmond paid his entertainers and the boys in the three-piece band two dollars each per night. You got that two dollars each morning at closing time. The tips the customers gave you were thrown into the kitty, and this money was divided, each entertainer and musician drawing down an equal share.

Edmond's was a small place and seated between 150 and 200 people, who sat at tables jammed close together around a handker-chief-size dance floor. It had a very low ceiling which Edmond John-son had decorated with paper chrysanthemums and streamers. The walls were covered with fading photographs of old-time fighters and Negro entertainers. Edmond was very proud of his decorations, par-ticularly the chrysanthemums.

Usually Johnny Lee was at the piano, but the first night I went there his fill-in man, One-Leg Shadow, was at the box. Wilbur, the guitar player, could play when he was fast asleep, never missing a note and stopping when the singer ended her song. Whenever people speak to me of the subconscious I think of Wilbur, the fast-asleep guitar player. He was all subconscious.

Georgie Barber was the drummer, but good, really good. He played like Sid Catlett does today. Other great drummers at that time were Diamond and Buddy Gilmore, and their drumming wasn't just noise that you applauded, hoping that would get them to stop.

When I started out at Edmond's Cellar there was an interesting and talented bunch of entertainers working there: Alice Ramsey, just a dancer, but she could kick high and good; Katie Griffin, a stoic, heavy contralto who tap-danced, and tapped very neat; Josephine Stevens, a tremendous soprano; and Edna Winston, who had no voice but gor-geous underwear. Edna did comic, eccentric dances, but her specialty was "showing her laundry." She could lift up her dress without any vulgarity, and it was a joy for all present to look at her underwear.

It turned out that One-Leg Shadow had known my father, and so he took a paternal interest in me. Shadow was a one-tune piano player. He was all right for filling in but didn't have a hell of a left hand. However, he sure knew his blues and could play fine to keep me shaking and singing the blues. There was a code of ethics at Edmond's that prevented one entertainer from poaching on another's repertory. But I was okay, as my blues and my shaking didn't conflict with the others.

I am no stoolie, but I don't think it can hurt anybody if I say there were many junkers, gamblers, and thieves down in that cellar at all times. And as at the Lincoln, I was amazed at how many people who listened to me had seen me before, at Gordon's.

I soon found out why. Whenever the lid was screwed down tight in New York, plenty of those customers would skip down to Philadelphia. They would stay down there until they got the word over the grapevine, "Come home. The district attorney has gone into his long winter's nap again."

At Edmond's I sang each night the numbers I'd done at the Lincoln—"Shim-Me-Sha-Wabble," "St. Louis Blues," Minor's Blues," and "I Want to Be Somebody's Baby Doll so I Can Get My Lovin' All the Time."

Though I often look back on that time as the happiest in my life, working in that cellar was like my tour. There was no set closing time, and once again I was working until unconscious. We'd report at nine o'clock at night and sometimes not get out of there until eight, or even ten, the next morning.

Yet we'd make only three or four appearances a night. We always had to wait for our turn to go on. But then we could stay out on that floor long as we liked if the tips kept coming into the kitty.

The customers took a great fancy to my blues by the time I'd worked there two weeks. One of their great favorites was "Chinese Blues." I made up my own words for this number, and in the song I acted out my life with Rocky.

I had Rocky down so vivid that the junkers in the crowd watching me would smile and say, "She's on that tip too." They were sure I had a habit. Thinking I was a smoker, I had access to their conversation and entree to their company.

The words I made up for "Chinese Blues" went like this:

Chinaman, Chinaman,
Washee laundry all day.
Chinaman, Chinaman,
Smokes pipe, they say.
He love little China girl
She likee him all right.
He love little China gal, too,
For he sing to her all night.
Sung Fung Lou, Sung Fung Lou,
Listen to those Chinese blues.
Honey Gal, I sing to you.
Won't you open up that door and let me in?
China gal, China gal,
Won't you open up that door and let me in?
Chinaman, Chinaman,
I feel my habit coming on.
It makes you feel happy
And makes you feel lighthearted, too,
When you get those yip sing foo yung ockway Chinese blues.

I feel my habit coming on,
I haven't got a dime,
Yet feel like I could lay down,
Draw a pill a long, long time.
When you get those yip sing foo yung ockway Chinese blues
It makes you feel happy
And you feel lighthearted, too.
When a colored gal gets the blues
She gets drunk and starts to fight.
When a China gal gets the blues
She just lays down and smokes all night.
It makes you feel happy
And makes you feel lighthearted, too,
When you get those yip sing foo yung ockway Chinese blues!

Edmond had a heart of gold. But he was also an uncouth, illiterate man, set and stubborn in his ways. His favorite term for the girls was "Bitches!"

Because I didn't drink I'd sit in the corner reading whenever I wasn't working. They had a little alcove in the cellar, and I used that.

I'd established right from the beginning that I wouldn't do any hustling of drinks. I wouldn't drink either whisky or the colored water they served that looked like whisky to the girls who didn't want to get pie-eyed. I didn't want to sit out with customers who blew smoke in my face. I wasn't selling my physical health for anybody.

Edmond didn't let his girls roll the customers or chisel money from the customers. He considered that cheap stuff and unethical. When the customers wanted to buy me a drink I ordered, as always, milk. And just as at Barney Gordon's, the customer would usually yell, "I ain't buying no damned milk!"

But when somebody would break his lifelong vow and buy milk, Mr. Perkins, the friendly and fatherly bartender who worked there, would give me the top cream off the bottle. Usually I drank an average of seven or eight quarts of milk a day. That's how skinny and underfed I still was. I always had to laugh when I thought of Mr. Perkins pouring off the creamy tops of the milk for me. That meant when any customer ordered a whisky eggnog the milk he got in it was skimmed and very thin.

Edmond would be standing at the door when we entertainers came in. He'd yell, "Get down those stairs, you bitches!" and slap them over the backside as they hurried down the steps. But he didn't say that or hit me that way. Sometimes he'd look at me and say, "You're the craziest sonofabitch!" Edmond wasn't a naturally mean man, and the way he said that robbed it of something. So I didn't mind.

One night Edmond didn't see me come in. And after an hour or so I went out to a drugstore to buy something I needed. When I returned Edmond thought I was just arriving for work. He reproachfully hit me over the behind.

I bridled. "Don't you dare hit me," I told him. "If you do it again I'll kill you. You're not my father. You're not my man. So you have no right to hit me."

He was stopped in his tracks with amazement, but I wasn't satisfied. A few nights later I came in and found him downstairs. He had just bent over to pick something off the floor. It was the kind of opportunity I could never resist. I kicked him in the behind hard as I could.

Edmond came up, staring. "Now we're square," I said. "Shall I check out? Am I through?"

Mule Johnson just laughed, and from that night on he never cursed me out or laid a hand on me. But he started picking on me. While I was performing one night he came out on the little floor and stopped me in the middle of a song.

"I'm tired of your damn blues," he roared. "All I hear out of you is that yangedy, yangedy, yangedy. Get some new songs or get out."

"But, Mr. Edmond," I said, "these are request numbers I'm singing."

"I don't care," he insisted. "I'm running the joint. I don't care to hear those numbers, so you can't sing them here."

The whole room started emptying. As they went out the customers told Edmond, "We don't want to hear nothin' else but her blues."

By that time I had built up business so that Edmond usually had people waiting upstairs, behind a chain, most of the time. Each night the place was packed with people who had come to hear my blues. But that night Edmond wouldn't let me sing them.

"I guess I'm through," I said to him when I checked in the following night.

My boss shrugged. "To me," he said, "your blues stink. But if these people want to hear them, what can I do?"

A short while later he had to let One-Leg Shadow go because my father's old friend couldn't read music. He was good for me, but he did kill off the other entertainers.

Shadow was replaced by Lou Henley, a truly wonderful pianist who always called me "Waters." Lou kept telling me I ought to learn other-type songs so I could do request numbers for the other girls when they didn't show up.

"I don't want to learn nothin' new," I told him.

But Lou kept at me, and I finally agreed to rehearse with him. But I warned him, "It's the story told in the songs that I like. If I don't like the stories in these songs you're pesterin' me about I won't sing them."

However, after that I'd go to Edmond's early. Lou Henley got me to sing the popular ballads of the day—"Dear Old Pal of Mine," "My Buddy," "Rose of Washington Square," and "A Pretty Girl Is Like a Melody." To my surprise I found out that I could characterize and act out these songs just as I did my blues.

I had heard Mamie Smith singing ballads like those at the Standard in Philadelphia. "I'm Always Chasing Rainbows," Maceo Pinkard's

"Mammy O' Mine," and "You're Mine" were other sentimental songs Lou had me work on. I still use "You're Mine."

Fanny Brice just then was making a sensation downtown with "Rose of Washington Square." But I didn't know anything about the white theater. At the time I didn't even know who Fanny Brice was.

Now many critics have praised my voice, but I've never thought I was a good singer. That I not only was able to please that brass-knuckle crowd of regulars but began to draw the sporting men and downtown white people I credit to the fact that I had spunk and was also an enigma. I was a kid, yet my mind was so old and raw that neither the public nor my co-workers could figure me out.

I also believe that they were intrigued by my characterizations which I drew from real life. I'd hear a couple in another flat arguing, for instance. Their voices would come up the air shaft and I'd listen, making up stories about their spats and their love life. I could hear such an argument in the afternoon and that night sing a whole song about it. I'd sing out their woes to the tune of my blues music. One song, for example, went like this:

> My man's trial was to come off at half-past one,
> My man's trial was to come off at half-past one,
> And he sent for me to see if I would come.
> I went to the lawyer and asked him
> To get it set for half-past two.
> I said, "I ain't a hustlin' woman
> But I'll get out and see what I can do."
> I went out and came back with fifty dollars in my hand,
> I went out and came back with fifty dollars in my hand.
> Don't ask me where I got it,
> Don't ask me where I got it.
> I give that to the lawyer and said,
> "Now bring me back my man."
> But soon as that man got out of jail he didn't treat me right.
> He stayed out with another woman that very same night!

Other verses of blues ran:

> She said that when I saw the blinds pulled
> And the curtains pinned

> That she had my man there
> And I better not come in.
> I said, "What she's telling me
> May be true without a doubt.
> What she's telling me
> May be true without a doubt.
> But if I can't come in
> She and my man better not come out!"

And here are two short ones:

> Love is like a faucet that turns off and on.
> The very time you think you got it
> It's turned off and gone.

> Some men like me because I'm happy,
> Some because I'm snappy.
> Some say I'm funny,
> Lots think I've got money,
> Others tell me, "Mama, you look
> Like you're built for speed."
> Put all together that makes
> Everything a good man needs.

I also began singing "After You've Gone" and a song I'd heard Gally Gaston sing in the South. This was "It's Right Here for You and if You Don't Get It, That's No Fault of Mine." Mamie Smith later made a record of that number.

White society folks began to come in to hear me. They were entertained by Negro society folks like Marjorie Sipp, Palmer Jones and his wife Florence, and Broadway Jones.

Mississippi, the old ex-fighter who was the only colored man allowed to drive a horse hack through Central Park, also brought rich white slumming parties to Edmond's Cellar. 'Sippi would get out on the floor and entertain his customers with his own little dance.

Our kitty pot began to spill over. Sometimes each of us would take home as much as twenty-five or thirty dollars for a single night's work. And that wasn't all. If somebody liked you particularly well he'd give you a dollar for the house kitty, then slip you a five-dollar bill for yourself. You'd put that fin in the kitty only if you were dumb enough. And I wasn't dumb enough.

One night in the week the hookers had off from their professional love-making. That night each sporting man would take his stable of women to Edmond's. Sometimes they'd take over the house, telling Edmond, "Lock the doors!" And then they'd vie with one another, seeing who could throw out the biggest tips.

Among the numerous free-spending men who brought their bank rolls down to Edmond's were Johnny Carey, Pop Steele, and Pop Lewis. Also such well-known gamblers as Jerry Preston, Rudolph Brown, Des Verney, Bub Hewlett, and Gershwin Meyers. In addition, there were colored acts like Leighton and Johnson and other people who'd never hung out along Fifth Avenue before. Fashionable Seventh Avenue had been their street until then.

They all adopted me, God bless them. They all adopted me and made me their pet.

Working such long and exhausting hours left me little time for recreation. But whenever I could I'd spend an afternoon in the peanut gallery of the Alhambra. And it was there I saw for the first time the standard Negro acts that had been playing the white time for years —Bill (Bojangles) Robinson, Moss and Frye, the dancing Dotson. I also heard many of the popular white singers: Belle Baker, Sophie Tucker, Blossom Seeley, Eva Tanguay, and Trixie Friganza.

That first year at Edmond's was sure a happy, busy one for me. There was hardly an evening when something interesting didn't happen in that cellar. Edmond was something to watch when there was a fight. He'd signal to the band to play and everybody to come out and sing their loudest. In all the din he'd pick up the rambunctious drunk like a baby—and this he could do regardless of the size of the rum-bunny—then carry him up the stairs and drop him none too gently on the sidewalk outside.

Edmond, of course, wasn't the most brilliant man in Harlem or even downtown. In fact, on no Skid Row would he have stood out in the crowd of bums as A Brainy One. But when he saw the different class of people I was drawing into his low-class dump, he realized I was a real attraction. I'd changed the clientele, making Edmond's Cellar a high-class dump.

I was pulling in so many of the money people that some of the other Harlem spots had to close up. Not only had their customers stopped making personal appearances at the tables, but their entertainers were also leaving in wholesale droves. Hoofers and singers from all over Harlem wanted to work in our place so they could get their cut of our big kitty. Edmond Johnson, the old Mule, found himself in a position to pick and choose whoever he wanted.

I'd been afraid to dance all that winter at Edmond's for fear my leg wound would open up. But one night, on an impulse, I just lifted my dress, showed my laundry, and started to hoof. My leg was all right! I was a kicker—with a difference; I could kick good with both legs. And after that, whenever I got mad at Edmond I would kick off the low ceiling those paper chrysanthemums that he thought so much of.

In the summer Edmond's Cellar became a furnace that could melt your bones—and our boss had to close up for the season. So when the hot weather came Edmond went down to Atlantic City and leased the Boathouse, a big club.

Now in small places like his in New York you could get away with a three-piece band. But in Atlantic City the people liked to dance and you had to have a full orchestra. Knowing this, I told Edmond, when he asked me to continue working for him down there:

"I'll only go if you'll hire a real band."

Edmond was not only stubborn, but he couldn't read or write. With his heart of gold and head of wood, he couldn't understand that in every summer resort everyone was out to get everybody else's hide. And they had to get it fast because their season lasted only three months. I pointed out that without a lot of band he'd be competed right out of business.

Edmond had invested every cent he had in the Boathouse lease, but he wouldn't get more musicians. He put in, instead, just three pieces. It was a big place with a big dance floor and, as Edmond's drawing card, I was on the spot. Nobody wanted to dance in that large barn to only three pieces.

I quit when Edmond wouldn't give in. That week end I worked at Egg Harbor, one of the big entertainment spots for colored people at Atlantic City. The other two were the Pekin and Philadelphia House.

Edmond came to see me at Egg Harbor. We stood face to face and he showed his muscle. He told me to get out of Egg Harbor—or else. The people who watched that big man thought he was going to crush me like a walnut. But I wasn't scared. I stood right up to him, and it turned out to be just another tongue-lashing contest.

After the week end I was invited to sing at Rafe's Paradise, a big club with mostly white patrons. I was scared to death. When Rafe offered me fifty a week I asked:

"How much do the other girls get?"

"Thirty-five."

"That's what I want—thirty-five," I told him. "I don't want to be paid more than everyone else."

This will give an idea of how much I still dreaded backstage contentiousness and professional jealousy. Remember, at all times I could protect myself. But I knew what snappishness, backbiting, and dirty whispering would go on at Rafe's Paradise if I drew down more pay than the other entertainers. I'd had non-stop fighting all my life at home and outside. It seemed to me that sacrificing fifteen dollars a week meant paying a very short tab for a little peace in my life.

Some first-class headliners played the Paradise that summer: Frankie Jackson and Edna Winston, Mary Stafford, Matty Hite, Izzy Ringgold, and the superb Charlie Johnson was the man at the piano. Show business is a small world, and Harry Waters, my uncle, turned out to be the mandolin player in the band at Rafe's Paradise.

It was there I had my first build-up as an attraction in a good spot. The shimmy had been banned in Atlantic City, but after looking over the one I did the authorities said it was artistic and decent and that I could go ahead and shake to my heart's content.

Before going into the Paradise I made Rafe understand that I didn't hustle drinks, sit and drink with the customers, or go out on any arranged dates. All my life I've found it is best to establish that before starting work in any night club.

But I did love to dance, so I danced with the customers. White men often were eager to dance with the performers. The other Negro girls in the show just wouldn't dance with them. Most colored people can't bear to dance with white folks. Invariably whites dance in a broken rhythm, don't listen to the music and count. They're off the beat most of the time.

Besides dancing with the white customers, I worked in the ensemble numbers with the chorus. My leg had completely healed, but there was still that inches-deep gash there which I concealed by wearing long opera stockings. My big solo song numbers at Rafe's Paradise were "The Japanese Sandman" and "Rose of Washington Square."

Many famous performers, both colored and white, who'd heard about the reputation I'd won in Harlem came to see me in Atlantic City. Bert Williams, the Negro star of *Ziegfeld Follies*, came three times because friends had told him I was a girl singer with his droll quality. After listening to me he sent word for me to come to his table.

"Young lady," he said, "you have the makings of a great artist."

Sophie Tucker was playing at the Beaux Arts that year and she, too, came several times to catch my act. This Last of the Red-Hot Mammas was then called a "coon shouter," an expression whose passing from the common language none of us laments.

Miss Tucker paid me a little money to come to her hotel suite and sing there for her privately. She explained that she wanted to study my style of delivery.

When the season ended I went back to Harlem, and the first showman I called on was Edmond. He warned me not to try to work for anyone else.

"This is not Atlantic City, Ethel," he told me. "And I'm not going to let you get away with it."

I just laughed at him because I had no intention of working in any other Harlem club if he still wanted me. I'd come to love that gruff, big man almost like a father. And that winter the really top names in the colored show world came to see and applaud me. Among them was Bill Robinson. Florence Mills, then with the Tennessee Ten, was at the ringside every night with her husband.

Now it occurs to me that people who read this may think I've been posing as a sissy and angelic because I've boasted that I've never touched anything alcoholic. I've mentioned drinking beer and liking porter as a child. On growing up I found that a couple of bottles of beer would give me a lift, but the third bottle would sober me up.

It was at Edmond's that I got stiff—for the first and last time. The drinking people there night after night were appalled and disgusted to see me swigging milk. I never told them that I was getting all the cream off the top of the bottles from Mr. Perkins, not wishing to expose him to abuse.

One night at Edmond's one of the girls persuaded me to drink an eggnog. It tasted wonderful—and harmless. I liked everything about it, the egg in the milk, the way it smelled, and the little crumbs of brown nutmeg that floated around the top. I had a lot of them.

That night when I got out on the floor to do my shimmy I put my hands on my hips. The crowd there was waiting to see me, the terrific hip-shaker, rattle my bones like castanets as I always did. But I stood there stiff and perfectly still. I didn't move. But I had the idea that I was shaking like mad. They applauded and said I looked cute. But I didn't know I hadn't moved a muscle until the next night.

The cops out on the morning beat all knew me, and when they saw me come out of Edmond's they asked me if I felt all right. "Sure," I said. "I feel great. I've been drinking eggnogs."

I guess they were men who liked their little nips themselves when off duty, because they said, "Wonderful, Ethel, that's wonderful."

Getting home, I walked up to our landing, then I walked *down*, but backward! All the way to the bottom without missing a single step. Terrified, I went up again, but this time crawling on my hands and knees—and made the door. They had stone stairways in Harlem houses in those days, and a fall could have been fatal.

I never drank eggnog again. And the only time I've touched alcohol since has been when my doctors have ordered me to drink wine or beer.

Rufus Greenlee and Ethel Williams were a first-rate name act I'd seen at the Alhambra. Ethel was a truly gifted dancer, and their turn had played all of the Keith houses around New York. Everybody in Harlem was shocked to hear one day that Ethel Williams had got blood poisoning in her foot from pricking her toe accidentally with a nail file.

When that foot was operated on she watched the doctor cut it, and developed a sciatic condition in her leg out of her pure fright. The rest of her Keith time with Rufus Greenlee was canceled.

Ethel became so melancholy that her mother began to stop people on the street and ask them, as old friends, to come and see her despondent daughter. Tash, one of the Four Dancing Demons, thought he could cure Ethel by constantly massaging her foot and baking it. He did everything possible to encourage her to start hobbling around a little.

But Ethel was in despair. She wouldn't come out on the street. She was afraid of how people would look at her and what they'd say. Because of my accident I well understood the kind of paralyzing fear that had her in its grip. I was scuffling around in my mind for some way to help her, when I remembered that Ethel had never seen me dance.

I went to see her. I told her I was eager to learn how to dance and did some steps very clumsily in front of her. Ethel Williams, being a born dancer, became impatient with me. The thing worked out just as I'd hoped it would. She'd forget momentarily, in her excitement, that she was crippled and would get up and show me the proper way to do the simple steps.

I'm no psychologist, but this experiment, I think, helped her gather the courage to go out on the street on a cane and one crutch. Ethel was really a stylish girl and she walked like a dancer. She was encouraged when she found out how glad everyone she met was to see her up and about. At every street corner people stopped her to tell her how hard they'd been rooting for her to get well.

After this had gone on for a while I told her, "You got to break the ice someday. Why not try night-club work for the present?" On talking her into considering this suggestion, I had to make the big pitch with Edmond. I explained to him that Ethel needed somebody to give her a chance. But he said he couldn't use her.

By that time I'd fought my way up to thirty-five dollars a week at Edmond's, and I said I'd make a deal with him. "If you'll throw in a ten-dollar bill each week, you can cut my pay ten dollars a week. That will make up the twenty you can pay her," I told him.

"Ethel, you're the damnedest fool I ever heard of," my boss said, "but I'll put her on week ends."

When Ethel Williams worked those week ends I'd go on first and do some of her steps as a challenge. That would make her so mad she'd get out on the floor and do those damn steps better.

But even then Ethel didn't regain full confidence in herself. About that time in Harlem they were casting a show they were calling Mayor of Jimtown. Miller and Lyles and Sissle and Blake were writing and producing it and were also going to appear in it. They hoped to send this show downtown. When Broadway finally saw this all-colored production it had the title Shuffle Along, and it was the fast-moving musical that made theatrical history and opened the trail for all the successful Negro musicals and big revues that followed.

I was trying to get a job in that show. I wanted to get away from smoky night-club work for a while, even if I was only to go in the chorus or in a walk-on part.

One day the producers sent for Ethel Williams and explained they had two or three spots in the show for her great dancing specialties. "I ain't dancing up to par," she told me when she came back. But that isn't what she said to the producers. Instead she told those men, I later found out, that she wouldn't join the troupe because I wouldn't let her—unless they gave me the job I wanted.

Well, if I'd had any chance of getting into that stage show, that sure would have settled my hash. And a little while later Snow Fisher, a friend of mine who was in the show, said:

"Don't go down to see them no more, Ethel. They say you're not the type."

Snow was giving me the right steer. The *Shuffle Along* producers still classed me as a Fifth Avenue honky-tonk performer. Unlike downtown, where Fifth Avenue is considered elegant and very brownstone, in Harlem it was the street of about-to-be-forgotten entertainers.

This baffled me because so many great Negro acts continued to come to Edmond's to see me, people like Earl Dancer and Cora Green, who were playing the white time; Butterbeans and Susie, already a solid standard act; Radcliff and Radcliff; Buck and Bubbles, who were about my age but already sensational with the Keith people; Billy King, who was then handling Gertrude Saunders, the comedienne slated for a big part in *Shuffle Along*; Ada Brown, the Kansas City pianist, and Amanda Randorf.

Later the careers of all those people were to be interwoven with mine one way or another. I was meeting them also at Eva Branch's boardinghouse, where so many theatrical folks ate their meals and gathered to chew the trade-talk fat. I did not like Earl Dancer at first sight. He was and is a smart showman, but I considered him egotistical and loudmouthed. Yet he was one who played a really big part in my professional life not long afterward.

During that winter I made my first appearance on Seventh Avenue when I was asked to appear at one of the special Sunday-night shows at the Lafayette Theatre, the Uptown Palace. Those Sunday shows were events. Harlem's dictys got their first gander at my work that evening. They knew performers and they decided that I had a future bigger than my present or my past.

Getting into a stage show somehow had become my greatest ambition, next to becoming a lady's maid and globe trotting with her. I was determined to show the *Shuffle Along* men they'd made a big mistake in rejecting my able services. Traveling shows were being put on by Whitney and Tutt, colored producers, and by Frank Montgomery, the performer.

Montgomery got Ethel Williams to go on tour with his troupe. Though still shaky about working in a sparked-up Broadway musical like *Shuffle Along*, Ethel realized she wouldn't need such flash stuff in a little traveling show.

Frank said he could use me for blackface comedy. That meant working in burnt cork. The name of his show, I think, was *Hello, 1919!* I sang and did a crow-jane character with Brown of Brown and Gulfport. In this I played a sort of blind-date bride whose groom refuses to marry her after getting a good look at her face. I also did a dance in the show. The white audiences thought I was white, my features being what they are, and at every performance I'd have to take off my gloves to prove I was a spade.

The big and memorable feature of the *Hello, 1919!* tour was that we show girls were forced to live in whore houses in each town, no other accommodations being available. As we hit each city the management would register our names with the police so the cops checking up on the red-light district would know we weren't "house girls." Each night when I came home from the theater I'd walk past the parlor where the men were making their nightly selections.

The madam in one of these whore houses was very superstitious. Whenever trade got slack she believed she could bring in customers by sprinkling her doorstep with pepper and a mysterious, also ill-smelling, water.

However, this madam insisted that her charm wouldn't work if anyone in the house spoke while she was at her sprinkling. Not knowing about this, I came down one night and saw her at her hocus-pocus rite. When I asked what was going on, the girls nervously hushed me.

A few minutes after the madam came back into the house five young sports walked in. "See, it's working," said the madam, rubbing her hands together. But the boys merely put a couple of nickels in the player piano, bought one round of beers, and then left.

"Who spoke?" angrily asked the madam. "One of you girls must have said something while I was sprinkling!"

None of the house whores wanted to lose their jobs, so they told her I'd broken the no-speaking rule. "Get out of here, you ignorant thing!" the madam told me—and I had to move to another whore house.

The *Hello, 1919!* company was stranded in Akron, Ohio, and it was good-by pay check. When I told the madam there of our hard luck she said:

"Look, dear! This is a five-dollar house I'm running. Why don't you become one of my girls?"

When I told her I wasn't interested she was utterly amazed. "Not interested in making five bucks a throw so easy?" she said. "I can hardly believe it."

It had been my misfortune always to come into this particular whore house, as in others, while the place was jumping with men. They'd see me, get interested, and want to come upstairs with me. They always complained bitterly to the madam when I refused to let them. I was put out of that whore house too.

I went to live with Louise Brooks, a woman who ran a restaurant in Akron. I soon got a job in a local night club, where I worked as an entertainer just long enough to get the money together to pay my fare to New York.

Once more I went to work in Edmond's Cellar. My real career was about to begin, though I didn't realize it.

10

The first Negro woman singer to make a phonograph record was Mamie Smith. My first was made for the Cardinal Company and had "New York Glide" on one side, "At the New Jump Study Ball" on the other. You'll find Bojangles Robinson's favorite word—copesetic —in the "Jump Study Ball" lyrics. I'd heard it all over the South.

The same talent scout who dug me up for Cardinal worked for other record companies. After catching my act at Edmond's a second time, he asked if I would care to make some records for Black Swan, a new company just started by Harry H. Pace and W. C. Handy, the two grand old men of Negro music.

The Black Swan office was, I think, in the home of one of the owners. The day I went there I found Fletcher Henderson sitting behind a desk and looking very prissy and important. Fletcher had come up from Georgia to study chemistry at one of the big New York colleges. But he was making side money doing arrangements and musical backgrounds for the company. He also made band records for them.

There was much discussion of whether I should sing popular or "cultural" numbers. They finally decided on popular, and I asked one hundred dollars for making the record. I was still getting only thirty-five dollars a week and tips, so one hundred dollars seemed quite a lump sum to me. Mr. Pace paid me the one hundred dollars, and that first Black Swan record I made had "Down Home Blues" on one side, "Oh, Daddy" on the other. It proved a great success and a best seller among both white and colored, and it got Black Swan out of the red. In those days you sang down into little horns just like the one you see in those ads of His Master's Voice. My second Black Swan record had "There'll Be Some Changes Made" on one side and "One Man Nan" on the other. Like all the other early records I made, these are now collector's items.

Pace and Handy then suggested that I go out on tour with Fletcher Henderson's band, which was called Fletcher Henderson's Black Swan Jazz Masters, with Fletcher as my accompanist. They said such a tour would sell a lot more of my records. They didn't call such trips personal-appearance tours in those days. I don't know what they called them; I guess they didn't call 'em anything. They just had 'em.

I didn't like to give up my steady thirty-five dollars a week and tips at Edmond's to go out of town, but the Black Swan people talked me into it.

Fletcher Henderson wasn't sure it would be dignified enough for him, a college student studying chemistry, to be the piano player for a girl who sang blues in a cellar. Remember those class distinctions in Harlem, which had its Park Avenue crowd, a middle class, and its Tenth Avenue. That was me, then, low-down Tenth Avenue.

Before he would go out Fletcher had his whole family come up from Georgia to look me over and see if it would be all right. They not only put their stamp of approval on me but they all fell in love with me at first sight. For advance man, Black Swan hired Lester A. Walton of the New York World. He was the first Negro reporter ever hired by a great white daily paper. Years later he became United States Minister to Liberia.

Interesting things kept happening, though, before we left on that tour.

One day I was coming back on the subway from Jersey, where I'd gone to make a record. It was a hot day and, feeling sick, I got off the subway downtown to get some air. I was dressed as Salvation Nell, as usual.

For some time I'd been thinking of buying a fur coat. Being a normal girl and in her right wits, I had settled on a mink. Now many Harlem people don't bother to go to the stores themselves when they want a fur coat. Instead they arrange with someone to get the kind of coat they want out of these same stores. The people who make a business of getting these coats charge you only about one third of what you are nicked in the better shops. I had just decided to get my fur coat through them.

I saw a big crowd of people on the street when I came out of the subway that afternoon. Joining them, I saw that they were all looking at some beautiful fur coats in the window of a store. There was a big-mouthed spieler there giving out with the old familiar line: "Why not pay a tiny fraction down and make sure of getting one of these wonderful coats? You can please the little woman if you are so unfortunate as to be a married man. And, ladies, we will be happy to put away one of our lovely de luxe coats, if you care to put down a small amount and pay the rest by Christmas."

Well, I looked in the window, and there was one hell of a mink coat there for only $425. I was thunderstruck, and the spieler noticed it. He started to address me directly. I was the only Negro there, and I guess he thought the idea of trying to sell a poorly dressed colored gal a fur coat would amuse the crowd of whites.

So he started working on me. It was the price tag on the mink coat that had surprised me. "Look how they gyp you uptown," I was thinking. "This should be a good lesson to me. Those thieves charge this much for a *stolen* mink coat. Shoplifters sure can't be trusted. And this is one wonderful store. I don't know how they do it."

The spieler soon had the whole crowd smiling at me. I could see them nudging one another. "Go on in, young lady," he kept prodding me. "I am sure you will find what you want."

"Have you other coats like that mink inside?" I kept asking.

"Of course we have," said the spieler, showing his big swindler's smile. The crowd was laughing. A poor Negro girl with the crazy dream of buying a mink coat was a great belly laugh to them.

"If I can't get one to suit me, I won't buy anything," I told the spieler, and went in. Some of the other people went inside with me. A few of them wanted to try on fur coats themselves; others hoped to enjoy more laughs at my expense.

So I led quite a parade inside and up to the fur salon on the second floor, where they had those fancy lights which make it impossible for you to see whether you are buying cat, dog, or mouse. I told the salesman I wanted a mink just like the one in the window. He showed me half a dozen other coats, none of them like the one outside.

"Do you really intend to buy a coat or are you just shopping?" asked the salesman petulantly.

"I do want a coat," I told him, "but why not let me try on the mink in the window? Just to see if it fits."

To my delight, he got the mink out of the window and let me put it on. I guess he thought that if he humored me he'd be able to con me into taking one of the phony coats.

The mink fit me perfectly. "This is the one I want," I told him. "I want to go out of here with this one on my back."

The salesman got pale as milk. Other salesmen and the owners of that gyp joint all came running over to his rescue. But the white people who had come in with me also gathered around. And when they saw what was happening they got over on my side.

I refused to take off the coat. The store men would have taken it off by force if it hadn't been for their other customers being there. The salesmen and owners tried charm, sneers, good-fellowship, everything but hypnotism—but I kept the coat on.

Then the salesman thought of something—and smiled. "All right, madam," he said. "We will be happy to hold this coat for you. How much did you wish to pay down?"

"The whole thing," I said. "I trust I understood your man outside correctly when he said I could have this mink for only $425. I think these good people here"—I nodded at the other customers—"will confirm that."

They started all over again showing me the other coats. I kept the mink on and refused to try any of the others they had in stock. It was a hot day, and I was melting in my fur Turkish bath.

Then an inspiration struck the salesman. "Have you the full amount on you—in cash?" he asked.

I'd been worrying about that. I had that much in the bank, but I didn't know whether I could get there in time. I'd gone into the store at noon, and it was almost three o'clock, closing time for my bank.

"If you'll send one of your people with me," I said, "I'll take him to my bank, get the money out, and give it to him."

Because the other customers were on my side, they didn't know what to do. And they sent one of their lady buyers with me to the bank. I still was wearing the mink. We got in a taxi, and I never saw anyone so happy as that disloyal woman employee of theirs. She told me the coat I had selected cost twelve hundred dollars to make up.

"It is a thrill to me," she told me on the way to the bank, "to see you give those people I work for the screwing of their lives. It is heartbreaking, day after day, to see poor workingwomen come in to get a good coat. They pick one out, but that is not the coat they get after they pay the installments. They all get robbed."

We made the bank just before closing-up time. I drew out the money for the coat and ten dollars extra, which I gave the lady buyer as a tip. Then I had just fifteen dollars left in my savings account. And I wore that beautiful mink coat for years.

Also before I went on tour, Jack Goldberg, a white agent, had been coming around to Edmond's. He must have recognized in my singing whatever it is that the world since has called artistry. Mr. Goldberg wanted me to sign a contract with him. He said he'd guarantee me seventy-five dollars a week for the first six months, with big boosts coming so fast that by the end of two years I'd be making five hundred dollars a week. He wanted to put me on the white time and drove me all over town to show me the wonderful-looking Keith theaters I'd play in under his careful management.

I refused to sign the contract, knowing that Jack Goldberg couldn't possibly pay me a nickel unless I delivered, and if I delivered he would clean up plenty on my work. If I was worth more than he paid me, I wanted it all. I would have been willing to pay him the usual agent's ten per cent, but that wasn't the deal I was offered. I had horse sense, and I believed that if I had something the public wanted it would be discovered sooner or later.

When Jack Goldberg asked me why in the world I was being so stubborn and shortsighted when I was only dragging down thirty-five dollars a week and tips, I told him:

"Lincoln freed me too."

I was learning a lot in Harlem about music and the men up there who played it best. All the licks you hear, now as then, originated with musicians like James P. Johnson. And I mean *all* of the hot licks that ever came out of Fats Waller and the rest of the hot piano boys. They are just faithful followers and protégés of that great man, Jimmy Johnson.

Men like him, Willie (The Lion) Smith, and Charlie Johnson could make you sing until your tonsils fell out. Because you wanted to sing. They stirred you into joy and wild ecstasy. They could make you cry. And you'd do anything and work until you dropped for such musicians.

The master of them all, though, was Lucky Roberts. Everybody calls him Pop, but reverently. He now runs a restaurant up on the hill in Harlem. I don't call it Sugar Hill. I don't use that kind of language. Any night you can go up to Pop Roberts' place and hear operatic arias sung magnificently by the great singers who are waiters and waitresses there.

Fine singers! People I know, people I admire, people I've worked with! But they are Negroes and have to wait on tables because they can't get any work in show business. They are colored. Period.

We had a jolly bunch of musicians in Fletcher Henderson's Jazz Masters. The trumpets were Joe Smith and Gus Aiken. Gus's brother Buddy and Lorenzo Brashear were the trombones, and a boy named Raymond Green was at the drums. Our clarinet was Garvin Bushell, who now has an eating place up in Harlem. He also plays the oboe in the New York Civic Opera Company, being the only Negro musician in that group.

We were stranded everywhere on that trip, though we had a lot of fun. The boys all adopted me as their sister, but when they played badly I told them they sounded like Jenkins' Band. This was the famous kid band sent out by a Charleston orphanage. That band has developed some first-rate musicians, but as kids they didn't toot any dream symphonies.

Being brotherly buddies of mine, all the Jazz Masters thought it right that they should use me whenever they wanted to get out of dates. No matter which musician it was, he'd tell the unwanted girl that I was his girl friend. He'd even get me to bawl him out in front of her. I'd say:

"None of that good-by stuff. Where do you think you're going? You're coming right home with me. Hear?"

The spurned girls talked together, and word got around that I was sleeping with the whole outfit. My name began to be besmirched as their wholesale mistress.

But they had not that kind of interest in me, nor I in them. None of them wanted me for a sweetheart, yet they would all get very jealous and start muttering if I responded to any town boy who got stuck on me. Just as a warning they would play a little lousy while I sang. That's when I would tell them they sounded like Jenkins' Band and German curbstone musicians.

I kept having arguments with Fletcher Henderson about the way he was playing my accompaniments. Fletcher, though a fine arranger and a brilliant band leader, leans more to the classical side. On that tour Fletcher wouldn't give me what I call "the damn-it-to-hell bass," that chump-chump stuff that real jazz needs.

All during the tour I kept nagging at him. I said he couldn't play as I wanted him to. When we reached Chicago I got some piano rolls that Jimmy Johnson had made and pounded out each passage to Henderson. To prove to me he could do it, Fletch began to practice. He got so perfect, listening to James P. Johnson play on the player piano, that he could press down the keys as the roll played, never missing a note. Naturally, he began to be identified with that kind of music, which isn't his kind at all.

Even today, almost thirty years later, I practically have to insult Fletcher Henderson to get him to play my accompaniments the way I want.

When Fletch is in form he is fine for me. When he doesn't play good for me I say, "Fletch, stop playing that B.C. music of yours."

I know what B.C. is, and A.D. too. What I referred to was the way he played so long ago that it seems to have been before the earth was discovered.

I can't read music, never have. But I have almost absolute pitch. My music is all queer little things that come into my head. I feel these little trills and things deep inside of me, and I sing them that way. All queer little things that I hum.

The funny part is that lately Fletcher Henderson, from playing the music I make him imitate, is once again becoming identified and well known for this sort of music instead of his own.

There was so much music day and night on that tour with the Jazz Masters that even Bubbles, my Pekinese dog, developed a sensitive ear for it. The last song on my program was "Down Home Blues." On hearing me finish that number Bubbles would know it was time for me to come off. He'd trot out of the dressing room and onto the stage, pawing at my dress to be picked up.

One reason that we got stranded everywhere—in spite of having the ace journalist and future State Department diplomat Lester A. Walton smoothing our way for us—was that we made the mistake of booking the show through various colored organizations. These organizations had never heard that peace is wonderful and were forever battling each other. They were jealous of one another and would knife and boycott any attraction not booked through their lodge.

So everywhere we went we were told we were wonderful but had made the ghastly error of booking through the wrong organization. If we worked through the local colored Elks, we were informed that next time we should contact the Knights of Pythias. If we were doing business with the Knights of Pythias in the next town, it should have been the Elks. It was as though they said:

"Next time, instead of contacting the sons of bitches, work with us, the bitches of sons."

We staggered back to New York, finally, after six haphazard months, and with Lester Walton still in advance.

It was summer.

Once again I went to Atlantic City to work at Rafe's Paradise. While there I was offered the two biggest chances of my career up till then—and passed both up. Morris Gest, the most extravagant producer of Broadway spectacles of the time—came to see me. He warmly praised my work and asked me to sing in his big show, *Chu Chin Chow*.

I told Mr. Gest that I was sorry but I was booked up solid for two whole years. I was scared to work for white people. I didn't know very much about them, and what I knew I didn't like. The very idea of appearing on Broadway in a cast of ofays made me cringe in my boots.

Another Broadway producer, one of the Selwyn brothers, came with his wife three or four times to see me work. He also wanted me to appear in a downtown show. I promised to see him in September—but I never made it. I never had any intention of showing up at his office.

Near the dance floor at Rafe's there was a little ring of seats for the performers to rest in while they weren't doing their numbers. One evening while I was sitting there quietly a noisy and drunken white man came along. I didn't like the looks of this white party. He seemed primed and ready for trouble.

I got up quickly and went to the bar. Ethel Williams and Frankie Johnson were doing a dance turn on the floor. They stayed out there so long that I couldn't figure out what was going on. Several times the music stopped, and I could hear money hitting the floor—then they'd do new encores.

So I went back, and Ethel and her partner were still on. And there was this drunken ofay s.o.b. sitting in my chair. I watched him for a moment, and there he was with his hand in my pocketbook, which

I'd left hanging on the rail. He was digging into my pocketbook and coming up with my money and throwing it out to Ethel and Frankie!

"You're not supposed to do that," I said, running up to him.

"Get away from me, you nigger bitch," he yelled, and he called me a lot of other names.

I raised my fist. I had two diamond rings on my hand that I wore for decoration and also, in emergencies, for both offensive and defensive work. He started to get up from his chair, and when he was off balance I hit him. I can hit short and I can hit long. He went ass over teakettle, as they say in café society.

When I saw he was trying to get up I picked up a beer bottle. My victim was a burly fellow, but I don't think he minded when peacemakers jumped in between us.

"She hit him with the beer bottle," said one of the spectators.

"Beer bottle nothing," said those admiring me from tables close by. "She hit him with her fist."

It was quite a victory. A few nights later the same fellow came back and made another disturbance. When Rafe tried to put him out he beat up my boss. And Rafe was quite a healthy and husky proprietor.

The day after scoring my knockout I went out on the beach. A few men greeted me respectfully as "Miss Johnson"! I turned around. It was some of the gangsters from Philadelphia who were giving me the same name as Jack Johnson, the former heavyweight champ.

I don't fight people with my fists any more. But I could get in shape if the occasion arose.

That fall I again worked for Edmond. Adelaide Hall, who was then rehearsing for *Shuffle Along*, came to see us almost nightly. She would do a number on the floor. Adelaide had a lovely, soft voice, and after singing a sentimental song she'd go into a flatfoot-time buck with much beating and stomping. Also in the show was Chippie Hill, who was so recently "discovered" by a lot of Johnny-Come-Lately Columbuses. Poor Chippie was killed in a car accident only a few days before I wrote these words. Her acclamation, unfortunately, came too late to do her much good.

That was the great time of "drags" in Harlem. In these affairs there would be fashion parades for the male queers dressed in women's clothes. Those who came to Edmond's would beg me to let them wear my best gowns for the evening so they could compete for the grand prizes. And they did win many first prizes in my clothes.

One night I lent my black velvet dress, trimmed with ermine, to one of these he-she-and-what-is-it types. But he got to fighting with his "husband" at the affair and was locked up in a cell.

And with him to jail went my expensive black velvet dress trimmed with ermine. The dress smelled of carbolic acid, the Chanel No. 5 of the cell blocks, for months, and I couldn't wear it. I would not have been much more humiliated if I myself had been thrown into the poky.

All this time I stayed cooped up but contented in the black belt. I was hearing quite a bit about the shows on Broadway but wouldn't go down to see them as I didn't care to sit up in the peanut gallery.

The only place outside of Harlem that I really liked to visit was Coney Island. I loved to play the sucker games and visit the freak shows and go on the rides. I got a thrill out of winning the gold ring on the merry-go-round. When there are no merry-go-rounds in one's childhood a person likes to make up for missing them. I'd like to go on all the Coney Island merry-go-rounds right now. But I know that a tall girl like me wouldn't look right on such a childish ride. And people would think I was doing it just for the publicity.

Whitney and Tutt, the Harlem theatrical producers, had a show called *Oh! Joy!* that they were booking to follow the tour of *Plantation Revue*, starring Florence Mills. They sent for me because they had no Negro performer in her class. Whitney and Tutt had refused to consider me for their shows before I made a big stir with my records.

I'd heard that they already had hired Sarah Martin to be their lead. Not wanting to put Sarah out of a job, I refused their offer. But somehow or other they fixed things up with her. I think they paid Sarah a salary even though she was out of the show. She told me it would be all right with her if I took her place.

Oh! Joy! was the show in which I first appeared as a name performer. But when Whitney and Tutt asked me to play Boston I didn't want to go there. I thought I could get out of it by asking for too much money and I said I wanted $125 a week. But they said they'd pay that.

This thing of asking what I considered an impossible salary when I didn't want to work for someone has boosted my pay again and again. That is one reason my pay got so big later on.

However, there is a bad angle to this. Whenever I was paid more than I thought I was worth I would always have to go out there and work my head off—so I wouldn't feel guilty and a thief.

When I planned my routines for *Oh! Joy!* I wanted to make a different kind of entrance than other well-known record singers were using. They were going in for flash and class, one of their favorite entrances being coming out on the stage through the door of an ornate phonograph. Just before my first entrance in *Oh! Joy!* Ethel Williams would go out on the stage.

"Where's that partner of mine?" she'd ask the orchestra leader. "Where's that Ethel Waters? What can be keeping her?" And she'd look all over the stage for me, behind the curtain, in the wings, and, for a laugh, under the rug. She'd mutter, "How can I start our act without that gal?"

After all that build-up I'd come out—in a funny hat and a gingham apron that was a gem. I was slim, and when Ethel would ask, "Are you Ethel Waters?" I'd answer, "I ain't Bessie Smith."

Those two lines would wow the audience. Then I'd sing the plaintive and heartbreaking song, "Georgia Blues." The number told the story of a Southern gal who felt lost and homesick up North. Georgia was home to her, no matter what else it was, and the piece had universal appeal. It was like the cry from the heart of all wanderers everywhere. And on the stage I was the bewildered, little colored girl who couldn't feel at peace and at ease so far off from the scenes of her childhood.

Ethel Williams would come on then and dance—and she was always a brilliant performer. The show went over well, and there was talk of bringing it to Broadway.

We played the Arlington Square Theatre in Boston. While there I got a new idea for my entrance, and Whitney and Tutt put it into the show. Now, when the curtain went up, you saw on the stage a boxcar. The door was closed and there was a sign on it that read, "All points South!" So after Ethel looked for me the door would be opened and the audience would discover me there, looking forlorn in my pathetic gingham apron and funny hat.

In Boston, though we were playing in opposition to *Shuffle Along*, the ofays who saw the show loved it. But there was not happiness unrestrained backstage in *Oh! Joy!*

In shows like that one, operating on short, sometimes non-existent, bank rolls, the producers often had to resort to legal but devious devices when payday rolled around.

You'd be called in by the management. "We have your money, Ethel," they'd say, and they would very kindly show you your money. "But if we pay you off in full, sugar, we can't pay the others. And if we can't pay them, we'll have to close the show. And you wouldn't want to throw all those other poor, hard-working actors out of work, would you?"

So it would end up with you taking what you could get, fifty dollars or so to pay your room rent and other expenses. Now this routine always amused me. I can't say it made me hysterical with laughter, but I'd leave smiling.

The other actors, waiting outside to talk to the producers, would see me with that smile on my face. And if the management told them I had insisted on being paid in full and consequently they would have to take a cut, they'd believe them. And they'd blame me for being selfish. At first I wouldn't know why my fellow performers jumped salty on me, but later on they told me.

Or when a show had rocky financial going the bosses would assemble everyone backstage and give them (instead of eating money) that old refrain, "If you can only hang on a little longer, we'll pass the danger point and have a hit."

When a producer decided to cop that plea he talked on and on. I'd never stay to listen, knowing that the only important point he was going to make was that we weren't going to get our money in full and toto. Such apologies and explanations bored me.

If we'd been playing to crowded houses the producer would swear on his children's bones that the house was almost all paper. If he wanted us to work our heads off he'd pass the word around that the Shuberts were going to take over the show, making us all rich and famous. And "Mr. Shubert" was catching the show that very evening!

He would pull in any frowzy-looking, ragged old white bum he found on the corner. He would dress the bum up, sit him in a box, and that would be "Mr. Lee Shubert" for that performance. The actors would then go out and kill themselves.

I was in another car accident in Boston. I was still leery of riding in automobiles, but one night some of the cast coaxed me into letting them drive me to Roxbury, where I was living. Our car hit a big truck at Forsyth and Ruggles. I was taken to the hospital. My injuries were not nearly so serious as the ones I'd suffered down in Birmingham. I had a hurt knee, though, and my face was cut. There was such a big lump on my cheek that I couldn't open my mouth. I still have a small scar on my face from that accident.

While recovering I stayed in Boston and testified in the lawsuit. I refused to blame the truck driver for the collision, but the owner of our car got some money, anyway.

When I got to New York, Whitney and Tutt said they were opening *Oh! Joy!* downtown and wanted me to rejoin the company. But when I went downtown I found out that the show was opening there all right—but in a tent set up in an empty lot.

"Here in New York," I was told, "a tent show will be a novelty."

"It ain't no novelty to me," I said. "The days when I worked in a tent are over forever. I have slept with horses for the last time, I trust."

I didn't go back into the show. And that tent was soon closed up like the tents of the Arabs. With Fletcher's boys I was booked into a Philadelphia theater. We were billed: "Extra Added Attraction—Ethel Waters and Fletcher Henderson's Jazz Masters!"

Jack Johnson was the headliner. Jack had just come out of a federal prison where he'd done a year for violating the Mann Act.

Jack, still enormously popular, was playing a return engagement. His dressing room was right next to mine. I always looked the other way when I passed his dressing room. I felt I meant nothing to him and gave him distant respect. Now this wasn't because I didn't admire that great fighter who had battled his way up from the docks of Galveston, Texas, to become the first Negro world's heavyweight champion. In fascination I would stand in the wings to watch him do his sparring turn. But I didn't think we could possibly have anything in common, personally.

I was in my dressing room between shows one day when Jack's valet came in and said, "Mr. Johnson wants to see you."

"All right," I told him, "it is exactly the same number of steps from his dressing room to mine as it is from mine to his. So tell him to drop over."

The valet got an odd look on his face. I guess no colored person had ever responded like that before to an invitation from his boss. When Jack Johnson said "Come!" they all came running. Especially the girls. But in a few minutes Jack himself knocked on my door and asked very politely if he could come in. He said, "May I ask you something?"

When I nodded he asked why I was so unfriendly and standoffish with him.

"I always speak to you, Mr. Jack, don't I?"

He invited me to have dinner with him that night. He was surprised because, unlike other colored girls, I didn't get blown over when he spoke to me. I thanked him and shook my head.

"But why not?" he asked. "Why won't you have dinner with me?"

I told him I wanted to make myself clear. "That white girl I see hanging around the theater, Mr. Jack—isn't she your wife?"

"No, she's just a friend."

"But I never see you with any colored girls."

"I have nothing against colored girls," he said. "And I'd be proud to be seen out with you, Ethel."

But I wouldn't have dinner with him. And Jack Johnson was intrigued. I don't think he had met one other colored girl since becoming famous who didn't try to track him down.

Jack Johnson and I were good friends to the end of his life. He regarded me as one of his buddies, and whenever we were in the same town he'd come to see me. Once in a while he'd say, "I could like a woman like you, Ethel."

But I'd only have to say, "Now, Jack," and we'd both laugh and go back on the more satisfactory buddy-pal basis. Once I said to him, "It's universally known, Jack, that you have the white fever."

"I like colored women," he told me. "I could love a colored woman. But they never give me anything. Colored women just won't play up to a man the way the white girls do. Look at you. What do you tell me? You fluff me off. No matter how colored women feel toward a man, they don't spoil him and pamper him and build up his ego. They don't try to make him feel like he's somebody."

I guess we Negro girls could take lessons from white women and light-colored women. We might learn a lot about flattering the vanity of our men, catering and playing up to them more.

I have noticed this same difference even in women of the underworld. Pimps very seldom had trouble with the white girls in their stables. The white girls almost always did as they were told. They obeyed. It was the brown-skin whores who made all the hell, were the rebellious and independent ones, and showed they had minds and wills of their own.

When the Black Swan Company dissolved, Fletcher Henderson's band broke up and the musicians went their separate ways. But there was a tremendous demand in the independent Negro houses for my act because of the popular blues records I had made for Black Swan.

A Chicago agent had jived Mr. Johnston, a white man who ran the Grand Theatre in Chicago, into thinking I would go out there for a return engagement.

But I wouldn't go. On my tour with the band I hadn't always been paid off and I was scared to go out on my own. So once again I asked a salary I thought no one would pay—five hundred dollars a week, plus transportation for three persons. I stipulated that I would want a good pianist and Ethel Williams in my act, and that I would only go out on a two-week guarantee.

I was flabbergasted when the tough deal was accepted. Why Mr. Johnston was willing to pay me big money like that, I later found out, was because he had to compete with big Negro musicals like *Shuffle Along*. They were drawing a lot of his regular trade away. The people who usually went to his colored theater were going into the balcony of the white theaters where the Negro musicals were booked. They wanted to see Florence Mills and the other top colored stars.

I had quite a time finding a pianist. I tried several established people with no luck, then got a good man. I paid him and Ethel Williams fifty dollars a week each. Mr. Johnston was a fine and courteous man. We had two very successful weeks at his house, the Grand, and when I was finishing there he said:

"Ethel, you have proved you can hold my customers uptown in opposition to Negro musical shows. So why don't you book your act into other cities? Towns like Detroit and Cleveland?"

"I don't know enough about the business side of my work to do that," I told him.

"Well, let's do it this way, Ethel. If you care to let me, I'd book you into the other towns. I'll guarantee you a salary of two hundred and fifty dollars a week and expenses and pay for your dancer and accompanist. I'll also buy two beautiful drops for the act."

I liked that offer. But my male accompanist had other commitments just then. I had to go back to New York to find another pianist. I had heard of a girl named Pearl Wright and got her to join our act.

Pearl was very good at the box. She was a nice girl, too, refined and very well educated. She was to be a mainstay to me for years, and my very good and dear friend.

Besides buying me two beautiful drops, Mr. Johnston paid for all the other new props we needed. That was a good deal all around. Sometimes he got six or seven hundred dollars for the act, and he had no trouble getting lots of work for us at that price. I kept the colored patrons out of the balconies of the white theaters where the Negro revues were playing and damn near starved some of those shows to death.

At the end of the week I'd take out my salary and expenses, pay off Pearl and Ethel. But as my salary increased, so did my personal expenses. As a headliner I had to buy plenty of expensive clothes and I got a lot of bites from my family and many luckless professional friends. I always liked to help people, feeling that, after all, it was God who brought me the good money and that He would be pleased if I spread it around.

The colored theaters had recently been organized into the T.O.B.A. (Theater Owners Booking Association). Milton Starr, a Nashville theater owner, was president, and Charlie Turpin, who ran a theater in St. Louis, was vice-president.

I really dressed in beautiful gowns for that act of ours. For my closing number I sang "Shake That Thing" and did a dance for the encore. That was a big surprise to my public, which, because of my records, thought of me only as a singer.

After Detroit and Cleveland we played all of the Eastern cities except New York. When I went into Charlie Turpin's house in St. Louis, Butterbeans and Susie, my old friends, were also on the bill. Stringbeans had died, and now Butterbeans and Susie were the top standard act on the colored time.

I had a new record out, "That Da Da Strain." It was a big hit, and people liked me to sing it. But Susie of Butterbeans and Susie had been doing a terrific patter with the same song, and it had stopped shows for them everywhere.

Butts and Sue were worried over what I'd do about the number. I was the headliner and I could claim the right to sing any song I wanted to. But I never believed in weakening the rest of the bill. The people might come in to see the headliner, "Ethel Waters of Black Swan Records," but they also wanted the rest of the bill to be good.

I've always wanted the whole bill that I was on anywhere to be good.

I told Butts and Sue, "You do 'Da Da Strain' your way. If the public asks me to do it, too, I'll sing it again." Butterbeans and Susie were on ahead of me, and they were one tough act to follow, even without that sure-fire number. But it worked out okay.

Bill Robinson, who just called himself Bojangles then, was playing in St. Louis when I was there. As I'd mentioned, he had come to Edmond's often, and he was annoyed when I didn't remember him. Ethel Williams knew people like Bojangles, having played on the white time with them. She could talk to them fine, but I couldn't. They used a different language, and I didn't understand it or know what to say to them. Business at Turpin's house was terrific when we were there. The lines of waiting people stretched so far that Charlie Turpin was way down at the railway station with his pistol and money satchel.

Harlem was crazy about Bojangles. They would yell "Bo! Bo!" when they saw him. The last time I saw him at Edmond's he had been barred off the white time for some misdemeanor or caper. But E. F. Albee, the head of the Keith circuit, who was usually sterner than a whole Southern Baptist convention, loved Bojangles and reinstated him so he could again play the B. F. Keith and Orpheum time.

Everybody in Harlem said Bojangles was a magnificent dancer, and they were certainly right. I would be the last one to take anything from Bo as an artist who had genius in his feet. But I wasn't knocked over, because I had seen other great Negro dancers who could challenge Bill Robinson or any other hoofer, including Fred Astaire, at any and all times. Two of these men were King Rastus and Jack Ginger Wiggins. Ginger Wiggins could do two hundred or three hundred different intricate dance steps without repeating. White people never saw them, but that's the white folks' loss.

So anyway, when Bill was at the Orpheum in St. Louis he was nice enough to come over to the Washington Theatre to see us. He invited us all to a party he was giving in his hotel rooms. I promised to come. I forget what happened, but at the last minute I couldn't go. I'm sorry to say that Bill never forgave me for what he took to be a slight. He always disliked me after that.

Maury Greenwald, a white producer, had seen me work in Chicago and for weeks during this tour kept pestering me to sign up with a Negro musical he wanted to send to England. He'd heard that Lew Leslie was planning to ship his *Plantation Revue* to London, and Mr. Greenwald figured that if he got there first with *his Plantation Revue* he'd clean up, a Negro show being then an unheard-of novelty around old Piccadilly Circus.

Greenwald had already signed up James P. Johnson and said Jimmy would be my accompanist. I told Greenwald I wouldn't take Johnson and insisted I must have Pearl. But this was only to get out of going, because the one and only Jimmy has always been one of my idols. And it proved a perfect out for me.

My real reason for not wishing to go was that I still had deep doubts and fears about working for a white manager in white theaters before white audiences. As it turned out, it was just as well that I didn't go to London with that show. It failed there, though the Florence Mills revue was a staggering success.

We started to play the Southern time in New Orleans. When last there with the Jazz Masters, I'd done a broadcast with the band over the *Times-Picayune's* radio station. We were the first colored entertainers permitted to broadcast from that station.

One day an old, ragged colored woman approached me on the street in New Orleans. For some reason she reminded me of my grandmother, Sally Anderson. "Daughter," she said, "I'm hungry. Please give me a nickel for some coffee."

I gave her a quarter, and she told me that she'd had an operation. Then she gave a vivid description of how the doctors had cut her.

"I'm still sick," she whimpered. "If you don't believe me, come home with me."

Touched because of her resemblance to Sally, I did go home with her. She was living in a hovel, but she kept it clean and neat.

I got attached to her, and she began to worry about what she'd do when I left town. I told her I'd send her a few dollars each week, which was all she needed to live on. The old lady couldn't read or write, and she said she would have to mark an X on the money orders I sent her.

Some time later, when I got the receipt from one of the money orders, I noticed that the character of the X scrawled on them had changed. I suspicioned that something had happened to the old lady and that someone else was taking the money orders.

I had a friend in New Orleans investigate to see if the old woman was dead. They reported back to me that she had indeed died recently and one of the neighbors had been taking the money orders and signing for her. So it's true that you can identify any person's X, just as you can a full signature.

When we arrived in Macon, Georgia, and went to the theater we sensed something grim and forbidding about the place. The people around the showhouse were the same as usual, except that they didn't say anything. It was as though a sorrow too profound to express hung over them.

We weren't there long before we were told the truth. A colored boy had been accused of talking back to a white man. For that he'd been lynched, and the white mob that murdered the youngster had flung his body into the lobby of our theater.

They threw it there to make sure many Negroes would see it.

As it turned out, the house I was boarding at was next door to the house of that dead boy's family. His people told me he was guilty of no crime. He had had no trial nor any chance to defend himself.

I became friendly with that grief-torn family. I sat with them, prayed with them, and tried to comfort them. But what is there to say to the mother of a lynched boy?

Like the other colored mothers of the South, she had not found it easy to bring up her son. She had done her best, tried to teach her children to smile good-naturedly when reviled and abused and laughed at.

But in the end this beloved son of hers had "talked back" to a white man. The sentence of the white man's mob had been death.

And what was there to say?

Should I have whispered, "Cry softly, little Negro mother. Put your work-cracked, tired hands before your face so the white men who killed your son won't be reminded of their shame and their crime.

"Hide your grief. Clutch tightly at your tormented heart so its wild beating will not be heard, mother of the Negro boy who has been lynched. Stifle your groans, little mother, as you follow his slashed and broken body to the Negro cemetery. Even though this boy you are burying was once the sweet little baby you fed at your breast and went hungry to feed and clothe. Yes, this is the little boy you dreamed of someday sending to college, the same boy you were so proud of.

He is no more, little mother, but don't cry out loudly. Hide your grief and your outraged heart. You are a Negro, Mother, and don't count for anything in this white man's world."

I sat and prayed with the family of that lynched boy while I was in Macon. But there was little I or anyone else could do for them. At least so it seemed to me then. I never dreamed that some years later, in a gay and sparkling Broadway show, I would have the chance to tell the story of their misery and their impotence in a great song called "Supper Time."

After we left Macon I became even more impatient with the two kinds of ostracism we were running into everywhere we traveled in the South. The dictys in each town were shocked that Pearl Wright, who had been a schoolteacher and was a member of one of the oldest Southern Negro families, had debased herself so far as to become the accompanist of a blues singer.

We were playing colored theaters, but the white people wanted to see me and hear my songs. When your act went over good in these showhouses you gave two performances at midnight for exclusively white audiences. If your act wasn't so hot there was only one of these midnight shows during the week. We had to do two of the extra shows in every town we visited on that trip.

So we found ourselves applauded by the ofays in the theater and insulted by them on the streets.

In Nashville, Tennessee, where the Bijou, the theater we played, was run by Milton Starr, president of the T.O.B.A., I got another kind of surprise.

Mr. Starr was a young, soft-spoken Southerner and a Jew. I will never forget him because he was the first white man who ever addressed me as "Miss Waters." He treated me as though I were already a star, and I like to think he recognized the talent I had and foresaw that the world would one day acknowledge it with rich rewards.

Other things I found in Nashville were less pleasant. The rats there were heavyweights. They were game as bulldogs and big enough to climb ladders. Going into a washroom one day, I saw one of these huge rats drinking at the washstand. He turned, looked at me indifferently, then continued drinking. I actually, on one occasion, saw another drinking from a Coca-Cola bottle which he held up in his two front paws. Their cockiness gave me the chills.

When George White, the Scandals producer, brought the black

bottom to Broadway, he was merely introducing to New York a dance that had come out of Nashville originally. This memorable backside-wriggling number got its name from the toughest section in town. The Negroes who lived in the Black Bottom neighborhood in Nashville were so bad, aggressive, and hurly-burly that the bravest white coppers didn't dare invade their streets.

If the coppers had a warrant for one of the criminals who lived in the Black Bottom they'd send word in for him to come out and report.

Nashville's undertakers were also an aggressive lot. One day while backstage I heard shots fired on the street. I ran out and learned a Negro boy had been shot. There were two funeral parlors on that street, and I watched morticians run out of both of them, carrying their baskets. They raced each other to the dead boy's side, and the man who got there first claimed the job of burying him.

In the Little Rock theater we played, no special performances were given for whites. But the many white people who had bought my records insisted on seeing me in person.

The manager finally agreed to set aside a section of the house for them. But they weren't the best down-front seats. These were kept for the colored patrons and, for once, the dominant race found itself segregated, and in the rear.

Playing theaters of the type we were working in, performers constantly had trouble getting the stagehands to co-operate. These stagehands are usually relatives or favored pals of the owner. Sure of their jobs, they spit at the actors and paid them little mind.

This caused me great trouble in Bessemer, Alabama, the coalmining town. For a number called "When You're Lonesome, Telephone Me," I was wearing a radium dress that showed up luminous when all the lights were put out.

On opening night there in Bessemer I instructed the theater's electrician to put out all the lights. "I will wave my fan," I said, "before I begin that number. That will be your signal to switch off the lights."

But that evening he left two lights burning, spoiling the whole effect of my radium dress, which didn't light up good when the theater was only half dark.

I sure pitched a bitch with that electrician. When he said it was the manager who had messed up the lights-out cue I jumped on that man too. I explained how important the dress that shone in the dark was to my number. "Your people have never seen anything like it," I told him in my rage. The white man just gave me a hostile look and walked out without answering me. When he stayed away from backstage all week the other girls in the show got more and more nervous. But I had no more trouble about the lights.

One of the girls who had heard me give that manager the bawling out of his life, said one night, "Oh, Ethel, you're in bad trouble. Our people just don't talk salty to white folks. This is not New York. It's Bessemer, Alabama."

Everybody agreed that my difficulties with the manager would come on Saturday, when we were through there and he came backstage to pay us off.

And sure enough, when he was paying me off on Saturday night he said, "I want to talk to you, girl."

"Oh, oh!" I thought. "Here it comes: Mr. Trouble wearing spiked shoes."

But the white man astonished me by saying, "Any time you want to play my theater again, Ethel, you can. Never in my life did I ever think I'd find myself taking what I did from you or anyone of your kind."

Then he went on to talk tenderly of the Negroes who came to his theater. Most of them worked in the mines, and they were always so eager to see the show that they didn't wait to wash the coal dust off their faces. They didn't even go home but came straight from work to his theater. I'd noticed all week how they gaped at us up on the stage as though they thought us creatures from another world.

"Ever since Monday night," he explained, "I've been thinking of what you said to me, Ethel. It so happens that I love these niggers who come to my theater. I love each and every one of them. And I know them. I know what they are and how they think and feel about things.

"And what I kept on thinking all week was that you must love these humble people the same way I do. That's why you couldn't bear the thought that they weren't seeing your radium dress light up. What mattered to you was that they weren't seeing the wonderful sight they had paid their hard-come-by money to see."

I was hardly able to answer that man. I just looked at him in wonder. He was a white man who had spent all his life among my people in that Southern town, and he loved them, so he had been able to read just what was in my mind and understand why I'd become so furious with him.

In his mouth the hated word "nigger" was almost a term of affection. I've thought a great deal about that. And the reason, I guess, we have come to detest that word "nigger" is not for itself but for the way it is usually used and by the kind of white people who throw it at us in burning contempt.

11

Charles P. Bailey, the tough-bitten old Georgia cracker, was still running the theater at 81 Decatur Street in Atlanta. We played it because it was the T.O.B.A. theater there.

Bailey had feuded, though, with Lonnie Reed, at whose boarding-house he had made us stay when we worked for him before. But now Bailey gave strict orders that we must not set foot or finger in Lonnie's. Our official residence was now in a little hotel run by Old Man Howard, as everyone called him.

As usual, Pearl Wright went over to the theater on Monday morning to run through my numbers with the two boys in the pit. Eddie Heywood, Sr., was still house pianist at No. 81 and had only a drummer with him. There was a man tuning the stage piano, so Pearl came home. She made a second trip but soon was back at the hotel again.

"I don't know what to do, Ethel," she said. "I can't play on that piano because the man tuned it in two different keys. I told that to Mr. Bailey, but he says it doesn't matter."

I went over with her to the theater and tried to explain to Mr. Bailey that Pearl couldn't use a piano with the bass tuned in one pitch, the treble in another. "You'll have to do something about that," I said.

"I don't have to do nothin' about it," he told me. "Your girl can play on the pit piano."

I looked down at that piano in the pit. It was half shoved under the stage. "I can't go on if you don't get the stage piano tuned right."

"What's this?" he asked, as though thunderstruck.

"I said I can't go on. You see, Mr. Bailey, during my act Pearl and my dancer talk to each other. How can she talk with Pearl sitting down there in the dark and almost out of sight?"

"Did I hear you say you can't go on? You will go on. And that girl of yours will play in the pit."

"I am willing to pay to have the piano tuned again or for the rent of another one."

"Who do you think you're talking to?"

"If I'm not mistaken, I'm talking to Mr. Charles P. Bailey."

"That's right, and look, you. No Yankee nigger bitch is telling me how to run my theater."

That was too much for me. I told him, "And no Georgia cracker is telling me how to run my act."

"I'm Bailey," he said, becoming all venom and white supremacy. "I'm standing on my grounds as the owner of this theater. And if you don't do what I say, I'll kick your ass out of here."

"I'm Ethel Waters," I told him, "and I'm standing on my grounds. And you or no other cracker sonofabitch can tell me what to do."

After that I just sat down and waited. The first show started at one o'clock. Two shows went by, with me sitting and still waiting. And at four o'clock another piano arrived at the theater.

Bailey didn't say anything more to me.

"I don't like this," I told Pearl. "I know Bailey."

I had good reason to think Charles P. Bailey must be cooking up something. I'd heard what he'd done to Bessie Smith after they'd had an argument. He'd beaten Bessie up, then had her thrown in jail.

On Tuesday, the day after the argument, Bailey's handy man, Mose, said to me, "You're lucky. The chief didn't beat you up."

It burned me up. Mose was head foot-kisser on Bailey's staff, but he was one of my own people. And he was taking sides against me. I bawled the hell out of Mose. I couldn't see that I'd done anything wrong. I'd only asked Mr. Bailey to have the piano retuned. I'd even offered to pay for that.

You got paid off in an odd way at 81 Decatur Street. Half of your week's salary was given to you on Thursday night; the rest, with your advance for transportation taken out, on Saturday.

A colored fellow who worked backstage came to me on Wednesday. He looked all around to see if anyone was watching or listening. Then he whispered, "Miss Ethel, I want to tell you something. You look like a person a man can trust."

I told him he could indeed trust me.

"I hope so, Miss Ethel," he said nervously. "In telling you what I'm gonna, I'm riskin' losin' my job, maybe gettin' beat up or killed." He took a deep breath, then went on:

"I heard the way you talked to the chief and to Mose. I'm afraid Mr. Bailey is gonna do somethin' bad to you, Miss Ethel. But you'll know that in advance."

"How?"

"You'll know when they come around with the pay tomorrow night. If they don't give you nothin', then for the first half of the week, watch out. That will mean Mr. Bailey ain't gonna pay you at all. Because he wants you to make a fuss. That will give him his excuse for beatin' you up and maybe puttin' you in jail.

"I'm no brave man, Miss Ethel. I'm only tellin' you this because you are one of the few colored women who's worked here and not messed around with white men. Mr. Bailey—he took my wife away from me. There ain't nothin' I can do about that, and I guess she's as bad as he is. Now I know you won't say nothin' to anybody about how I talked about the chief. But, remember! If you don't get no money tomorrow night, you can expect trouble."

"And if I do get paid?"

"That will be the sign that Mr. Bailey ain't intendin' to do nothin'. Nothin' bad will happen to you."

I was really scared. But I said nothing to Pearl or Ethel about this conversation. I couldn't see any use in getting them nervous.

Early on Thursday the stouthearted and husky coppers of the Atlanta Police Department started coming in and out of the theater. They kept that up all day long. They were across the street, in the lobby, and backstage. One of these Southern-type storm troopers stopped me. He asked:

"Which one of you blues-singing gals is Ethel Waters?"

"I am."

He looked me over from head to toe. "Just wanted to get a good look at you," he said, "so I'll know you when I see you again."

That night Mr. Fulton, Charles P. Bailey's assistant, came around with the half week's pay. He gave everybody else their money. But he passed me up. When I asked him about it he said:

"The chief says you are to get yours in full on Saturday."

I knew then that I had to get out of Atlanta fast. I wanted to take along everything that belonged to me. There was one break I got on that. At No. 81 you changed your act in the middle of the week, and I used this as an excuse to carry home most of my costumes.

But when I tried to buy tickets at the railway station I found out the man at the window had orders not to sell me any. I got another bad shock when I got home. Two policemen were watching Old Man Howard's hotel from across the street. And there was another one around at the back.

I began to feel trapped and lost. I knew that Old Man Howard disliked Mr. Bailey, so I asked his advice. It turned out he knew all about my spat with the cracker theater owner.

"Bailey is powerful in this town, Ethel," he said. "You've found that out already. And he's ruthless. He'll stop at nothing. But I can at least ship your costumes out in boxes. The cops will think it is stuff that belongs to me."

He thought for a minute. "Ethel, if you could only get to some railway station on the outskirts of town you could get away from there. I'm sure those station agents haven't been warned not to sell you tickets."

I had him call up one of these suburban stations to find the times the northbound trains came through. I thought I knew of a way I could get to such an out-of-the-way place.

All week a young light brown fellow had been coming around to my hotel. He, too, had heard about my tiff with Bailey and had complimented me on the way I had stood up to him. When he came around that night I told him, "I don't want to stay around here one minute longer than I have to. I gotta get away."

He very kindly offered to help me make a getaway. "I'll get a car," he said, "and drive you to some place far off where you can catch a train. After all, I'm colored too."

By that time, of course, Pearl, who was in the room with us, and Ethel Williams knew all about what was going on. I'd had to tell them.

While we were sitting there talking to this young brown-skinned fellow I saw Old Man Howard out in the hall. He signaled me to come out. I excused myself very quietly.

"Do you know who that feller is?" Mr. Howard asked.

"I know his name."

"What else do you know about him?"

"Nothing."

"I thought so. Ethel, he is Charles P. Bailey's chauffeur. That's all."

That was tip-off enough that my brown-skinned friend was working in cahoots with his boss. It was like Bailey to send him to Howard's to make friends with us and offer to help us escape. He would have driven us right into Charles P. Bailey's waiting claws. But when I went back into the room I said nothing to him. Instead I spoke to Pearl.

"I have changed my mind, Pearl. I'm not gonna run away. Not even Mr. Bailey can scare me into running out of town. After all, there is such a thing in this country as justice."

The chauffeur, who wanted to double-cross us, left soon after that. To report to his white master, I suppose, that I was asleep in the deep, and naïve.

The three of us waited up all night for those cops to go off duty. We watched them standing there across the street from behind our windows. But they didn't leave their appointed station across the street.

I did some of my best and hardest praying that night. I got down on my knees and kept repeating the same plea to God I'd been saying for days.

"O Lord! I know you're not gonna let anything bad happen to me down here in Atlanta. You'll let me die—or escape. . . ."

I never in my life have used fancy language while talking to Him. I always figured that God likes simple words straight from the heart.

I was in the most terrible fix of my life, and it was asking a lot of Him to get me out of the jam. The whole big city of Atlanta, Georgia, was in back of Charles P. Bailey, if he could call out the cops and make railroads refuse to sell me tickets. I felt very little and helpless.

I wasn't a blues singer and an actress that dreadful night. I was just a young colored girl sick with fear. Walls I couldn't see were all around me.

The clock ticked on—one o'clock, two, three—but the cops didn't move. I could imagine them over there, laughing and kidding each other. Or maybe they were grumbling about being kept out all night to watch a dumb nigger gal who hadn't the sense not to talk back to a white man. The little boy in Macon had been lynched for talking back to a white man. I couldn't forget him and his family.

I did have plenty of cash money on me. On that tour I usually packed three or four hundred dollars with me. In other towns I'd changed my money into traveler's checks. But with all the turmoil I'd been going through in Atlanta, I hadn't had time for that.

The clock ticked on—four o'clock, five—and we three—Ethel Williams, Pearl Wright, and I—prayed hard and watched the cops. But it wasn't until 5:30 A.M. that God made His move. He must have put into those coppers' heads the idea that we were sleeping in all innocence—and they all went off together to get themselves a cup of coffee.

The moment the cops got out of sight we slipped out of the side door. We didn't have any idea how we could get a ride at that hour, unless the Lord kept on the job and sent us something on wheels.

And he did. Just as we three got out of that door, holding our breaths, an old man driving a horse and buggy came by. I hailed him. Knowing how my people love funerals, I told the old man that we girls had just lost a dearly beloved relative and had to get home so we wouldn't miss the services. He agreed to drive us to the out-of-the-way station for five dollars. We had no trouble buying tickets to Nashville there, but the station was so small, the through trains didn't stop there ordinarily. The stationmaster had to go out and flag down the train, which was not long in coming through. I thanked Jesus all the way to Nashville. In fact, I'm still thanking Him for helping me out *that* time.

I was going to Nashville because I wanted to get to Mr. Starr, head of the T.O.B.A., with my story before Charles P. Bailey put in his report, which I knew would be all lies. On reaching Nashville, I couldn't help doing one thing before calling on Milton Starr. Going into a Western Union office, I sent off a telegram to Mr. Charles P. Bailey of Atlanta. It read:

WHO GOT EFFED THIS TIME?

Mr. Starr was in his office and very cordial. I had just begun my story when he said:

"I don't want you to hold anything back, Miss Waters. I want you to tell me everything. We've had complaints about Mr. Bailey from other acts."

Before I'd talked long the phone on his desk rang. It was Charles P. calling long-distance from Atlanta. Mr. Starr listened. I listened too. Bailey was yelling so loud about black bitches and nigger whores that no ear-straining was necessary.

"Now just a moment, if you *please*," said Mr. Starr in his soft, low voice. "I know Miss Waters, and I hardly think it necessary to use that kind of language in discussing her. I will get her side of the story in due time, Mr. Bailey, believe me.

"As a matter of fact, she is sitting right here in my office now. So she'll tell me her version. I'll insist on that."

"*Her* version!" exploded Mr. Bailey. He was jumping with rage and frustration, and he sounded as though he was coming right through the phone. "That nigger's got no version. And I'll tell you this right now, either you'll take that black bitch off the T.O.B.A. time or I'll pull my theater off your circuit."

"That is an excellent idea, Mr. Bailey," said Mr. Starr, "and it would be perfectly all right with us. Yes, perhaps it would be better if you made other booking arrangements."

"Other booking arrangements!" screeched Bailey.

"Why, yes, Mr. Bailey," said Mr. Starr quietly. "Didn't you know that we were having great difficulty getting any Negro acts at all to play your theater?"

And while he had Charles P. Bailey on the ropes and gasping and grunting, he added, "It seems to me, sir, that something must be very wrong with the way your theater is run. I'm sure that otherwise nothing could have made a fine artist like Miss Waters walk out, leaving her costumes and scenery there."

Naturally, I was swept away with gratitude to Mr. Starr for his generosity and his complete faith in me. But I was even more impressed by the way he dealt with that situation without once raising his voice. I never did get my costumes back—or Mr. Johnston's props and drops —from No. 81.

I did get interesting firsthand accounts later of the ranting and raving Bailey did that day he learned I had slipped out of his noose and beyond his knuckles forever.

In his uncontrollable frenzy he seemed about to have a stroke. He worked the other acts on the bill to exhaustion, running around in his rage and calling them black sons of bitches. He threw out the usual feature movie after each show and ran his terrible advertising lantern slides over and over to put the audience to full rout.

As almost always happens after some ordeal I've been through, I soon got a little belly-laugh relief. For example, the Louisville theater we played in on the way home had a three-piece orchestra that had delusions of grandeur at every performance. They opened the show by playing such high-brow pieces as "Poet and Peasant" and the "Overture" to *William Tell*. But they had one bad handicap besides their lack of talent. It was very drafty in their pit, and their sheet music was always blowing off the piano stand. When that happened the drummer would carry on with *William Tell* all by himself, while the piano player and the other musican leaped and scrambled around after their fugitive sheet music.

And at the end of the week the manager there paid me off in pennies. He must have thought I wouldn't have the patience to count all those thousands of pennies. But he was underestimating your friend and mine, Ethel Waters, star of Black Swan Records. Counting those coppers, each and every one, I got penny-drunk. But I found the old swindler had gypped me out of ten dollars. A whole sawbuck!

Staggering back to his office with all the pennies, I made him count them again. I stood over him while he did it, and blasted the thousand extra pennies out of him.

When we got back to New York, Ethel Williams quit our act to marry Clarence Dotson, the dancer. I had some money, also some records to make, and decided to loaf in Harlem for a while and get some rest.

Nights, Ethel Williams, another girl, and I would go to bars and night clubs up there. I'd pick up the check and was glad to. You had to order whisky or some alcohol drink in those places. The girls did that drinking for me, and I could have my soda in peace.

Jerry's Place, on West 135th Street, was a favorite of mine because it had a good band, entertainment, and dancing. I loved to dance still just for fun, and I liked Jerry Preston, who ran this spot.

Earl Dancer had become part owner of the Golden Gate Inn just across the street from Jerry's. He dropped in on our party there one night and bought some drinks. As always, he asked me, "Why don't you ever come to my spot, Ethel?"

But I'd never go. I just didn't like Earl at that time. He was intelligent, a sound showman, and he knew the theater. But as I had done at Edmond's, I'd insult him every time he tried to talk to me.

That night he got Ethel Williams in a corner and pleaded with her to get me over to his night club. "I don't know why it is," he told her, "but whatever I say to her turns out to be the wrong thing. I don't mean to rub her the wrong way. Won't you tell her that I admire her work and would like to be her friend?"

She did tell me, and we went to Earl's place later on that night.

Another time, when I ran into Earl, he told me he had caught my act at the Lafayette. "I was amazed," he said. "You are a truly wonderful artist. You got something the whole world is crying for, the ability to make people laugh and cry.

"And, Ethel, believe me when I say you don't belong on the colored time. In those theaters you're playing now, your public will get fed up with you in two or three years. But if you would only let the white people hear you sing, they'd love you for the rest of your life." He shook his head and added, "You're a genius, Ethel."

But I still wanted no part of the white time.

I started making records for Columbia that summer. They paid me $250 apiece, or $125 per side.

But I began to have trouble keeping Pearl with me. Her two young daughters were living with relatives in Chicago, and Pearl went out to see them. She had the idea that if she didn't work she could get her husband to support the children.

I was booked into the Monogram in Chicago and another theater out there. I talked Pearl into playing those dates with me. I also had in my act James O'Brien, a colored violinist whose playing could make your heart dance—or break.

I have already mentioned the Monogram. That was the theater where you had to dress way downstairs with the stoker and come up to the stage climbing slave-ship stairs. While working there I took sick from the migraine headaches I'd had off and on for years. The air was very bad down there where the stoker was.

Somebody told me that Earl Dancer was in town and one night he came to see me. He had a dream-crammed look in his eye.

"Remember us talking together a long while ago in Harlem, Ethel?" he asked. "Remember me telling you then that you oughta go on the white time?"

"Yes."

"Well, why don't you let me go now and see about getting you an audition in a white theater?"

"No white audience would understand my blues. I'd be a complete flop."

I'd sung the blues at those midnight performances given for whites

—but that had been in the South, where the white people are hep to everything about the Negro, his blues, moods, and humor, particularly his humor. But, as I pointed out to Earl, that wasn't so with Northern whites.

This, by the way, is no longer true, since Northern whites have been educated to the blues. Today you can sing your blues to them just as to a Negro audience and go the full limit. I argued that I never exaggerated or overemphasized my characterizations. I said that most of the Negroes who were getting by on the white time were like caricatures of human beings and portrayed buffoons who were lazy and shiftless beyond belief.

"And I ain't changing my style for nothing or nobody," I told him.

But Earl Dancer just wouldn't shut up. He kept picking at me, kept insisting that I would be a sensation on the big time.

"Have you ever seen Fanny Brice work?" he asked.

"No."

Then he told me how Irene Bordoni had brought the song, "My Man," to the United States and sung it in French. Brice did it in English, he went on, in the *Ziegfeld Follies*. "She did it almost as a satire, and the people who heard it called it the blues," he said. "That's only because they've never heard the real blues, the kind you sing, Ethel."

Well, the yapping went on, with me insisting white people would be puzzled by my blues, and also bored to death.

Earl argued, "You don't have to sing as you do for colored people, verse after verse after verse of the blues. You can break it up: sing some blues, then talk the story in the song, and end up with more blues. They'll love it. Why should an artist like you have to dress down in a dirty old coal cellar, Ethel? They'll never treat you like that on the Keith time. You won't get migraine headaches because the air is poisoned. You gotta give yourself a break."

When I consented to do a break-in date on the big time it was only to shut him up. I wanted to get rid of Earl's big talk and dreams. I was sure I'd flop even after he'd arranged for the tryout at, I think, the Kedzie Theatre there in Chicago.

With malice and impatience I looked forward to the joy of cussing him out for leading me into the humiliation of flopping in a white theater.

It was the first time I'd worked on the stage of a big-time vaudeville theater. We were getting only forty dollars for the three-day engagement, but any act was willing to take a nominal fee on a so-called break-in date, the whole object being to showcase your routine to the bookers.

Earl went on and did the "Where is that partner of mine?" patter. Then I appeared in my gingham apron and funny hat and sang "Georgia Blues." I did other songs, and Earl did his specialty number. There was applause when we finished, and I went upstairs to our dressing room.

Earl took one look at my unhappy face and asked, "What's wrong, Ethel? What's the matter?"

"What's the matter?" I cried. "You know we took the flop of our lives just now. Those people out front applauded us only because they wanted to be polite. Nobody stomped as they always do in colored theaters when I finish my act. Nobody screamed or jumped up and down. Nobody howled with joy. On account of you I have the first and worst flop of my whole life."

Earl said the people out front had been crazy about our act, but I told him I didn't want any more of his jive. I was sure I had failed in front of my first Northern white audience.

I was on the verge of tears. I was still bawling out Earl Dancer when the manager came back to see us. He was smiling with excitement and elation.

"We'll keep you on for the whole week," he said, "and pay you $350 for your act."

I didn't know what to say. I was even more speechless when the reviews came out. One critic called me "the ebony Nora Bayes." There was no mistaking what that meant. Nora Bayes was one of the most popular of the white vaudeville singers. She had elegance, dignity, class. She was the great lady of the two-a-day, so I liked being called "the ebony Nora Bayes."

Dozens of people in show business say they discovered me. This always irritates me. Edmond's piano player, Lou Henley, was the first one to get me to sing different types of songs. Earl Dancer pushed me into the white time.

Talent can be developed, but no one in show business discovers it. Only the public can do that. It was the public who discovered me every step of the way—from Jack's Rathskeller, through my season with the Hill Sisters, at Barney Gordon's and Edmond's, to Broadway and Hollywood.

But I'm grateful to Earl Dancer for egging me into going on the white time. He got me my first break-in date, laid out our act, and helped me in other ways. Whatever it is you have, though, it is always the public that finds it. If it isn't there for them to applaud, you are not behind the footlights for very long.

Yet I've never understood what in hell people are talking about when they call me "an artist."

An artist, it seems to me, should be complete mistress of her medium. Many critics have been kind enough to say that about me. But if I was mistress of my medium I wouldn't be so scared each time I walk out in front of an audience. Before each performance I tell myself the same thing:

"They don't have to like me, those people out there. They are not my friends. My job is to make them like me. I have to make these strangers my friends."

As a dramatic actress all I've ever done is to remember. When I act I try to express the suffering—or the joy—I've known during my lifetime. Or the sorrow and happiness I've sensed in others.

And I never neglect to pray to my God before I step out there. I ask Him to be my prompter and stage manager and to make the people out front like me. But I've also found out that He likes to help only those who help themselves. So I go out and always kill myself. It's the same thing whether I'm working on Broadway or the Bowery. I just never could learn how to cheat, or coast, or take things easy.

Toward the end of that break-in week in Chicago, Earl's professional representatives, the Pat Casey Theatrical Agency, sent for me.

"I don't want to go," I told Earl. "You go down there and ask them what they want."

Earl came back that day looking crestfallen and very sad. When I asked him what the trouble was, he said:

"There is no use in my stalling on this or building a story. They want to give you $350 a week and a route, Ethel. My agents say you are sensational. But they don't want me in the act."

"I am not rat enough to go out as a single," I told him. "I just couldn't do that after you harangued and browbeat me into trying the white time. And I need you, Earl. You know the score on this kind of vaudeville. I don't. The act has to be Waters and Dancer."

I told the Pat Casey office that. They said, "But you'll get as much money as a single, Ethel."

"It's gotta be Waters and Dancer."

And I stuck to that.

When Earl Dancer and I had worked our way back to New York the Pat Casey office there urged me to drop him, just as their Chicago boys had. But when I explained why I couldn't do that, those bookers understood. They had no trouble at all getting five hundred dollars a week for our act, then seven hundred and fifty.

One of the Keith houses we played was Proctor's Fifty-eighth, where there were continuous performances and a feature movie. You did a matinee show, one at dinnertime, and another in the evening. On Saturday and Sunday you did four shows.

The other acts hated the dinner show because the audiences were so small. They would clown and ad-lib through their routines and act indifferent to the people who had paid their good money to see them.

But, as I say, I couldn't work that way. I had to give out with everything I had—even if only two people were there, both uncles of the doorman and in on passes.

One dinner show at Proctor's Fifty-eighth Street Theatre, unknown to us backstage, two of the biggest booking agents on the Orpheum time slipped in to catch the show. Those two Orpheum bookers didn't think much of the other acts, but they gave Ethel Waters and Earl Dancer the sugar-coated route over their circuit right to the West Coast. The Orpheum time we played was straight two a day, and we traveled first class, which is as classy as you can get. It was my first trip to the Coast. Out there my work seemed to remind people of many different white singers. But I preferred being called the "ebony Nora Bayes" because she was the one who never gave out with any unladylike shouts and growls but sang all her songs with refinement.

Everywhere we played the people seemed to like my singing, and the style was brand new to them. But I was so accustomed to the Fourth of July type of reception I'd always got from colored audiences that it took a long time to convince me I was getting over.

I began, though, to draw colored patrons into the balcony. And when those good folks upstairs heard authentic blues sung on a white stage for the first time they went mad with joy.

I opened up in my gingham apron for "Georgia Blues," did a smart eccentric dance, then a comedy routine with Earl to build up for my comedy number, "Mama Goes Where Papa Goes." Earl then would do his specialty number and he was always good at selling a song.

His suggestion of how I should sing "My Man" proved invaluable. After the announcement that I'd sing Fanny Brice's song "as a little girl from Georgia might do it," I'd come out in a simple black dress and a paisley handkerchief around my hair and sing it—with blues interpolated.

The blues I sang after one verse of "My Man" went:

> Trouble, trouble,
> I've had it all my days.
> Sometimes I think the trouble
> Will end carrying me to my grave.
> All because I love my man
> And he won't treat me right.
> He has other women
> Every time I'm out of sight.

The song pluggers began to come after me to sing their numbers. I'll never forget one of them. His name was Ben Black and he came to my dressing room when we were playing the Orpheum Theatre in Los Angeles.

Ben Black told Earl he was crazy about the way I sang "My Man," also "She's Funny That Way," which I did "*He's* Funny That Way," as a reverse switch.

Ben wanted me to try "Eïli, Eïli [Oh, God! Why Hast Thou Forsaken Me?]" during my act. He said that another Negro performer, George Dewey Washington, who was then with Paul Ash's Band, was getting wonderful results with it. I heard Washington sing it in his deep and beautiful baritone, and it was something indeed to listen to.

Ben Black taught me the Hebrew words in that great lament. He said them for me and made me repeat them, syllable for syllable, after him. I didn't understand one word of what I was singing. I always used the simple Sophie Braslau version of that work.

"Eïli, Eïli" moved me deeply, and I always loved to sing it. It tells the tragic history of the Jews as much as one song can, and that history of their age-old grief and despair is so similar to that of my own people that I felt I was telling the story of my own race too.

Jewish people in every town seemed to love the idea of me singing their song. They crowded the theaters to hear it, and they would tell one another:

"The *schwarze* sings 'Eïli, Eïli'! The *schwarze!*"

We were always penciled in as a No. 2 act on the bills. That meant we went on after the acrobats, the trained seals, or the juggler in the show. But the house manager had the authority to shift around the order of the acts as he saw fit, and invariably Waters and Dancer would be shifted, after the Monday matinee show, to the next-to-closing spot, which is usually reserved for headliners.

During my big-time vaudeville days I played on bills with some of the most gifted and well-known star acts—Van and Schenck, the Pennant Winning Battery of Songland; Jack Benny, Ted Healy, Pat Rooney and Marion Bent, Olsen and Johnson, and Charles (Chic) Sale, who I think was the funniest vaudeville performer I've ever seen.

Though I liked many of the white vaudevillians, I never got to know any of them well. I didn't fraternize with them. For one thing, as a No. 2 act, I was not as yet in their class as a performer. Familiarity brings attempt, as well as contempt. And I had the sense to know I was colored. The white actors and I didn't eat together, we didn't sleep together, and I thought it wisest to keep everything on a casual "Nice day, isn't it?" basis.

As I gradually became better known as a performer who could draw crowds on the big time, the house managers made it tougher and tougher for Earl Dancer to get adequate billing. The name "ETHEL WATERS" was printed in ever larger and brighter letters and "earl dancer" very small and delicate. One day Earl looked at his name on a three-sheet poster and said:

"My God! I never knew they could print so small."

When we were back in Chicago from our tour to the Coast, Mr. Johnston, the theater owner who had personally booked my act over the T.O.B.A. time, sent for me. He explained that Maury Greenwald's *Plantation Revue* had been playing in his Grand Theatre for two weeks.

"It's a hot, fast show, Ethel," he said, "but something is missing. Would you go in there and help out as an extra added attraction?"

"You were pretty good to me once, Mr. Johnston," I told him. "I think you'll find me a grateful person."

"How much are you getting for your act, Ethel?" he asked.

"Seven-fifty a week," I said.

Mr. Johnston whistled. "Could you possibly come into our show at a cut? For five hundred dollars? It's just for two weeks."

I told him I'd do this gladly on condition that he keep the cut a secret between us. "I will even pay my agent, whom I am not going to take into my confidence, his ten-per-cent commission on $750 a week," I said.

I guess it's no news that cutting your salary in show business is like cutting your throat. People in our trade take it for granted that there is only one reason a performer takes a cut: because he's no longer in demand. Once that sad word gets around, your pay can dive fast to ten thousand feet below sea level, and you are "at liberty" from then on.

Mr. Johnston said he would keep the financial part of our deal dark. The *Plantation Revue* billed me as their "Extra Added Attraction," like a circus with Sarah Bernhardt. The whole place was bulging with customers the night I opened, but none of the other players would relinquish their dressing room to me, though I was the extra added attraction who was expected to save their show. I suppose one of the girls would have shared her room with me, but I decided to dress backstage under the stairs, with a sheet hung in front of them to conceal my fatal charms from the rude stares of the husky stagehands.

Though I'd been playing the white Keith and Orpheum time, the women stars of that revue still looked down on me as just a T.O.B.A. singer.

Suddenly, on the night I opened in the fast-flopping revue, all backstage began buzzing. There was much excited talk and whispering before the curtain went up.

All the whispering went, "Do you know who is out front? Ashton Stevens! *Ashton Stevens!* ASHTON STEVENS!"

I'd never heard of him, so I said, "Well, who the hell *is* Ashton Stevens?"

The whisperers were astounded. "You mean to tell us, Ethel Waters, that you don't know who Mr. Ashton Stevens is?"

"No, I don't!"

Then they told me that Mr. Stevens was the great earth-shaker among the Chicago newspaper critics, that he could doom a show with a printed frown or make a hit with a pat on the back published on his dramatic page.

"Ashton, girls, is all yours," I said. "All I want to know is: are my people out front tonight? I am speaking of my stockyards people, odor and all. Yes, you can have Ashton Stevens, and I will keep my people. If they are out there I am all right, even if Ashton goes home sick and disgusted."

That night I didn't come on until ten forty-five. Everything else, including the big chariot race from *Ben Hur* (figuratively speaking), had been on ahead of me. We used the "Well, I ain't Bessie Smith!" entrance, and there was terrific laughter. And we stopped the show, Earl and I.

The next day everybody in the show, including the backstage porters, was out on the street early to buy up copies of Mr. Ashton Stevens' paper. He seemed either to be still meditating or smitten with writer's cramp, because nothing was in. Not a word about any of us. Not a cheer or a bellow. The next day all the actors were out buying copies again. Still nothing. That kept happening all week. But on Sunday when his paper came out there was a headline that made the sweetest reading I'd ever had. It was printed right across the page in the biggest type the printer could lift. And it said:

ASHTON STEVENS FINDS
YVETTE GUILBERT OF HER
RACE IN ETHEL WATERS!

"A new star discovered on State Street," Mr. Stevens wrote. "Ethel Waters is the greatest artist of her race and generation."

When my two weeks were up Maury Greenwald wanted me to continue with his show, but I went back on the Keith time, and we headed home to New York.

Ashton Stevens' wonderful love letter of a critical review was re-published in newspapers all over the country. And when I played the Keith theater in Cleveland, Archie Bell, the most respected critic there, caught our bill. When he went back to his office he forgot to review the headline act.

Mr. Bell wrote a lot about what a great artist I was and added that if I were white I would be a Raquel Meller and a Duse. He took cracks at the local Keith theater manager because he said you could hardly find my name on the program and said it was only because I was colored.

We made another coast-to-coast trip, Earl and I and Pearl Wright. I think it was on the second one that we had Pearl's two sweet daughters along: Catherine, then nine, and Vivian, seven and very tall for her age.

Pearl couldn't afford to pay half fares for them. All the way to California and back we made those poor kids scrounch down in their seats whenever the conductors came around collecting tickets. You have to be under five years old to ride free, and the girls not being midgets, the conductors were ever suspicious.

"You mean to tell me those children are only three and four?" they'd ask. "Where's their father? Where's their mother?"

Earl was very fastidious, but we made him pose as the girls' dear daddy. We made him sit with the kiddies, and he didn't like that.

We all had to watch Vivian and Catherine. If we didn't, they'd be reading high-powered magazines like the *Cosmopolitan* and the *Saturday Evening Post*, high-powered books like *The Sheik*, which was supposed to be for mature minds only.

We never could get those kids to pretend they were just looking at the pictures. And in the dining car, the girls would grab the menus and start reading aloud to each other the names of the good things they wanted to eat. We had to snatch the menu cards out of their hands when the conductors hove in sight.

I loved having those children with us. Pearl always favored Catherine, so I built up Vivian's ego by paying her little attentions.

Like me, Vivian promised to be tall—and I knew what that meant. I had never found any happiness in being too big to fit.

12

In 1924, while I was doing good for myself in vaudeville from coast to coast, Florence Mills had become the sensation of New York. She had done such big business at Sam Salvin's Plantation Club at Broadway and Fiftieth Street that the management wanted to keep open all summer.

But Florence insisted on touring, and Mr. Salvin started to look for a colored name to replace her. Earl Dancer, always a great one for getting about and talking to people, heard they'd tried out several girls, including Katherine Yarber, a choir singer who'd been in *Shuffle Along*   .

"They're still auditioning," he told me. "Why don't you go down there?"

I shook my head. I felt that Broadway and all downtown belonged to Florence Mills. I also thought our singing styles were too similar for me to follow her at the Plantation. But Earl, who never got tired of nagging me, went on and on about it.

"It won't hurt you none, Ethel, just to go down there and talk to those people."

In the end I did go down, but only to shut him up. Florence Mills was vivacious, a cutie, and a whirlwind when it came to selling a song and dance. But she had a small voice. They had been using a choir around her to get volume, and then Florence would come in and sing the punch line. However, she was a public idol, and I didn't think that following her at the Plantation was going to be easy. But I went there for the tryout, and in those days I was as trim and shapely as Florence or anyone else.

Mr. Salvin, along with Harry Akst and Joe Howard, who were

writing the songs for that floor show, was there for my audition. They asked me to do a couple of my own numbers, and I started off with "Georgia Blues." I could see that Sam Salvin was tremendously impressed. After I finished my own songs Harry Akst and Joe Howard asked if I'd try a new one they'd written. And they sang it themselves for me, doing it fast and corny.

"Is that the way you want me to sing it?" I asked.

Akst and Howard looked at each other.

"Why not sing it your own way?" they said. "Take it home. Work it over, kid, then come back and let us hear your version."

Now I've always had a strict rule about this. I'll do any new number the way I'm asked to sing it. But once you say, "Do it your way, kid," I sing it my way and won't try any other style that is second-guessed on me.

So that day I took that song home and worked on it with Pearl. "This is a nice little number, Pearl," I said.

That nice little number was "Dinah."

After I sang it in my style for Mr. Salvin and the boys who wrote it, I won the wooden apple: the uphill job of following Florence Mills at the Plantation—and this through the hot weather when most sane New Yorkers dash off to the beaches and mountains to get much-needed air-conditioning.

It was a fine night-club show, though, that Sam Salvin was putting together that summer of 1924 at the Plantation. He'd hired lots of first-rate creative talent. Leonard Harper and Bill Seabury did the staging, and Bill Vodery contributed his *Swing Mikado*, the original jazzed-up version of the Gilbert and Sullivan operetta.

Now this was fifteen years before Michael Todd got the critics' kudos and love and kisses for his *Hot Mikado* and the same idea. Mike Todd, who was hailed in 1939 as Broadway's brilliant boy-wonder producer for bringing in that show, must have been a tiny street gamin who was playing with his toy balloons back in 1924.

"Dinah," with your girl Ethel singing it in her own way, made history from Tin Pan Alley to Tokyo because it was the first international song hit ever to come out of an American night club.

With Jimmy Ferguson, now known as Baron Lee, I also sang "Mama Goes Where Papa Goes." But I think I loved best working in the satire of that show, a take-off on *White Cargo*, a Broadway hit melodrama.

People would laugh at White Cargo today, it is often said. Well, lots of people were laughing at it then because it was hokier than a horsecar full of comics.

There was a South Seas native girl in White Cargo who just had to say "I am Tondeleyo!" and the Englishmen in the play were dead ducks. One look at Tondeleyo's curves and they started growing scraggly beards and getting seedy. They went native when she shot out her heat waves. They forgot home and England and threw off their white man's burden. In other words, they became bums.

For our take-off eight of our most attractively stacked girls came out dressed like Tondeleyo, and I came out in the same half-concealing, have-revealing outfit.

The chorus girls shook in competition and showed me all kinds of wriggles. But I had plenty of wriggles left that they didn't know about, and I was Tondeleyo.

For the late show I sang colored songs like "Go Back Where You Stayed Last Night." Such crowds came that Sam Salvin stopped wondering if he could keep open all summer.

At the Plantation there were three of us in the same dressing room —Josephine Baker, Bessie Allison, who later married the manager of the Savoy Ballroom in Harlem, and me.

Josephine was in the chorus, but she stepped out of the line to do her specialty once during each show. Josephine was a mugger with a great comic sense, and she had a beautiful form. She could dance and she could clown joy into you. She could also play the trombone.

I'd met her while touring the South. She was like an orphan then and was with one of those Negro kid gypsy bands they have down there.

I worked through all that hot summer at the Plantation, but in late August or early September they closed me out because Florence was coming back. And Florence Mills came in on my smoke.

But, after all, it was her show and it had been built around her. So I had no beef. The world loves a winner, but you have to be a hell of a good loser, too, in show business.

Before I closed, Mary Louise Howard asked me to go to Europe and appear in Paris. I said I preferred to see America first. So I asked for five hundred dollars a week, which was like asking those French for all their Chateaubriand steak and world-famous fried potatoes.

They do not part happily with a buck, those French, and five hundred dollars a week! *Sacrebleu!*

Mary Louise Howard took Josephine Baker, who didn't want so much, to France. Josephine ended up with a château, an Italian count, and all Paris at her feet permanently. Again, *sacrebleu!*

Every once in a while I'd run into Edmond, formerly of the well-known cellar of the same name. Poor Edmond had lost his club and he was working as the big-muscled doorman of somebody else's spot. But until Edmond died I called him only one thing—Boss—whenever I saw him around Harlem. I can only hope that made him feel a little better.

Around this time I was co-starred at the Palace as a single with the McCarthy Sisters, an act that had been in George White's *Scandals*. They told me I was the first Negro woman who'd ever shared top billing there.

For a long time Earl Dancer had wanted to be a producer. "Someday you will see in lights the words, 'Earl Dancer Presents . . .' Oh, if I could only get hold of a backer," he told me.

"You got no material for a show, Earl," I'd say. "You have no money for a show."

But Earl got Donald Heywood, the song writer, to start working with him on little tab shows. Sam Salvin, meanwhile, suggested that I go out in a tab version of his summer Plantation show and offer it to both the white and colored time. I could always fill in for different spots. In that little show I made entrances as five or six different characters. The dancers, Ralph Cooper and Eddie Rector, were in this show too.

I didn't stay with that troupe long, quitting when we closed at the Lafayette Theatre. Some of the other performers began to kick up, and I just wouldn't be bothered. It was easier to leave than to stay and bicker it out. That backbiting and conniving backstage always make me sick. After I quit they had to hire five other girls to take over all my parts.

Earl Dancer then suggested we do *Miss Calico*, a tab show. I rehearsed the girls for this and staged all their numbers. I danced with them and I opened the show and closed it. I filled in all the gaps.

I also did a take-off on *Lulu Belle*. That was another Broadway hit, starring Lenore Ulric, that Edward Sheldon and Charles MacArthur wrote. I had met David Belasco, with his collar turned backward, who produced it. In the play Lenore Ulric played a Negro trollop who works her way up to a count and a boudoir in Paris by her diligent whoring. In my take-off on Miss Ulric I sang "You Can't Do What the Last Man Did," and this take-off was later in *Africana*.

We'd work such a tab show like this: We'd have eight chorus girls, a seven-piece band, two dancing boys, two comics, and the name, which was me. We had that great, great man, William Grant Still, in the pit.

I toured with this show all through the South. When we'd go into the bigger towns up North we'd add a few more girls and some extra acts so we'd have a full-length show. We not only called it *Miss Calico*. We called it the *Follies*, the *Scandals*, the *Vanities*, or anything else we felt like calling it. Once we brought up North with us, from New Orleans, Willie Jackson, the singer, and Zutty Singleton, the drummer. And it was the first time they could be lured up out of the balmy South.

On one production number the chorus girls posed in a living-statues tableau. This was called "Just a Picture of You on the Wall," with the girls standing perfectly still on their pedestals. The flash came when the curtains parted and there stood a girl painted in silver or gold and absolutely nude. But the enraptured audience didn't get much of a gander. The curtains parted and she was revealed—but only for a second or two. Then the lights went out.

In Detroit they have rats as big as the heavyweights down in Nashville. One came running out on the stage during our living-statues number, and the girls ran in all directions, screaming hysterically.

Funny things were always happening while I was with Earl Dancer. About the biggest laugh I ever got, though, came one night when we were riding into Chicago in the day coach. We hadn't taken berths because we were to be on the train only an hour or so.

Earl, Pearl Wright, and I were the only Negroes in that day coach. Like the white people, Earl and Pearl had gone to sleep. But I was awake and sitting near the ladies' washroom waiting to get in. A white woman was in there so long that I thought she must be ducking the conductor.

So I was sitting there, rather impatient, naturally, and I was studying the expressions on the faces of those sleeping people. I tried to imagine what they did for a living, where they lived, and what they were dreaming about.

All at once a stench worse than one of the devil's own stink bombs filled our coach. I knew what it was as the conductor soon came through. He said with a wink:

"We just ran over a skunk. Ain't it awful, this smell?"

The skunk odor began waking up the white people. They rubbed their eyes, twitched their noses—and then they looked straight at me. The moment they got a whiff their eyes seemed automatically to fasten on me, the innocent colored woman in their midst.

Well, I started to laugh. I knew what they were thinking. They were shaking their heads, their eyes still on me, and thinking that all the stupid stories about colored people smelling terrible must be true. The whole carful of them was soon staring at me with reproachful dismay and disgust. I didn't move, but laughed all the louder. I was never a girl to stifle her giggles and guffaws. That made them furious. They thought I was taunting them with my ability to stink up the car.

Then the white woman who had been in the washroom so long came out, and all their bitter eyes turned on her. Now they were blaming her for being responsible. That made me hysterical.

But soon the conductor and his brakeman came through and put plugs under the car's doors to keep them open. The conductor made a little speech, saying:

"Ladies and gentlemen, we have to keep the doors open for a little while. We have just had the misfortune to run over a skunk, and his odor seems to be traveling along with us. I wish to apologize on behalf of the railroad, my train crew, the engineer—but most of all for the skunk."

Now none of those white people who had stared at me so angrily apologized when they found out I was not guilty. I guess they thought they didn't have to apologize for what they were just thinking.

We did okay all over with *Miss Calico* and the other tab shows while we stayed in vaudeville. But Earl couldn't get that "Earl Dancer Presents . . ." out of his head. And in Chicago he booked us into a theater run by the Shuberts. The Shuberts took over all the money we drew for their rental and wouldn't give us any of it back for our pay roll. So we were stranded in Chicago.

It was after this, and in New York, that Earl's big dream of becoming a Broadway producer came true. He got Otto H. Kahn, the banker-philanthropist, to put up ten thousand dollars so he could do a full-length revue. This was *Africana*, my first Broadway musical, and it was patched up from all the different little tab shows we'd been doing. It was a good, fast show and gave the theater-going ofays of Broadway their first long look at me.

Africana opened at Daly's Sixty-third Street Theatre, where *Shuffle Along* had its long run. I was the star, and the *Variety* reviewer wrote:

" . . . Ethel Waters is the kick of *Africana* in her specialty. She started with 'My Special Friend Is in Town' . . . the first-niters ate that one up. She also sang 'Shake That Thing,' 'Dinah,' 'Take Your Black Bottom Outside' . . ."

I also sang "I'm Coming Virginia," and the Broadwayites loved it. I'd just made a record of that lovely song with "He Brought Joy to My Soul" on the other side. But it was the first time the ofays had heard "I'm Coming Virginia" in a theater.

So Earl at last saw his "Earl Dancer Presents . . ." in lights over a Broadway theater. Donald Heywood wrote the music and lyrics and Louis Douglas, fresh from Paris, staged the dances. Louis was the son-in-law of Will Marion Cook.

Africana had a good run and afterward we took it on the road, playing the Midwest cities and closing in St. Louis with a bang. I was to hear echoes of that explosive closing for many a sad, long day.

While I was playing in *Africana* on Broadway I had a Locomobile and a love affair. I should have kept them well separated. But I couldn't drive, and my love affair could, so I put him in charge of the keys and the steering wheel.

Now I had a very liberal attitude and I told him, "Look, I know you are messing around with other girls. That is okay if you obey two simple rules. Don't fool around the little chorus girls in my show. And I won't have you taking any chorus girl, or a girl of any other description, joy-riding in my car."

The idea that he was using my expensive Locomobile, not to mention gas, oil, and the usual wear and tear, to promote on-the-side romancing was just too much for me to take.

So one day I was in a taxi going down Seventh Avenue, when I saw my big beautiful Locomobile parked in front of an apartment house where I knew two of the little show girls in my show had an apartment. I got out of the taxi and went up there.

"Who is it?" asked one of the girls when I rang their bell.

"Western Union," I said.

She opened up.

"My boy friend is here, or maybe I should say our boy friend," I told her.

She looked scared. "Oh no," she said, "he isn't here, Miss Waters."

"All I want is my car keys," I said. "Get them from him, will you?"

"But he isn't here, Miss Waters!"

"My car is parked downstairs, so I know he is here. Now get the keys."

Though she continued to deny he was there, she led me through the apartment so I could look for him. But there was one room with the door closed which she didn't show me. So I knew he was in that room.

Now this fellow of mine was a very nosy and inquisitive type. I had a hunch that he would be standing right there behind the door, listening to what I was saying.

I went to the door and pushed it open. I slammed it back hard against the wall. And he was hiding there all right. I crashed him so hard against the wall that he gurgled for breath and began to search himself all over for broken bones.

The other *Africana* chick was in the bed. She looked terrified, but I told her, "I don't intend to beat you up—today. But I'll get you some other time when I'm more in the mood. And it will be me and you. So you can relax—for the time being."

Then I got my car keys from him and left. It was now raining in the street, and the top of my Locomobile was down. I had never driven a car before. But I was so mad that day I got behind the wheel and drove it off right down Seventh Avenue.

Everything went better than I expected until I came to 126th Street. At that time the Fifth Avenue busses that went up Seventh Avenue turned there at 126th Street to go downtown again.

As I approached the corner I could see that a bus was turning. The Irish driver was swinging it wide. I yelled to him, "Get out of my way."

But that stupid Irish bus driver was stubborn, and he wouldn't stop. I guess he thought I knew how to stop, or at least turn the wheel. And all on account of his pigheaded stubbornness I crashed into him, wrecking my car.

An officious white copper, also Irish, of course, came rushing up. He was as dumb as the bus driver.

"And will you be getting your wreck of a car out of the way of my southbound traffic?" he yelled.

I remained cool and very much the lady. I just took the keys out of my ignition and handed them to him.

"I'll tell you a little secret, officer," I said. "I don't know how to drive."

"Will you listen to the talk of her?" he said to the bus driver. "She doesn't know how to drive! And is it news you're telling me, madam? As though I couldn't see that with the foine eyes the good Lord gave me. So get your car out of the way before you tie up traffic all the way to Poughkeepsie!"

I kept trying to hand him the keys, but he ignored them. I found out later the reason was that he didn't know how to drive himself, that dumb cop. But he wouldn't admit he didn't have the know-how. A big crowd was all around us, laughing, and the other car drivers who couldn't move were honking their horns like it was Armistice Day.

"Officer!" I said. "You are the one who wants the car moved. So you can move it. I own this car and I have my owner's papers right on me. I give you permission to move it. Or if you don't want to move it yourself, get somebody to do it—and I will pay him."

Nobody in that big crowd volunteered his services. Harlem people are like that. They were enjoying all the yelling, the cop's frustration, and the confusion too much to want it to end. I wasn't having such a bad time myself. I had bruised and rattled the bones of my two-timing man and I was glad I had wrecked my Locomobile—because now he couldn't drive any little girls around in it.

At the height of all the uproar, who should come along in a taxi but my battered, depressed Romeo himself. He got out, and when he saw the wrecked Locomobile he almost sobbed. But I made him get in and drive it and me off Seventh Avenue and down a side street where the repair people could get it. I was laughing at the top of my lungs.

And he could read what was in my mind. Not only had I wrecked the car for a long time, but I was gonna whip him when I got him home. However, when we did get home he got out his gun—and I had to about-face on the whipping for the time being.

I went out of there in a hurry. And when I returned to my apartment Pearl Wright called to say he was down at her place and to come and get him. I went and got him and gave him the whipping at home when he was defenseless.

But that was not the end of my revenge. With Betty Hardy and Tony Salemme, the sculptor, I dropped into the Nest, a place Mel Frazier was running on 133rd Street. And the little chorus girl who had been in the room with my boy friend that day was an entertainer in the show there.

In Harlem night clubs they have ways and means of protecting their entertainers. So I did nothing for a whole hour. I wanted that chorus girl to relax and think I wasn't going into action. She was small like all the girls this particular boy friend had two-timed me with.

Between shows I noticed that she was sitting at a table only a few steps from the ladies' room. And I waited—until the dance music started up and the customers were dancing. I knew that everyone else would be watching the dance floor.

Then I started for her. I gave her one of my short, hard lefts to the chops, then dragged her into that ladies' room. I locked the door, then just beat the living hell out of her.

I told her what I always tell girls who mess around my boy friends: "There takes two people to make one of these love affairs. And my pain goes along with his pleasure."

Then I'd whip 'em to illustrate my point.

Now when my love affair heard about my whipping one of his on-the-side girls he didn't take it in silence. And once he said, "But, Ethel, you just can't go around beating up everybody you don't like."

"No," I answered him, "but I can whip anyone you like. Because you like only little chorus girls. I'll whip 'em every time I catch you messin' around with them. And I'm gonna make you respect me if I have to cripple 'em all."

I was playing in Baltimore one week when I heard he was messing around with a popular Plantation chorus girl in New York. After my last show that Saturday night I took the train to New York and a cab from the station to the Plantation, giving the driver five dollars to wait for me.

"I'm waiting for my cousin," I said.

But before I could go inside she came out of the club. I rushed over and slugged and disabled her. Then I got back in the cab and told the driver to take me back to the railway station.

I was working at the Everglades Night Club on Broadway when Earl Dancer maneuvered me onto an all-star bill for some big Catholic charity that was being staged at the Palace Theatre. The backstage was jumping with big names, and I had to go on following *Will Rogers*. Rogers was No. 23 act on that bill, I was No. 24, and Singer's Midgets were coming on after me.

That big crowd had sat there for hours listening to the biggest and best entertainers in the whole world—and Will Rogers. Yet they waited to hear this little brown-skinned girl sing. Following the unmatchable Rogers was like going on during an earthquake. I got a big hand, and that was one of the most heart-warming compliments I've ever had.

Another was the review one of those tough Chicago newspaper critics wrote: "When Ethel Waters sings 'Dinah' she is beautiful. When she sings 'Eili, Eili' she achieves greatness. But when she sings 'Shake That Thing' she is incredible."

By this time, of course, I was beginning to meet more and more white people. One of the first ones I understood was Antonio Salemme, a sculptor who made a bronze bust of me that Carl Van Vechten later bought.

Tony lived down in Greenwich Village, and he took me around to meet his friends and to Romany Marie's and the other Village places. Those bohemians were like my own people, and I liked them. Your color or your bank account made no difference to them. They liked you for yourself. They were doing work they loved, kept what hours they pleased, and didn't care what Mr. and Mrs. Buttinsky down the hall thought of them and their odd ways. That all made sense to me.

I also met Paul Robeson for the first time at Salemme's studio, where Tony was making a full-figure nude of him. Paul was a wonderful young man in those days. He'd been a brilliant college student and a football star. Now he was on the eve of sailing for his first concerts in London. His boy, baby Paul, had just been born.

I went to see Paul's wife, who was still in the hospital, the day Paul sailed for Europe, and then went down to the pier to see him off. I gave him a picture of me, inscribing it "from one black bottom to another."

Rex Stout and his first wife and Jo Jo Coffee were other interesting white people I met through Tony Salemme. Rex happened to be in the hospital on his birthday that year. The birthday present I gave him was to dress up as a nurse. When he pressed his bedside button I went into his room, carrying his breakfast tray. I waited on him all that day, wheeling out his chair to the balcony when he wanted to sit in the sunshine.

The best of all my white friends I met one week while I was playing at the Lafayette with a unit. Business was so big that Frank Shiffman, the manager, gave me a bonus, making it a happy week for me.

The call boy there told me one night that a white man named Carl Van Vechten wanted to see me. The name meant nothing to me, though I'd heard of his book, *Nigger Heaven*, and had condemned it because of its obnoxious title—without reading it. Later I read this novel and thought it a sympathetic study of the way Negroes were forced to live in Harlem.

When Carl came up he told me he'd been catching my act for years and he invited me to have dinner at his house. I didn't see any reason for going. White people generally bored me, and we didn't speak the same language.

If whites bored me, it was because they bored themselves. They seemed to get little fun out of life and were desperately lonely. Often when I worked in night clubs I'd look around at those pale faces and weary eyes and I'd think, "They are only here to kill time." In spite of the countless advantages they enjoyed as the master race they looked fed up with everything and as though they hated life itself. When you worked in front of them you had to do the whole job.

But in the Negro night clubs the customers worked with you. They had come to the spot to cut loose, and even if you were lousy they had a good time. High spirits weren't forced on them. They came in with bounce and éclat, checking their troubles at the door.

As far as I could see, the white man was full of mental pains and psychic aches. He had all but forgotten what it was like to breathe freely and with pleasure. If he came to night clubs it was only to escape whatever the hell it was that ailed him. And I couldn't help wondering, if he was really like that, what good were all his fine homes and jobs, trips to Florida, silk hats, and his poses of superiority?

When Carl Van Vechten talked to me that evening in my dressing room I sensed that he was more like my Greenwich Village friends than the night-clubbing crowd I'd watched. He was rich, but that hadn't got him down. Carl had great life in him and enthusiasm.

Before he left he persuaded me to come to a big-time dinner at his home. When I got there it was filled with beautiful things—paintings, rare old books, sculptures, and antiques. But none of those things meant a damn thing to me. They still don't. Nothing in my life has geared me to like or appreciate works of art.

Carl had the bust of me there that he had bought from Tony Salemme, and I must admit I liked that. Working with his fingers in clay, Tony had brought out much of what I'd been like as a girl and was now like as a woman. It was my portrait in bronze shaped by affectionate and intuitively wise and sympathetic hands.

I made no secret that I didn't care for the food they served to me that first night I went to Carl Van Vechten's house on Park Avenue. It was rich white folks' food, and they started off with borsch. *Cold borsch!* That is nothing but beet soup and clabber. Served cold, it is enough to chill your gizzard for a week.

I told Carl that the caviar looked like buckshot to me and didn't taste much better. I had worked enough in service around Philadelphia to know what caviar was, and it is sturgeons' eggs. But I never cared to eat those little round gray-black balls even then, when I had the extra fun of eating them on the sly.

But Carl and Fania Marinoff, his wife and a good actress, became my dearest friends. Sometimes it seems to me that Carl is the only person in the world who ever has understood the shyness deep down in me. To others I seem not shy but aloof and indifferent. But I'm not.

I have reason to be shy. I have been hurt plenty and don't want to be hurt any more. Carl summed up my character as well as anyone ever has, I think, when he said once:

"Ethel, you never ask anyone for anything—and you never thank anyone for anything."

From time to time I met a great many white celebrities at the Van Vechtens' home. Eugene O'Neill; Sinclair Lewis and Dorothy Thompson; Alfred and Blanche Knopf, the book publishers; George Jean Nathan, the Grim Reaper among American critics; prissy but brilliant Alexander Woollcott; and Heywood Broun, the shaggy and unkempt columnist. I also met there Cole Porter and Noel Coward and Somerset Maugham. They were all at the top of their fame.

Carl Van Vechten was credited with knowing at the time more about Harlem than any other white man except the captain of the Harlem police station.

But he said that other colored people were never quite themselves when he was around them and that I was the only Negro he'd ever met who was completely natural with him. I told Carl that was because he'd been hanging around mostly with dictys who tried to be as much like white people as possible.

"But what *do* you like to eat, Ethel?" he asked one evening when he became convinced I didn't care for the expensive food in his house. I made a date with him to come to my home for a meal, and I cooked that dinner myself—baked ham and string beans, topped off with iced tea and lemon meringue pie.

Carl loved that dinner and our informal way of living. My house, I guess, was a great novelty to him. There was not one towel in my bathroom that matched the others. They came from different hotels, and the Pullman Company was more than adequately represented. We had no silver set of our own or fancy tablecloths.

Carl Van Vechten, the rich white writer whose ambition was to be the historian of my Harlem people, reveled in it. For many, many years after that Carl sent me a pair of antique earrings on each of my opening nights on Broadway.

Meanwhile I was getting the first hints that theatrical fame was not all pie à la mode. I often read that such-and-such an actress has changed completely since she got in the big money, and stories like that made me wonder if she has changed half as much as her friends. When you become a celebrity some people act as though you have turned into a walking Christmas tree. They try to pick presents and annuities off you.

Around this time I opened at the Café de Paris in Chicago, where business was good. But I didn't get the money I was entitled to. I told one of the men who ran that place:

"You have made an awful mistake in trimming me. You started out as a hat-check man and you're going to end up that way."

He did become a hat-check man once more later on, and it is unfair for me perhaps to prophesy such disasters because they generally come true.

Going back to New York, I worked as a single act. I was living on West 137th Street, and some of the actors in the *Africana* troupe who hadn't been paid began to yell from across the street, "We didn't get paid! We want our money!"

Despite my growing earnings, I had little money just then and I wasn't responsible in any way for the debts run up by that show. That all was proved later when others tried to put the legal bite on me on that same score and their cases were thrown out of court.

Harold Gumm of Goldie and Gumm, theatrical lawyers, was trying to disentangle the financial troubles of the deceased *Africana*. The show had closed, but the subsequent arguments and lawsuits were in for a long run. Mr. Gumm said he would handle my part in the mess if I would give him five per cent of my earnings exclusive of my pay for vaudeville dates. We sealed that deal with a handshake.

Mr. Gumm was very successful in helping me, but the actors picketing outside the door (none of the true-blue troupers who had been in *Africana* were among them) upset me so I didn't care to go out on the street. I was having stomach trouble, and all that hullabaloo made it worse.

Butts and Sue asked me to come down to Philadelphia with them while they played a date. I was glad to. Besides everything else, I was on the verge of splitting up with Earl Dancer and also the Love Affair. Earl came running down to Philadelphia and he had a let's-forgive-and-forget-and-start-all-over-again routine, but I let him slide.

In Philadelphia, Clyde Edward Matthews appeared out of the nowhere. I'd met him in Cleveland a few months before, and it was quite a surprise when he slithered back into my life. When I first met Eddie, the girl he was romancing told me he was interested in me, but I didn't believe it. I paid him no mind, but in Philadelphia Eddie started picking up the checks. He wined me and he dined me, and most graciously. He had an air, and when he heard I needed money he would say:

"Here is a couple of hundred, Ethel. It's just a loan."

I accepted the loans, but inside I was leery of him, and I didn't want to be wolved. But just like Rocky had, Clyde Edward Matthews worked the sympathy racket on me. I was a tonic, according to this sweet talker, a breath of fresh air, and just what the doctor ordered for him so he could get on his feet.

Being sick, I fell for it, though, and some time later Eddie Matthews and I were married. He came up with me to New York—Butts and Sue were along—when I went there to fill some vaudeville dates. I was amazed to find that the show people in Harlem had turned on me for quitting Earl Dancer. The truth is that our association had been mutually profitable.

The work I enjoyed most at that time was making records for Columbia, though that company had not yet seen fit to identify me in its catalogue as a Negro singer.

Then and later I made records with such wonderful white musicians as Benny Goodman, Tommy and Jimmy Dorsey, Joe Venuti, Ruby Bloom, and Manny Klein. It was a caper and a delight doing those records with those fellows who could ad-lib my music with me. If the bosses wanted changes, we'd make them on the spot without any hesitation—and those changes would be right.

The Palace Theatre in Chicago wanted me, and I asked $1,250 and transportation, more than I'd ever dragged down before. It turned out to be the same old story. I asked that big money because I was sure I'd never get it. I wanted just then to stay around New York. But I got the boost and had to go.

King Vidor was making Hallelujah, a great all-Negro, movie, in Hollywood and wanted me for it. This wasn't anything picked off the grapevine because he later told me so himself.

They have queer and dizzy ways in Hollywood. The talent man King Vidor sent East to wave gold bags at me was stalled on the job by colored theatrical people unfriendly to me. He reported that he was unable to find me. But I never was so small and inconspicuous that picture people can't locate me, particularly when the price is right.

Harry Akst, who'd written "Dinah," came to my dressing room while I was playing the Orpheum in Los Angeles. Harry said he was working on the score for a new musical Warner Brothers wanted to make. They needed a song hit, and Harry thought he had it. He had brought the lead sheet to me so I could work on it with Pearl.

So we worked on it, and the song was "Am I Blue?" When we were ready Harry brought me to the studio and introduced me to Darryl F. Zanuck, who was production chief, spark plug, and the all-around hot young man at Warner Brothers.

Mr. Zanuck listened to my interpretation of "Am I Blue?" said "This is it," and asked what would I nick him for two weeks' work on his spacious and sunny movie lot.

"Well, Mr. Zanuck," I said, "I have commitments on the Orpheum time, but I will see if I can postpone them."

It so happened that Pearl Wright, my accompanist, was suffering from a tumor. So I used that as an excuse to get out of the commitments, saying I would prefer to wait until my pianist had recovered her health. The Orpheum people were nice about it and said they would rearrange my bookings. Then Pearl said she would like to take advantage of this breather to have her tumor removed at a local hospital. She did, the operation was a success, and I paid Pearl her regular salary while she was in the hospital.

Meanwhile I'd talked salary to Mr. Zanuck.

"How much do you get?" he asked, and I gave him an honest answer, telling him the truth, which was $1,250 a week. "However, Mr. Zanuck," I added, "between Pearl's operation and having my two-a-day schedule rearranged, I will probably lose more than two weeks of my valuable time. So if agreeable to you, Mr. Zanuck, I would like to have a four-week guarantee at $1,250 a week, which will come to a nicely rounded five thousand dollars."

"You drive a pretty good bargain for yourself, Miss Waters," he said, but with a friendly smile, and that was our deal for the picture, which was On with the Show.

I was traveling with Clyde Edward Matthews and I met his relatives on the Coast. One was Gertrude Prescott, a sweet, lovely person, and another, Uncle Albert Bauman, who was in the real estate business out there.

I also met Stepin Fetchit, the lackadaisical colored comedian, who was making his debut in Hallelujah, and was introduced to King Vidor. When that director heard of how he had been double-crossed out of my services he raised merry hell with his staff.

I worked my way East after finishing On with the Show. In New York I made some new records, among them "Trav'lin' All Alone," which Kate Smith sang later and Al Jolson did in Wonder Bar. I had the great pleasure and privilege of being accompanied on that recording by James P. Johnson.

But my throat, which had been troubling me for some time, had got worse, and my worried New York physician recommended a long rest. When I asked whether I could rest in Europe, while seeing all the sights, he suggested I consult, while in Paris, the greatest throat specialist on the Continent, a Dr. Weisart.

13

We sailed for Europe on the *Ile de France,* and first class. I was incognito, as we had booked passage as Mr. and Mrs. C. E. Matthews and child. The child was my goddaughter, Algretta Holmes, whom I'd adopted when she was only eighteen months old.

The beautiful liner moved slowly down New York Bay that night. The ship news reporters were looking for me. Not knowing I was Mrs. C. E. Matthews, they couldn't find me. I was tired and wanted to stop being Ethel Waters, the blues singer, for a while. My life had been full and exciting, full of joys and sorrows and laughter and thrills, but I wanted a real rest from it.

That was all I wanted. I wished to live for a short time just as a human being. I was expecting to have the time of my life taking care of little Algretta, who was a plaintive child, almost white, and very beautiful. And I did have the time of my life on that trip abroad. I dressed Algretta myself, fed her, put her to bed, and gave her her two baths each day. My ambition was to bring Algretta up so everyone would love her as I'd never been loved as a little girl.

For once I wanted to do the little things that every other woman does each day of her life. I thought that being a wife and mother would convince me I belonged to the human race.

Being a mother is what makes a real life for a woman, not applause, your picture in the paper, the roses and the telegrams you get on opening night. A great many people who think of themselves as poor have that richness in their lives.

You are a person of the greatest importance when you are a mother of a family. Just do your job right and your kids will love you. And for that love of theirs there is no satisfying substitute.

In writing this I trust I will not be misunderstood by any of the people who have been so kind to me during my career. No performer was ever pulled up out of a childhood so dark and cold. And I am grateful to the public that helped me every step of the long, hard way, grateful to the bottom of my soul.

Yet I cannot help feeling I would have been happier with a husband and children of my own.

I was able to relax on that ship with Algretta all to myself to hold and play with. I'd adopted her because I lost my baby, Ethel, who was Genevieve's child, some time before. And I brought up Algretta until she was twelve. The experience was so heart-warming and rewarding that I have since brought up, or helped to bring up, about twenty other little girls.

Some of them are married now and have children of their own. They and their children all call me Mom, and there is no word I would rather hear.

When Baby Ethel, my namesake and niece, was three and a half years old I had Genevieve bring her up to New York for a week end with me. The day after they went back to Philadelphia the child caught diphtheria and whooping cough and was having spasms. The doctor they called was so alarmed they sent for me.

It was awful watching that darling little child trying so hard to get her breath. But when I held her in my arms she seemed a little easier. I have always had a way with children, and it seems to comfort them when I hold them.

But after a while the doctor said to Momweeze, "Why don't you let your daughter go back to work?" I think he knew he couldn't save little Ethel and wanted to spare me the agony and the pain of watching her die.

And before I got back to Harlem the yellow envelope, the telegram, was there with the news that the child I loved so well was dead.

After we lost Ethel I was bitter for a long time against God. I told Him He was unkind to take her because I would have brought her up good if He hadn't interfered.

But in the end, of course, I made my peace with Him. I forced myself to face the truth: Genevieve would never have let me have little Ethel for myself, no matter what I said or did. Yet that adorable Ethel had loved me better than anyone else in the world, including her own mother.

And because I wanted her so bad I would have quarreled with Genevieve for not letting me bring Ethel up. There would have been quarreling and dissension over her as she grew older, and she wouldn't have been happy. Maybe that was one reason God took her from me.

Perhaps He also knew I wouldn't go on with my work if I had a child. God must have known that in the years to come I would appear in many plays and motion pictures in which I'd have a chance to expound my deep religious feelings, using the evangelical tendencies I'd inherited from my mother. It could be that God thought that more important than my having Ethel or a family of my own.

Coming home from my last trip to Chicago I had stopped off at Detroit to see Mozelle Holmes, a girl I'd known at Edmond's. She'd come up to New York originally as a chorus girl in the Billy King show and lately she had written me from Detroit that she had a baby.

When Mozelle brought that angel down to see me Algretta was so small she fitted in the tray of my traveling trunk. Mozelle was always a fine cook, and while I was in Detroit I ate at her house. During our conversations she told me she had no money and was finding it hard to bring up the baby.

"I'd like to take Algretta," I said, "and I'll provide for her." I was thinking that it might be almost as good as having a baby of my own. I explained to Mozelle that there would be no papers. I said, "If, when Algretta gets older, she wants to go back to you, all right. But if she prefers me, Mozelle, not all the policemen and courts in this country will be able to take her away from me."

Every day when we were on the *Ile de France* I'd sit out in the sun in a deck chair with Algretta. A good many show people were on that trip: Jimmy Durante's partners, Lou Clayton and Eddie Jackson; Tess (Aunt Jemima) Gardella, who passed away shortly after I started writing this book, and many others. But the other first-class passengers didn't know I was Ethel Waters.

They'd see me in my deck chair with Algretta and wonder about us, but not enough to stop and speak to me. Except for being white, Algretta bore a great resemblance to me, which probably came from association. And Eddie Matthews is much lighter than I. So there were the three of us, and our fellow passengers couldn't figure us out. I guess they suspected there was a colored gentleman somewhere in the lumberyard.

Because Algretta had to eat early I always answered the first call to dinner. Whenever I approached the table the white ladies there would begin talking about how wonderful their Mirandy was and how nobody in the world could fry chicken like their little old Emmy Lou.

They were being as subtle as a night stick over the shins, but I just smiled and pretended I didn't know what in the world they meant. But I understood, of course. They were trying to let me know that they didn't think a first-class cabin was the proper place for a colored woman, and rightfully she should only aspire to mopping floors, putting out the garbage, and presiding over a nice hot stove.

I'll never forget one lovely-looking and beautifully dressed young white girl on that trip. If it was my misfortune to have to go to the ladies' rest room while she was there she'd get out as fast as she could travel.

I loved to stand at the rail and look down on the water, endless and moving always and slapping itself into a lather against the side of the *Ile de France*. This young girl came by one day while I was standing there and looking at the water. She spoke to a couple of people she knew. I turned around just as they left her and saw that she'd had an accident. Her white satin dress had split right up the back. You could see many of her assets and liabilities, the strong sea breeze blowing the torn pieces of dress this way and that.

I walked up close to her. "Don't turn around, miss," I said quietly, "but you're in trouble. The skirt of your dress has burst open. If you can stand it for me to get close to you, I'll walk behind you until you reach your cabin. Then you can go in and change your outfit."

And that's the way we walked to her cabin, with me close behind her so nobody could see how her dress had split up the back. When she came out again she looked for me. I was again at the rail, and she bubbled over with gratefulness.

I smiled, but I didn't unbend. "I'm the same person I was before. There is really no reason at all for you to treat me any different."

I don't know whether she understood that, but I bet it made her think some. I imagine she was puzzled to discover there were Negro persons who weren't interested at all in becoming intimate with whites.

I was very busy at the job of bringing up Algretta. She was a sweet, wistful child and could already laugh and talk. I had one great advantage in rearing her: that was being able to remember everything that had happened in my life since I was less than three years old. So I didn't have to waste any time talking to child psychologists and reading books on how to guide your kiddies so they won't grow up to be safecrackers or dope fiends.

All I did was try to figure out what would have been good for me as a child. I raised Algretta by that simple system of doing for her what should have been done for me when I was a kid. I just used my foster mother's heart, and it was enough.

Like myself, that little girl seemed to have been born hungry, and heaven knows I understood that. After Algretta had a good-sized portion of food she'd yell, "More! More! More!"

"You really want some more, Algretta?"

"Yes, Mommy."

"Well, then you'll have to eat all of it. You can't play with it or throw it on the floor. Or next time when you are hungry and ask for a second helping you won't get it."

Algretta was cute, playful, and beautiful, but I didn't spoil her. I've never been able to understand those parents who spoil children by giving them everything they want and then suddenly turn on the kids they've made into little brats when they, the parents, become bored or irritated with them.

I kissed and hugged Algretta plenty. But I was strict with her, too, and never overindulged her. I remember how as a child I'd imitated everything I saw my elders do, and I did my best to see she was exposed to no misconduct or bad language while she was around me.

Though the white ladies who were my fellow passengers ignored me, they were pleased and intrigued by my husband, Eddie Matthews, and his courtly airs. Eddie was a charmer, though I do not care to say what else he was.

From the day I stepped on the *Ile de France* one of the ship's officers, wearing a lovely white suit, paid me much attention. He had capulets, or epaulets, or whatever you call those things on his shoulders.

That officer came to our cabin every morning and inquired kindly how I felt and how Algretta was standing the voyage. Whenever he saw me during the day he'd again asked how I felt. That nice man, in fact, was so interested in our health that I thought he must be the ship's doctor.

The night before our voyage ended there was the usual ship's concert. This benefit performance is given for the widows and orphans of seamen.

The day before the ship's concert word was sent me that it would be appreciated if I appeared and performed. But I'd heard that the other theatrical people aboard had been asked by the purser, personally. I became very angry. I sent back word that if they wanted me to sing at their ship's concert the purser could come and ask me, personally, too.

I made quite a ruckus over this. I told Eddie Jackson and Lou Clayton and Tess Gardella. They were all on my side and furious at the slight to a fellow artist because she was colored. And we all raised holy hell.

But the next morning a big bunch of flowers was delivered to my cabin, along with a written invitation from the chief purser that was almost obsequious.

I graciously said I'd appear. And that evening as I dressed in my prettiest gown I thought of all those white women who had been snubbing me and talking about their wonderful Mirandys and Emmy Lous at the dinner table.

I knew what was going to happen when they saw me now. I knew how white people treated Ethel Waters when she wasn't incognito. So I didn't leave my cabin until just before the time for me to go on and do my act.

"And now," said the master of ceremonies, "I give you—Miss Ethel Waters."

I walked up and onto the stage—and there was a gasp. And you should have seen all those young female varmints and old harpies. After I finished they fluttered and flashed kindness and warmth all around me.

"Where you been, Miss Waters?" they asked as they crowded round. "Where have you been hiding yourself all the way from New York?"

Now I know how to fight and take care of myself, as you know. But sometimes not fighting is better and hurts the other fellow more. I just smiled and told them sweetly:

"Why, ladies, I haven't been hiding anywhere. I've been on this ship all this time, and in plain sight. I've been on the deck every day in my chair. Now that I come to think of it, I've seen you all each day, and I'm sure you saw me.

"But none of you spoke to me. Not one of you. Yet I'm the very same person as I was yesterday. I have the same face, same body, and same color."

The main number I had just sung as appropriate for the occasion was "Trav'lin' All Alone."

Maybe some of those first-class passengers and ladies always will remember how they heard it on the *Ile de France* that night.

But what I remember best about that whole incident is the ship's officer who escorted me into the big room on the evening of the concert. He was the same beautiful man who had been so solicitous about my health all through the trip. He wasn't the ship's doctor at all but the chief purser. And I'd made that big ruckus about his ignoring me!

Many of my friends were in Paris, and they tried to give me a good time. Valaida Snow was working there, and the Berry Brothers were playing in the Paris company of *Blackbirds*. And we also saw a lot of Lorenzo Brashear, one of Fletcher Henderson's old band men.

One day Brashear and I took Algretta to a circus in Paris. Brashear, who is very dark, had Algretta, who is so white, by the hand. We stopped to see the Ubangis. They looked at dark Brashear, copper-colored me, and almost lily-white Algretta and thought us a mama, papa, and baby group.

So we were looking at the Ubangis and they were looking at us. Their eyes would go from Brashear to me and then to Algretta. With their big saucer lips they didn't say anything. But their rolling eyes told the whole story of what they were thinking. They were making fun of him, "the papa," believing that I, "the mama," must have been playing house with somebody who didn't even have a sun tan.

I still loved to dance as much as I had when I was the world's champion shimmy shaker in Chester, Pennsylvania. And in Paris I danced quite a bit. On many nights my escort and dancing partner was Al Brown, who became world's bantamweight champion the following year. I met a lot of people in Paris, and Radclyffe Hall, the author of *The Well of Loneliness*, was the most interesting of them. I saw Florence Jones. In Harlem she had paid me twenty or thirty dollars a session for singing to her privately so she could study my style. She was becoming rich and famous with her Chez Florence, which was for many years one of the most popular spots in Montmartre. Josephine Baker was touring the other capitals of Europe while we were in Paris, so I didn't get to see her.

When we went out at night crowds would follow us around, comparing me to Josephine. I did enjoy myself there, and in the daytime I had Algretta to cuddle.

My homemade system of bringing her up didn't include letting her whimper her way out of punishments that she deserved. It seemed to me that when she did anything bad she should learn for herself how it could hurt her.

One day I caught her trying to light a cigarette. I got Eddie Matthews, my husband, to hold one near her and pretend not to notice when Algretta removed it from between his fingers and stole a puff. After she choked and spluttered a little I knew she wouldn't fool around with cigarettes any more.

Another time I found her trying to open a whisky bottle. I opened it for her and let her have a tiny taste. That burned her little throat and made her the youngest member of Alcoholics Anonymous.

We were still in France when I faced my biggest problem with Algretta. We were living at Maisons-Lafitte, just out of town, and I'd go in several times a week to get treatments for my throat from Dr. Weisart.

On these occasions I would leave Algretta with the Negro family we were living with. This family laughed at her capers and were particularly amused when she tormented Cyril, a handy man who worked around there. Algretta, a bright little thing, would turn the hose on Cyril and call him all sorts of names.

The family never told me about this until one day after she had called one of them "black." When I returned from Paris they reported this outrage and all her previous teasing bouts with Cyril.

"You didn't say nothin' before about what she had done to Cyril," I pointed out to them. "You only complained of Algretta after she called one of your own people a black. You thought she was cute when she called Cyril the same thing. So I am not going to punish Algretta for what she did to you but for tormenting Cyril."

I worried about what Algretta had done. She was so light she could easily be mistaken for white. And I knew there were Negroes in the world who would kill a person they thought white, even a child, for calling them black.

So I had a long, serious talk with Algretta. She was cagey. At first she would only admit that she had spit at Cyril. A little later on she reluctantly admitted that she had called him black.

"Your skin is very fair, Algretta," I said. "But I, your mommy dear, am black too. Just like Cyril. So is your own flesh-and-blood mother. And when you call anyone black, you are black, Algretta, but in a different way. There is something black inside of you that makes you say things like that."

Her eyes grew big with wonder. "Now I'm going to have you touch something black," I went on, "something black that you'll remember." I put a little black pepper on a spoon, made her taste it, and gave her a glass of cold water to wash it down.

Algretta screamed, cried, and leaped around. She is grown now and has a baby of her own, but I have never heard of her calling anyone black since.

Memories of my own childhood shenanigans were so clear that I could anticipate Algretta's every mischievous thought. She began to think of me as a mind reader, and I think that helped me keep her in line.

When Algretta was older I had several amusing and instructive experiences with her. She was still quite small the day we went to Coney Island. We went into a freak show, and my little girl was fascinated by a monstrosity on one of the stands. This unusual fellow had the body of what had started out to be his brother coming out of his stomach. Even the other freaks considered him a freak.

On the way home Algretta could talk of nothing else. When we were back in the house she said thoughtfully, for the hundredth time, "Mommy, that man has his little brother coming out of his stomach."

I nodded.

"Something about that man with his little brother coming out of his stomach reminds me of my mother and me," she said.

When I didn't answer, she asked, "Don't you think so, Mommy?"

I tried to distract her, but she repeated, "Don't you think so, Mommy? And do you know why that man in the show reminds me of my own mother and me, Mommy?"

"I'll tell you what, Algretta," I whispered. "Don't you tell me what you know about that. And I won't tell you what I know. Let's keep the whole thing a secret."

I was glad when I didn't have to whip her and could punish her in some other way. Whenever I whipped Algretta I made her apologize to me afterward for getting me so upset. And upset was hardly the word. It brought on an emotional crisis in me. Each time I'd whip her I'd get terrible headaches and have to put ice-cold towels on my head.

Being a smart, quick-witted opportunist, Algretta soon discovered how to use this to her own advantage. If she did anything wicked she'd tell the people who were caring for her, "Don't you tell Mommy I been bad or she'll get one of her awful headaches. You wouldn't want that to happen, would you?"

We spent three months in Cannes. We had booked passage home when an offer for me to play at the Palladium came from London. So we went there.

I became more alarmed than ever about my throat while I was appearing in England's most famous music hall. After the first show each day I could hardly whisper. My agents sent me to the Honorable Dr. Cyril Horsford, the great throat specialist.

Dr. Horsford examined me and said I had a nodule (in plain language, a wart) on my left vocal cord. He advised an operation, though he warned me it might be dangerous. When I heard his fee for such an operation was £150 ($750), I said I couldn't afford it.

He prescribed drops which at one time took my voice away. But the treatments of Professor Drysdale, a colored voice coach, who showed me how I could lift my voice, enabled me to sing in another range.

Dr. Horsford questioned me about my work and asked me to bring some of my records to his office. He wanted to hear how I'd sung before I'd had the throat trouble. I played "Trav'lin' All Alone" for him. Before that I'd been just another patient in his busy life. Like many people, he was attracted by my lower register and he now looked upon the saving of my voice as something specially important. He told me he had been Nellie Melba's medical coach.

Dr. Horsford went all out for me, and I was able to take an engagement at the Café de Paris. The night I opened there that plushy spot was jammed with bluebloods, lords, earls, baronets, and their titled ladies, also Spanish, Hungarian, Prussian, and Russian types of royalty, both ex- and present. We entertainers were almost the only commoners present, not counting the waiters. Linholm and Fairchild, a piano-playing team, played my accompaniments. As I came out to sing I saw that Tallulah Bankhead, the gorgeous yam from Alabam', who was then the reigning queen of the English stage, had a ringside table. It was an exciting night.

One of the beautiful hostesses at the Café de Paris was Estelle O'Brien, who looked like some sort of Javanese. I often talked to Estelle, who told me she reported for work early each night so she could hear me sing.

"Do you think I could make good in Hollywood?" she asked me one night. "Should I take the gamble and go there?"

I looked at her for a moment. She had almond-shaped eyes and olive skin, was sweet, charming, and had a lovely face. "I think you'll make good," I told her. "Go to America. Take the chance."

It was the best advice I ever gave anyone. Sometime afterward Estelle O'Brien went to Hollywood, and made good under her professional name, Merle Oberon.

The management of the Café de Paris reserved the same table for me each night. One evening I came in to find the Prince of Wales sitting there with a lady. He was incognito, and when he was told he had my table the Prince walked over to me and apologized.

I told His Royal Highness that it was okay. I didn't like it later when he abdicated as King and Emperor and ruler of the Dominions Beyond the Seas and all the rest. After all, he was the only king who had ever apologized to me for anything. The Prince came back once a week to catch my act during the ten weeks I played at the Café de Paris. He always nodded to me and I nodded back.

Dr. Horsford still thought I should risk the operation. He told me straight out that if the operation failed I could lose my voice and it might even be fatal. But he thought the operation would be successful and that my voice would be immensely improved, though I might have to lay off working for a while. This particular operation, he said, had never been performed before.

I decided I'd let God call the turn this time. I told the Honorable Dr. Horsford, "If I can earn one hundred and fifty pounds before I leave, I'll have you operate on me."

For a while nothing happened. The ships were crowded with American tourists going home from their vacations, and it was necessary to arrange for your passage well in advance. Finally I got accommodations on the *Aquitania*.

I was actually packing my things when my agents called with an offer for me to play a week at the Holborn Empire Theatre, another top music hall there.

"They are willing to pay one hundred pounds," the agent said.

"If you can get me one hundred and fifty pounds for the week, I'll take the date," I told him.

When the manager of the theater agreed to my terms, I felt it was God's way of deciding I should have the operation. I didn't think He would cross me up, yet I was scared to death. And my friends who had heard me sing at the Holborn Empire told me I'd never been in better voice.

Leighton and Johnson, Maureen Browning, and the other friends of mine who were in England didn't think I should risk the operation. Just then I was living in Regent's Park with John Payne and his family. John was a protégé of Lady Cook, the philanthropist, and it was her home we were staying in.

To rest up, Dr. Horsford went down to the country the week end before that all-important operation. Then on Monday he put drops in my throat. On Tuesday I went to his office and signed a paper of release exonerating him from all blame if the operation failed.

As he watched me sign that paper Dr. Horsford told me, "The operation won't fail. Everything is going to be all right." With two of his colleagues looking on, he prepared me for the operation, warning me not to move or sneeze. Then he held his right hand straight out in front of him for a long time to make sure it was steady enough.

Next he applied the local anesthetic and got out his long instruments. Finally he put those long, thin scissors deep down into my throat—and snipped. It took only a split moment, and then he brought up the nodule. It was about the size of a grain of rice.

Dr. Horsford was sweating terribly, but he had nothing on me. "Don't talk, Miss Waters," he said, "but this operation has been successful." He repeated what he'd said before about it being the first time in medical history that such a nodule had ever been removed from the center of the left vocal cord. I thanked God for keeping the Honorable Horsford's hand steady while he was making new medical history with my vocal cord.

Once again I booked passage. A couple of my entertainer friends were in London, and the wolf had them. They were broke, stranded, and homesick.

"For heaven's sake, Ethel," they said, "don't leave us here."

So I got them both tickets—in the steerage. I was in a second-class cabin because that ship was so crowded, and my little steerage pals had the privilege of visiting with me any time they liked.

The first time I sang after my throat operation was at that ship's concert. It was one of the tensest nights of my life. But my voice, which for some years had had a certain husky quality, proved to have a clearer tone than ever before. I also could sing now in a higher pitch.

God once again had stayed in my corner, nobly assisted by the Honorable Dr. Cyril Horsford.

14

I had been away from the U.S.A. for eight long months. But not a single theater had closed up. No maddened mobs had threatened to lynch J. J. and Lee Shubert for keeping me out of sight and hearing distance.

So I lost no time getting vaudeville dates and making new records. Then Lew Leslie, who had never wanted me before, asked Goldie and Gumm if they could get me for his new edition of *Blackbirds*. Leslie had split up with Bill Robinson, his box-office ace in the hole, and Bojangles now had his own show, *Brown Buddies*. Adelaide Hall, Leslie's other star, was in Europe.

Leslie wanted me as his big name, and he had some good acts lined up: Flourney Miller, formerly of Miller and Lyles; Buck and Bubbles, Jazzlips Richardson, Mantan Moreland, and Eubie Blake's Orchestra.

That show started off by almost being stranded in rehearsal. Leslie was splitting up quarters each day among the cast so they wouldn't have to walk home to Harlem.

Blackbirds opened at a Forty-second Street theater right next to the flea circus. Our show was a flop, and the fleas outdrew us at every performance. The depression came in and made our business worse. But it didn't dent the take of the flea circus at all. It reminded me of the old vaudeville joke about the flea circus that became so prosperous each flea was given his own private dog.

My best number in that show was "You're Lucky to Me," a take-off on Rudy Vallee, then the crooner who was getting sighs from all young girls who didn't have any fellows, also many who had fellows but weren't satisfied. I had recorded that song with "Memories of You" on the other side.

Rudy, who always was a darling, loved that take-off on him and he had me as guest star on his radio program. Another girl on that broadcast was Alice Faye. She had won a contest in Atlantic City and was going to Hollywood for her first screen tests. And in Hollywood she got starred and, eventually, Phil Harris.

The *Blackbirds* shuffled off to Philadelphia, where business was bad, and then to Newark, where the troupe was stranded. The back of my car almost broke down under the weight of all the entertainers I drove back to Harlem with me.

The depression was in full swing, but Lew Leslie told me he wanted to build a show around me—with a choir and a stage band. And he was going to call it *Rhapsody in Black*.

But when I got to New York after a vaudeville tour I discovered that Lew Leslie had built his show around Valaida Snow. Valaida was also directing the stage band. And Eloise Uggins, a girl out of the choir, was singing "Eïli, Eïli" and another number I did.

So I asked Mr. Leslie, "What am I going to do? What does that leave me to do?"

"We'll open up in Washington," he told me, "and you'll come on and sing your songs, some of your off-color ones."

Your lawyer can be the United States Marines in a case like that. When I told Mr. Gumm, an expert on any lapses of the party of the other part, about this business of getting the business, he gave me his best lawyer's smile.

"Don't worry, Ethel," he said, patting my hand. "I'm afraid that Mr. Leslie hasn't read your contract very carefully. If he had, he would not have overlooked the clause which states that the material furnished you must meet with your satisfaction. He doesn't seem to have been able to find anyone who can furnish you with this satisfying material. So we will have to find him."

Mr. Gumm was not only a smart lawyer who was proving a good investment for me, he knew just where to look in the many cubbyholes and walk-up apartments of New York for song writers. The ones he came up with were a gifted husband-and-wife team, Mann Holiner and Alberta Nichols. They worked with Pearl and me night and day and they wrote socko songs for me. Even on the train going into Washington they worked with us on the four numbers they had created for me. The numbers were "Washtub Rhapsody," "Dancehall Hostess," "What's Keeping My Prince Charming," and "You Can't Stop Me from Lovin' You."

Thanks to Mann Holiner and Alberta Nichols, I was ready for the opening at the Belasco Theatre in Washington, but Valaida Snow, my old friend and European sight-seeing companion, wasn't up on her stuff.

My billing was so big I had to be good, or else. One critic down there in Washington compared me to Ruth Draper and Cornelia Otis Skinner, the monologuists, saying I was the first Negro woman entertainer to present monologues of that high quality. I also recorded those four numbers Mann and Alberta had written for me under such high pressure and short notice.

I had a very interesting dispute with Mr. Producer Leslie over my salary. I said I was willing to take $1,250, just half of my established vaudeville weekly salary. I wasn't doing any kind deed of benevolence for the management. Being in a Broadway musical always builds up your prestige and future earning power.

But Lew Leslie didn't want to pay $1,250. So my wily Mr. Gumm said we'd accept instead a $700 a week guarantee plus ten per cent of the gross box-office receipts. Lew Leslie leaped like a happy goat at that deal.

Rhapsody in Black ran through the grimmest days of the depression, usually dragging in from $22,000 to $24,000. But no week was bad for me. Even when the show pulled a comparatively miserable $17,000, I made $2,400—my $700 plus $1,700, the ten per cent peeled off the top of the horrified Lew Leslie's bank roll.

When Rhapsody in Black finished its long, profitable run Leslie condensed the show for the big time and movie-presentation houses. He got a tremendous weekly guarantee for the capsule production.

And when we came into the New York Paramount Theatre, I was not billed at all. But the other performers like Adelaide Hall and Avise Andrews were billed. Leslie had switched the show from Rhapsody in Black to Blackbirds to eliminate me.

Again I placed my troubles in the lap of Mr. Gumm.

"We won't worry about this, Ethel," he said in his quiet way. "We'll bring this gentleman to his senses. I will simply book you into the Roxy the same week they open at the Paramount."

The Roxy, of course, was the Paramount's biggest opposition house. When the Paramount executives heard I was going into the Roxy the same week they had the unit I'd been starring in, they hastily rubbed their sticks together and made a hot fire under Lew Leslie. Leslie had to pull out his whiskers fast and eat out of my hand.

My Roxy booking was canceled, and I was billed at the Paramount as their Extra Added Attraction and was paid twenty-five hundred dollars for that week by Mr. Leslie. I stayed with that unit through most of 1931.

Now for a long time the class spot in Harlem that drew the white trade had been the Cotton Club. It featured such sterling attractions as Cab Calloway and Duke Ellington. One evening they gave an "Ethel Waters Night"—and I must say I enjoyed myself immensely.

When we had played *Rhapsody in Black* in Chicago, Al Jolson was down the street from us in *Wonder Bar*, and Ben Bernie gave a night for him at the Sherman Hotel. Fred and Adele Astaire and other great stars from shows playing all around Chicago appeared as representatives of their various companies. I was sent there to represent *Rhapsody in Black*. And it was like an Oscar night with an orchestra playing your music as you arrived to the heart-warming reception. All those terrific people went on. Even Jolie himself went on before anyone thought of calling on Ethel Waters.

Jolie was never a slacker. Until he died, and for good reason, they called him "the world's greatest entertainer." From the day he first stepped on a stage Jolie always sang as though he expected the next note to be his last "wah wah" or "bebee mine" or "I loav you, honeh, loav, loav you" or "Californyah, heah I come, Golden Gate."

On his Chicago night Jolie sang everything he knew, playing everything from shoemaker to baker with his heart and his lungs bursting. He worked on the stage for an hour and a half, worked in a sweat until exhausted. And he wasn't the only one, because Jolie's singing is all uppercuts, and if anyone ever told him to restrain himself he gave them the deaf ear.

Al Jolson sat down, after having stunned and amused and mesmerized his audience for that solid hour and a half. Ben Bernie—whom I always loved, and he was the sweetest-natured of all entertainers—got up and said:

"But the evening would be hardly complete if our girl Ethel Waters didn't at least rise and smile."

Ben was trying to give me an easy out. Because nobody was ever expected to follow Jolie. The folks were supposed to stagger to their feet and go home. That's why acrobats were invented, to go on the stage and throw each other around after stars like Al Jolson are finished and the audience is starting for the doors marked "Exit! Walk, Don't Run, in Case of Fire!"

But I was never one to duck a challenge and I went on and sang seven songs. And Ben gave me a night only two weeks later at that same Sherman Hotel. There was never anyone tougher to follow than Jolie or Will Rogers. And if you don't believe me, ask any acrobat.

I had another exciting experience in Chicago when Al Capone and his brother Ralph wanted me to appear in a night club they were running in Cicero. I was scared to death. I was afraid not to accept and just as afraid to work for those kings of the Chicago underworld.

Jake Lingle, the Chicago *Tribune's* crack police reporter, had just been murdered out there by mobsters. I couldn't help thinking that if the boys didn't hesitate to knock off a police reporter what would they do to a poor blues singer if she gave out one sour note?

But I went there, and the whole Capone mob treated me with deference and respect. But my fears didn't quiet down. Whenever a car backfired outside the club they all had to come running to my dressing room and convince me that it wasn't a new gang war that was starting up.

If I was nervous from fear and trembling, Eddie Matthews was in a dithering panic. If someone knocked on the door of our Chicago hotel room Eddie would get the jitters and the bends.

"Who's there at the door?" he'd cry out, but in a broken voice. "I got my pistol right here and ready. What's that you say—a telegram? Shove it under the door."

I had bought an Elcar, and we noticed other cars following us a couple of times. They were mobsters who thought we were imported gunmen. Once two cars forced us to the curb, but when they saw it was just me they passed on and Eddie almost passed out.

As scared as I was, I had to laugh at his sweating with terror that way. The Capones paid me off in full, and my efforts were appreciated and applauded. But though I'm a child of the underworld I must say that I prefer working for people who never laid eyes on an Italian pineapple or a sawed-off shotgun.

I went back to New York glad to be alive.

One day Herman Stark suggested I work for him at the Cotton Club. I asked for a larger salary than they'd ever paid any other star. To my surprise, Herman Stark said okay.

Pearl and I went up there, and they had a new number that Harold Arlen had written. They were using a lot of mechanical devices to get storm effects. It was a wonderful number. But after listening to it I told them that the piece should have more to do with human emotions and should be expressed that way instead of with noise-making machines to interpret the rumblings and rattlings of Old Mother Nature.

"But let me take the lead sheet home," I suggested. "I'll work on it with Pearl. This song should be given a dramatic ending. I'm gonna see if I can't give it that. But if I do, I will only want to sing it at one show a night. I want to give it everything I got. That will take too much out of me if I have to sing it in more than one show."

The song, of course, was "Stormy Weather."

Singing "Stormy Weather" proved a turning point in my life. My love life, my marriage, was being stormy as hell just then. I felt I was working my heart out and getting no happiness.

"Stormy Weather" was the perfect expression of my mood, and I found release in singing it each evening. When I got out there in the middle of the Cotton Club floor I was telling the things I couldn't frame in words. I was singing the story of my misery and confusion, of the misunderstandings in my life I couldn't straighten out, the story of the wrongs and outrages done to me by people I had loved and trusted.

Your imagination can carry you just so far. Only those who have been hurt deeply can understand what pain is, or humiliation. Only those who are being burned know what fire is like. I sang "Stormy Weather" from the depths of the private hell in which I was being crushed and suffocated.

I was worried, a nervous wreck, when Ethel Waters singing "Stormy Weather" became the talk of New York. And one night Irving Berlin, the frail little Jewish man who has written the great love songs for two generations of Americans, came up to hear me sing that song.

The following day he got in touch with Goldie and Gumm. He told them he was writing the music for a revue that Sam H. Harris was producing.

"We're going to try to inject a serious note into this musical," said Irving. "We'd like to talk to Miss Waters about it."

I went down and saw Irving Berlin, Sam Harris, and Moss Hart, who was writing the book for the show, which they were calling *As Thousands Cheer*. Clifton Webb, doll-like Marilyn Miller, and Helen Broderick, the comedienne, were to be starred. I was only to be featured, but there were four big song numbers for me.

My doctor for some time had been urging me to take a vacation. When I closed at the Cotton Club I had two weeks before rehearsals began for *As Thousands Cheer*. I taught the new girls at the club all the routines, and I sent Algretta and Eddie Matthews to Atlantic City a week ahead, saying I would join them there.

"Dinah" had been the first international song hit to come out of a night club. "Stormy Weather," which might have been the theme song of my life, was proving to be the first dramatic song hit out of a night club. But I was in no physical condition to take pleasure in that.

After Algretta and Eddie had left for the beach resort I couldn't sleep. I was sick every night and suffering from psychic insomnia. I had the premonition that a new tragedy was about to close in on me.

And when I arrived at Atlantic City I found Algretta terribly ill. The doctor we got said my baby had infantile paralysis! I summoned a specialist from Philadelphia, and he prescribed treatments.

I attended to Algretta myself as long as I could. But I couldn't keep that up and rehearse and everything else. In the end I sent her up to Cambridge, Massachusetts, to live with my two dear friends, Myra and Joseph Webster. They, bless them, did all that massaging you have to do day and night. Often, while away from her, I was haunted by the dread that Algretta would be a cripple for life. I could close my eyes and see that mischievous little angel scampering over the decks of the *Ile de France*, and her humor and her pranks came back to haunt me.

I visited Algretta every chance I got. Eventually she recovered—thanks to the Websters' loving care. She went to school up in Cambridge, and I paid all of Algretta's living expenses until she was twelve. Mozelle then wanted her back and she was in a position to take care of her. So I gave my baby up but continued to see her.

I guess I was facing the most important test of my career as I started rehearsing for *As Thousands Cheer*. I had to compete in that show and hold my own with such top-ranking stars as Marilyn Miller, Clifton Webb, and Helen Broderick.

I must say, though, that I never had better material to work with. My four song numbers in that show were "Heat Wave," which turned out to be a tremendous hit; "To Be or Not To Be," "Supper Time," and "I've Got Harlem on My Mind," a take-off which I did with Hamtree Harrington, a perfect man to work with.

But from the very beginning it was "Supper Time" that most intrigued me. This was the serious note that Irving Berlin had spoken about.

"Supper Time" was a dirge. It told the story of a colored woman preparing the evening meal for her husband who had been lynched. If one song can tell the whole tragic history of a race, "Supper Time" was that song. In singing it I was telling my comfortable, well-fed, well-dressed listeners about my people. I only had to think of the family of that boy down in Macon, Georgia, who had been lynched to give adequate expression to the horror and the defeat in "Supper Time."

If they would only let me sing that song I knew I would be singing for all my people.

But "Supper Time" was one tough number to spot in a gay musical revue. There were the stars to think of and the effect the powerful and heartbreaking song would have on the routines with which they had to follow it. And when we opened in Philadelphia no one yet was sure of where it could be spotted or whether it should be kept in at all.

Mr. Harris came over to the theater in Philadelphia. He was the one who had insisted all along on the song staying in, and now he said:

"We will try out 'Supper Time' at the Wednesday matinee and evening performances. If the audiences like it, 'Supper Time' stays in."

There were some good Catholics working backstage, including Minnie Eisler and Jackie, the wardrobe mistress. And before that Wednesday matinee those people burned plenty of candles for me. After praying for help from Him I went on and sang "Supper Time." When I was through and that big, heavy curtain came down I was called back again and again. I had stopped the show with a type of song never heard before in a revue, and a number that until then had been a question mark.

"Supper Time" was in the second act. Marilyn Miller and Clifton Webb had to follow it with a flippant bedroom dance. They didn't like the idea of trying to be cute and amusing right after the people had heard that grim, overwhelming song.

"It stays in," said Sam. H. Harris, the producer.

Mr. Harris is gone for some years now from Broadway, but I would like to add here my little tribute to the thousands of beautiful words that were written and said about him when he passed on.

Like me, Sam H. Harris had come from way down low in the social scale. As a young man he'd been the manager of Terrible Terry Mc-Govern, the featherweight champ. Later he was the partner of George M. Cohan.

Mr. Harris was a little man with a big chin and sad eyes. He always put his own money in his shows, which few producers dare do today.

The point about him is that he was a showman who lived and died in the theater. Old-timers tell me that Sam Harris, a gentle man, broke down and cried like a baby when his Terrible Terry McGovern lost his championship title to Young Corbett. No one could console Sam Harris for weeks after that.

People never could understand why the sweet, goodhearted Sam Harris, who could never hurt his worst enemy, loved Terrible Terry, the great man-power destroyer in the ring, and very brutal and savage.

But I think I know. Terrible Terry McGovern was a great entertainer and crowd pleaser. He could thrill all who saw him. It was the showman in Sam Harris that worshiped McGovern, the killer. And it was the showman in Sam Harris that made him insist, over all opposition, that "Supper Time," a fantastic thing in a revue, stay in.

It was the emotional impact on an audience that Mr. Harris reveled in. That was his real pay, as it has always been mine. He was a true showman, and the money he made on his hits was only something he was glad to get because it meant he would be able to put on more shows. And if the theater needs anything today to cure its ills, it is more little men like Sam H. Harris, who was a gambler and no real estate operator.

As Thousands Cheer was a smash hit on Broadway. But the real test of the show came during the summer, when Marilyn Miller and Clifton Webb took their vacations. Sam Harris kept the show on even though there were only Helen Broderick and me as draw people. He said he wouldn't have to close it unless the box-office receipts dropped below twelve thousand dollars a week. And they never did.

That year I became the highest-paid woman performer on Broadway. My salary in the show was one thousand dollars a week. I doubled in a nearby night club for four weeks at twenty-five hundred dollars per. Also, the Amoco Gas Company hired me for their Sunday-night broadcast of Jack Denny's Orchestra at fifteen hundred dollars a shot.

Amoco originally signed me for three weeks, then three more weeks were added, and before they were finished adding time I was on the air for eighteen weeks. That made me the first colored performer to star on a commercial coast-to-coast show on a national network during the winter season.

When Jack Denny and his boys had to leave the show the sponsors asked me what band I wanted to work with. I said, "Jimmy Dorsey's," and they tried Jimmy out and kept him and his band on.

When I was taken off the Amoco program I was told that some of the stations in the South objected to having a colored woman on the air and were refusing to pipe my program in.

Marilyn Miller never came back to work with us in *As Thousands Cheer*, being replaced by the charming Dorothy Stone. During the summer in New York the billing had starred the show, and it read: "*As Thousands Cheer* with Helen Broderick and Ethel Waters." But when it was sent on the road I was starred along with Clifton Webb, Helen Broderick, and Dorothy Stone.

Webb quit after Chicago. Dorothy Stone also left the cast when we were on the road. Mr. Harris was planning to send the show through the South to the Coast. There was some doubt on Broadway whether Southerners would accept a musical with a Negro woman so prominent in a cast otherwise white. The tour of *As Thousands Cheer* marked the first time a colored person had been co-starred with white players below the Mason-Dixon line. But the people who came to see the show always received me warmly.

Finally we played the Coast, and in the end I was all alone as star and we came back East by another route and closed in Rochester.

I'd been with that show for two years, and it did a great deal for my career. After that my vaudeville salary soared to thirty-five hundred dollars a week, and in some theaters I was able to get four thousand dollars without much trouble.

But while I was in *As Thousands Cheer* I got a letter, and sometimes I think that letter, which asked for money and was from St. Theresa's Monastery in Allentown, Pennsylvania, opened as important a phase in my life as all the good luck and success I'd enjoyed with *As Thousands Cheer*.

15

It was a form letter, appealing for funds for St. Theresa's Monastery in Allentown, Pennsylvania.

I'd always contributed to Catholic charities, increasing my donations as my pay rose. But I'd never heard before of that monastery. And the moment you become well known in show business you are snowed under by requests for money from worthy causes and individuals.

Just a form letter, this one, yet there was something very special about it. As I read it I could almost see the little nuns in the monastery putting their heads together as they wrote it, wanting to find just the right words to move the people out in the world they knew so little about.

I sent three dollars. I was deeply touched by the letter of personal thanks that came from the Mother Superior. It rang true with sweetness and simple gratitude. I began to send the monastery five- and ten-dollar checks. Always I got a letter back that gave me a big lift. I began to look forward impatiently to these little letters of thanks. They did my heart good, and after a while I realized why that was. The Mother Superior's notes were full of that warmth and holy love that I'd found among the nun-teachers who had tried so hard to help me through my grim childhood in Philadelphia.

I needed something like that just then. How I needed it!

While performing in *As Thousands Cheer* I had separated for good from my husband, Clyde Edward Matthews. It was good for me, anyway. That is what I say. But I guess every woman knows that breaking up a marriage is never anything to celebrate. It is the toughest of all good-bys, even when your man is a louse. You have put in years trying hard to make your marriage work. When it fails, you, the wife, are the loser. I knew all this then, but it had become simply impossible to go on.

When *As Thousands Cheer* ran into the hot weather Sam H. Harris told us he could keep the show going only if the weekly gross stayed above twelve thousand dollars. I sent the monastery a contribution each week to pray we'd have good weather and not much rain. It rained very little that summer, and I have always credited the sisters of St. Theresa's Monastery for keeping *As Thousands Cheer* open all through that July and August.

After that I sort of adopted the monastery. Down through the years I often seemed to sense when they were pressed for money. Again and again one of my checks would reach them on the very day they got to the bottom of the coal pile in their cellar. And each time I was in trouble, personally, and didn't know who to turn to, I'd sit down and write to the Mother Superior. Always I found in her replies the loving sympathy and understanding that helped to calm me.

When I first crashed into the big-earner bracket I was amazed to see that money is only important when you haven't got it. Once in the chips, you can only give those dollars importance by what you do with them.

I have always lived simply. But I do like my comfort, and I have fur coats, jewelry, and big, beautiful cars. But the main reason I have for buying such extravagant objects is because a Broadway star cannot dress like a waif or ride in the subway. People will talk and you can say, "The hell with them!" but they are my customers and I gotta live and appear in public as they expect me to.

My earning power, though, has given me the chance to help twenty little girls grow up and to assist God-loving people like my Allentown nuns do His work. This is the only true satisfaction I've taken in collecting checks with the big numbers on them.

In 1935 I was co-starred with Beatrice Lillie in a Shubert show, *At Home Abroad*. That revue was Vincente Minnelli's first directing job, and he also designed the sets and costumes. The book and music were written by Howard Dietz and Arthur Schwartz "with a bow to Rosamond Knight." The first-rate supporting cast given Lady Peel and the former shining star of Edmond's Cellar included Eleanor Powell, the tap dancer; Reginald Gardiner, the Englishman who imitates everything from steamboat whistles to drunken goldfish; Eddie Foy, Jr.,

Paul Haakon, Vera Allen, Sue Hastings' Marionettes, and many, many others, as the bill posters say.

We opened at the Winter Garden in September, and once more I got the big hello and nod of approval from the alert critics. Mr. Brooks Atkinson of the stately New York *Times* wrote, and I quote: ". . . Ethel Waters, the gleaming tower of regality, who knows how to make a song stand on tiptoe . . . Her 'Hottentot Potentate' runs a high temperature . . . she has an enormous lurking vitality, but also knows how to wear clothes. . . ."

In January 1936 we moved to the Majestic Theatre, the big house where *South Pacific* is running now, and closed in March.

One day in 1936 I heard a rumor that Pearl Wright had died. I rushed to her house and her daughter, Vivian, opened the door.

"Where is your mother?" I asked.

"In the back room."

I went there, expecting to see Pearl laid out in her coffin. But she was sitting up in bed and she spoke to me as soon as she saw me. That kind of thing gives a person an awful start. And Pearl did die within the next day or two.

Her passing was a bad blow to me. We had grown very close together toward the end of her life. Whenever I was in a Broadway show in which she didn't appear I paid her three hundred dollars a month, her regular salary.

Pearl and I had long worked together through a sort of telepathy. I never had to tell her what I wanted. She understood my every mood and musical desire. She could interpret a number exactly as I wanted it played.

A clue to this instinctive co-operation lies in Pearl being a singer herself. An accompanist who can sing knows the effects you seek, and you can feel understanding and help coming out through her fingers, through the piano, to you. Reginald Beane, who has accompanied me so much in more recent years, has the same gift of knowing what I want before I have a chance to ask for it. But then Reggie is a singer too.

One hell of a good trumpet player named Eddie Mallory had accompanied me in some of my numbers in *At Home Abroad*. We got very fond of each other. When the show closed Eddie said he was ambitious to build up a band of his own and would I please help him. I said I would be very happy to assist.

Mr. Gumm had many thirty-five-hundred-dollar-a-week movie-house dates waiting for me. Instead of filling these I went off into vaudeville with Eddie Mallory's band and a unit. In the troupe I had my two old faithfuls, Butterbeans and Susie, and Whitey's Lindy Hoppers and Derby Wilson.

There is a great supply of amateur undertakers in show business.

These people couldn't understand why I should go out with such a small unit after having two big Broadway hits. "She is deteriorating," is the word they spread around. "Ethel Waters is on her way out."

They believed this because my whole unit was only getting fifty-five hundred dollars a week. They figured that after I paid off the acts, the band, and the traveling expenses I would not have much of a pretzel left for myself.

That was correct, but I didn't care. I held Eddie Mallory in high esteem, personally, and yielded to none in my admiration of him as a top trumpet player. He was the kind of man I thought should have a band. After we finished with the vaudeville time I arranged a route through the South.

I never could want any better company than musicians. They speak my lingo and language. Their high jinks and the scrapes they always get into make me hysterical. Musicians are as daffy and uninhibited as so many jolly little monkeys.

For the Southern dates we added some good acts: Sunshine Sammy and Sleepy Williams, the dancers; Daybreak and Joiner, comics; and Lily Mae Yuen. Elida Webb, one of the greatest dancers my race ever produced, came along as my personal secretary. Elida could supervise routines, too, having been for years assistant dance director at the Cotton Club.

Eddie Mallory couldn't get any discipline over the boys he had gathered together, so I had to be the policeman, complete with whistle and doghouse. We chartered a bus for the band and the minor performers to ride in. I traveled in my Lincoln with Eddie Mallory and a couple of the featured acts. Other of my featured acts rode in my other car, a Zephyr.

But I had to keep either close behind or right in front of the bus. Only if I stuck close to the bus could the much-bedeviled driver make any time. Every few miles somebody in the bus would holler:

"Stop! Help! Murder! I have to go to the can!"

So the disgusted driver then would have to stop once more at the next roadside tavern or lunch wagon so the frantic musician could pile out and race to the men's. Not only would he take his time there, but on the way back to the bus he would stop for an honest glass of beer or two. And there were whole cases of beer right on the bus.

Before long our schedule was getting so loused up, stopping all the time to let some trombone player or drummer use the men's, that I gave out an ultimatum, which was:

"We don't stop more than once in every fifty miles no matter who has to go."

The boys had all kinds of arguments against this edict of mine. The boys growled and grunted, but I said, "Save your lip for your horns. If there is any more rebelliousness I'm liable to make a new rule— one stop every *hundred* miles."

And at every town I laughed myself sick when I saw those cans and bottles being carried so carefully out of the bus.

Eddie Mallory was good company for me when he rode in my Lincoln. But after a while he got a little cute. I was annoyed to find young chicks waiting at every town we stopped at for "Mr. Mallory" to pull up in his big limousine.

"Oh! So you are *the* Mr. Mallory!" the chicks would say when he stepped out of my Lincoln. "What a beautiful car you have there, Mr. Mallory." There was much fluttering of eyelashes and bashful come-on glances whenever he arrived in my big ship.

Eddie quickly got puffed up about being the universally admired "Mr. Mallory." I, the owner and legal license holder of the Lincoln, got sick of those twitterings and dewy, dewy greetings. After all, it was I who had bought that luxurious car with my hard-sung-for money. I wasn't going to be just a passenger who "Mr. Mallory" was courteously giving a lift to.

So one day when "Mr. Mallory" had comfortably settled himself in the Lincoln to go on to the next town and more fresh young chicks, I told him to get out and ride in the bus with the other musicians. He tried to bicker and cajole his way back into the Lincoln, but I said the bus was a better place for him.

"There you can keep an eye on your boys," I told him.

After that there were no chicks waiting for him when we stopped. He wasn't "Mr. Mallory," "*the* Mr. Mallory," but just another tired little fellow getting off a dusty, crowded old bus.

Eddie complained he was losing a lot of prestige riding with the band. And his musicians didn't have any pity. One or another of them was always asking Eddie:

"How come, boss? Why are you riding this old bus with us boys? Why ain't you in your big Lincoln?"

Eddie never stopped complaining about his loss of dignity. I thought it was very funny. But I am still deeply grateful to him for taking me to the small town of Lexington, Mississippi, where I got a whole new and inspiring look at my own people and could see for myself the first-rate stuff they are made of.

More people live in one crowded Harlem block than you'll find in Lexington, Mississippi. We went there to see Eddie's sister, Ireana, who is an official of the Saints' Revival School of the Holiness Church.

Ireana had the kids in her school travel around and sing in various churches. Her girls were all sweet, virginal children, very innocent, and they could sing the heavy heart right out of you.

I found out that there were children in the Saints' Industrial School who walked five or six miles each way every day to attend their classes. Some of them who lived even farther out and couldn't get to the school by walking were housed in the dormitories that had been built for them. These only went home on week ends.

Their parents were all poor share croppers and they didn't have any money to pay for their kids' lessons. They paid off, instead, with sacks of meal and whatever else they could grow. And this meant food off their table and clothes off their backs.

I was flattened by how deep and intense was the hunger for education in those backwoods children and their parents. But when share-cropping time came, the white farmers who owned the land the Negro families worked on would come to the school in drays to get the kids. The children had to go off and help in the harvesting. And when that was finished the white farmers didn't bother to take the kids back to school. The children had to get back to Lexington as best they could, and they always made it. They made me proud of being a Negro, those children and their ignorant, overworked parents.

While I was in Lexington I went out among the colored people there. I found many old settled people, as well as kids, who had never seen a show in their whole lives, or even a movie. So we got the band up there and gave our show for them.

The night we gave our show the tears came to my eyes as I watched ragged and hard-working colored farm women humbly handing in to the school the cakes and other stuff they'd cooked. As they watched our show those people just sat there, awed and thunderstruck by everything: our clothes, the music, the dances. We might have been people from another world, with no blood or color or language in common with them.

But it was our turn to be awed afterward, when the girls of the school came on and sang. We were professionals and we had done our best, but those little girl singers put us in the twilight by the sea at high tide. The professional never lived who could compete with them.

It is hard for me to describe the emotion roused in my breast as I listened. For this was pure. Those little girls sang and praised their God, and it must have been how women first sang before there were teachers to coach youngsters how to imitate others.

When the girls sang there was nothing between them and their God. Nothing to stop their voices, rich and full of heart, from reaching Him. These were voices untampered with, and they were raised in song not to impress people or to earn money. They were singing to express something they felt and that they never could say in words if they went to all the Vassars and Howard Universities on earth.

It was the soul of the Negro that I heard that night, all his religion and simple faith, and that singing carried all the Negro's hope for happiness and a better deal in the next world. And I cried and I was proud again of my people and I loved them. I would have liked to hug and kiss every one of those girls. I wished I knew how to thank them because it was like rebirth. I couldn't help feeling that, until then, with all my fame and money and name in lights everywhere, I had been shut out of a most beautiful spiritual experience.

And I felt rich and refreshed and strong when I left Lexington, Mississippi, for having seen that school, the people who ran it, and the children who sat at the little desks.

I've never forgotten the Holiness Church and I am proud that, later on, I was able to do something for several of the child singers in the Saints' Revival School.

And now, as usual, we must go from the sublime to the ridiculous.

I had my half brother, Johnny Waters, playing the piano in Mallory's band on that tour. For years, whenever I would play Philadelphia, people asked had I heard Johnny, who they said was a whiz.

Johnny had only been a baby when our father died. But he was a full-grown man now, of course. I was also to find out that he had some of the bad habits of most males.

One time when Johnny was playing in a spot over in Camden I heard him. And my little half brother could play a wonderful piano, and the organ too. He could play to send you off in a dream, and I was deeply impressed.

Johnny was short and real dark. He asked could he visit me in New York and I said, "Yes." When he got to New York he asked, "Can I live with you?" and I said, "Yes."

I was just going on the road, and I let Johnny use my apartment while I was away. Johnny, though a terrific player, couldn't read one note of music. I said I would send him some money every week so he could learn to read.

I explained to my half brother Johnny that if he would only acquire technical knowledge of music he could play any sheet put before him. "With your original style," I told him, "you will become a top pianist —if you have also that necessary technical knowledge."

"Yes, yes, Sis." Johnny nodded.

The whole time I was on the road I sent my baby half brother money for lessons. When I got home I checked on the progress he'd made. Johnny set up the music for my ditties before him and played them, note for note. Not being able to read a line of music myself, I could only believe that Johnny had caught on awful fast.

Pearl had already got sick when I was playing a date at the Lafayette. I hired Johnny as my accompanist, generously paying his initiation fee in Local 802, the musicians' union.

The pieces Johnny knew, he played fine. But my new songs, which he hadn't had much chance to study, he played very sick and anemic. But I thought he had stage fright.

While I was filling a two-week engagement at the Keith theater in Washington, my accompanist collapsed. I put in a rush call to Johnny.

That's when I found out Johnny had taken no lessons and couldn't read music. If I hummed a tune to Johnny he could outplay Paderewski. But if I didn't hum the tune he would always play sick and anemic again.

The remarkable thing about Johnny was his licks. Pearl Wright and Reggie Beane could listen to Johnny's music and learn a lot about certain riffs only he could get for me. But they weren't licks and riffs anyone could catch to write down on paper. Yet Pearl and Reggie, once they'd heard them, could play them.

I got Johnny the job at the piano in Eddie Mallory's band. He got paid one hundred and twenty-five dollars a week, and during our lay-offs I would give him fifteen to twenty-five dollars a week so he could support his family.

Johnny is still playing his wonderful riffs and licks around Philadelphia. But he might today be famous all over the world for his music if he'd only learned to read.

It's just an old theatrical tradition that stars have to have a built-up entrance. I don't think any real actress has to have a built-up entrance. I think she should feel lucky to get on at all.

I could always open shows, perform through the middle, and close shows. I was slim when I was with the unit I had with Eddie Mallory's band. I could sing, and dance like a teen-ager.

Some of the critics didn't know who I was because I was now so streamlined, and the last time they'd seen me I was very fat. Later in the performance I would come back for my big numbers and I was Ethel Waters in evening clothes. And I would be greeted as though I hadn't been on before.

I got my kicks in two different towns when the critics there put the rap on me. They said I was fine but how about that newcomer in the opening number who sang and danced so well? Why didn't I give a gifted beginner like her a little recognition and billing instead of being so selfish and inconsiderate? They said they didn't like to see any star act that way. These boys were very surprised when I let them know that the beginner they were so happy to discover was Ethel Waters.

Whenever I played Columbus, Ohio, I dropped in to see my close friend, Ruth Thompson, a medium who had mysterious powers. Her Indian guide was Mohawk.

For years Ruth had been saying, "You are a medium, Ethel. You could help and influence people with your God-given gift of reading the future."

I always told her the same thing: that I wouldn't care to develop any powers I might have. I explained, "I might also develop the power to destroy someone who had wronged me and, Ruth, I'd do it—in a fit of temper.

"You can do a lot of good with mystic powers. But you can also do a lot of harm. And I notice that people with such gifts get power-drunk very quickly." I added, "When you dominate other people's emotions, it seems to me that the time has to come when you will have to pay, and heavily, for that privilege."

The first time I met Ruth Thompson she was a great beauty with finely chiseled features and lovely hair. But the day I stopped off to see her in Columbus—on my way to the Coast with Eddie Mallory's band—I saw that her beauty had vanished. The bridge of her nose had fallen in. I pretended not to notice it.

After Ruth went upstairs her mother told me that my medium-friend had suffered a blow a long time before and this had caused her nose to collapse now, years later.

"I'm afraid Ruth is going to die," she said. "It is terrible the way she shuts herself off from everybody. When anyone comes in she runs to her room to hide. She watches people, imagining they are talking about her."

"Do you think Ruth would go to California with me?" I asked.

Her mother thought such a trip might pull Ruth out of her melancholia. "If something isn't done about her, Ethel, she'll die, I'm sure, within six months."

I stayed at their home overnight, and in the morning I asked Ruth if she had ever been in California. "No," she replied, "but I'd like to go."

"Come with me, Ruth. I need you to take care of some of the business details of the trip. I could pay you something."

Ruth joined us later in Chicago, and on the train to the Coast she appeared to be on the verge of a nervous breakdown. I still had not mentioned her disfigurement. When we were in California she asked, "Why haven't you said anything about my face?"

I looked at my friend who had once been such a beauty. "I did notice that something about you had changed," I told her. "But that was nothing for my comment. The beauty I've always seen in you was never in your face."

I waited for a moment, then asked if she remembered our conversation of some years before. "I mean the day we talked about your power and how it could be misused."

She nodded, and I went on, "Now I'm sure everything you've done,

Ruth, has been with the best intentions. But you put yourself in God's place—and that was wrong. That's God's job, it seems to me.

"But I'll tell you something you may not believe. God can make you appear in such a way that nobody will notice your face. Your Twelve Guides have been unable to help you. But God can. I am not speaking of miracles. There will be no miracle. But God can help you mentally, and all of the beauty that has always attracted me and others to you will come through. That's if you believe God can do that for you."

I reminded her of the Bible story in which Christ fed five thousand people with five loaves of bread and three fish. "Those five thousand people didn't feel fed, physically. It was a spiritual thing that made them lose their hunger."

I explained how God had helped me in my work only recently. After years in white theaters I dreaded working with the unit in colored houses. The noise, the stomping, whistling, and cheering that hadn't annoyed me when I was young was now something I dreaded. There was also the familiarity of the colored audience to contend with. Certain men out front would sometimes shout vulgar and insulting remarks at you.

So before going on in a colored theater I had prayed, "O Lord! Please shut out those noises from my ears so I can do my work." And God did that for me—the screaming, stomping, and insults went on, only I couldn't hear them.

I had many such talks with Ruth Thompson while we were in California. She gradually found the courage to face people and didn't run away and hide. And a new beauty had come into her face, just as I predicted. Since then she has summoned enough faith to have plastic surgery on her nose.

Today Ruth does a great deal of Christian talking and thinking about God in the course of her daily work.

I stayed with Eddie Mallory's band and my unit much longer than I had first intended. I had the best of reasons. The most exciting prospect of my entire acting career had come up—the play, Mamba's Daughters, in which I was to prove I was an actress as well as a blues singer.

It took two whole years to locate first money, second money, and the other moneys needed to put on that show. I had given my promise to take no long commitments while waiting. And I remained with

Eddie Mallory's band and the unit during those two years, knowing I could step out of those dates to start rehearsing at any time.

That is a long time to wait, working for peanuts, for a role—yet not too long to wait for Hagar, my Hagar, the part that made my reputation on the American legitimate stage.

16

"Great tributes and new homage are coming your way, Ethel," Ruth Thompson, my medium-friend had told me one day. "I don't know when or how. But you should get out more, go to parties and see more people."

A while later Georgette Harvey, who had a good part in *Porgy and Bess*, invited me to a big party she was giving for Rouben Mamoulian, the director of that famous Negro folk opera. Georgette had invited the whole cast.

I decided not to go. I still felt like a wet blanket at such get-togethers, not being a drinking or smoking woman. At such festivities I always worried about the smoke in the room hurting my throat. And men resented it when I'd say politely, "Please, would you mind putting out that cigarette?"

That night I had started to go to bed when I changed my mind at the last minute. I don't know why, but I got dressed again and went out. A white couple were just arriving before the apartment house as I got out of my car. We went up in the elevator together, and the three of us sat down side by side on Georgette's couch.

The white lady asked if I remembered her. "Yes, I do," I said. She'd been a guest at a society tea where I'd sung some years before. Afterward she'd come up and complimented me on one of my songs, a take-off number on "Porgy" that Dorothy Fields and Jimmy Mc-Hugh had written.

I could even recall her exact words: "Miss Waters, it's wonderful how you manage to convey the whole story and meaning of 'Porgy' in that one little song."

The white lady seemed pleased that I remembered her so clearly.

"And what do you think of *Porgy and Bess*, Miss Waters?" she asked.

Like the play *Porgy*, the folk opera had been based on the novel, *Porgy*. I told her I preferred it to the straight drama.

"I wouldn't say," I explained, "that it wasn't good acting that Frank Wilson did as Porgy in the play. But I knew the original Porgy in real life, and he was a short, stocky man with no legs and enormous strength in his hands and arms. Frank Wilson just hasn't got Porgy's build or physical strength. So I couldn't believe in him when he kills a man with his bare hands.

"But I do believe in Todd Duncan, who plays the same part in the musical version. And there was one other thing about the straight play I didn't like. There was no 'I'm a bitch!' and 'I'm a whore!' in it. The characters in *Porgy* kept apologizing for being themselves. Like everyone else, I've known a great many bitches and whores in real life. They never apologize for being what they are.

"Watching that play was like seeing some society woman playing a slut on the stage. She hopes you'll think she's wonderful. But at the same time she is worried that you might think she is also a slut in real life. So she tries to tell you in her acting, 'Remember, I'm a society woman off the stage. I'm not really like this in private life. I'm just acting here tonight.'

"However, in *Porgy and Bess* the performers express themselves much more honestly and freely. They don't give a damn what you think they are like off the stage. All they want is you to believe in them. They're good actors, so you do."

"But this is very interesting, Miss Waters," said this lady. "DuBose and I——"

For the first time I realized I must be talking to Dorothy Heyward, who had dramatized *Porgy* with her husband from his book. And also that he was the man seated next to her.

"There was a book I read some years ago . . ." And I went on to tell her how and why *Mamba's Daughters* had held me spellbound. Yet I didn't know that DuBose Heyward had also written that novel as I explained that Mamba's family was just like my own, with Mamba herself almost the image of Sally Anderson; her daughter Hagar like Momweeze, and Hagar's daughter Lissa being a girl like myself, illegitimate and going out into the world to become a successful singer.

"To everyone else, I know, Mamba is the main character in the story," I told Dorothy Heyward, "but not to me. Hagar is the main one. Hagar dies in the middle of the book, but for me she lived right on through the last page, and ever afterward."

Hagar had held me spellbound. In Hagar was all my mother's shock, bewilderment, and insane rage at being hurt and her fierce, primitive religion. But Hagar, fighting on in a world that had wounded her so deeply, was more than my mother to me. She was all Negro women lost and lonely in the white man's antagonistic world.

Dorothy Heyward listened as I talked all about this.

"If we ever decide to dramatize *Mamba's Daughters*," she said, "we'll see you."

Then of course I knew that her husband had written the book. But it was quite a long time before the Heywards did make a play of it and sent me the script to read.

I was thrilled and I was scared as I read that play. I had visualized Hagar as quite a small part. But even if it had been only a walk-on role I would have given anything to play Hagar.

However, the Heywards had thrown away the other plots that had been in the book. The play was Hagar's, and she had the dominating role throughout. *Mamba's Daughters* now was a straight and simple melodramatic story, the story of Hagar, a lumbering, half-crazy colored woman with a single passion: seeing that her beautiful Lissa has a better life than she's known. The climax of the play comes when Hagar strangles Gilly Bluton, a sporting man who has raped Lissa and is planning to blackmail her.

I'd never played in a straight drama, of course. I'd had offers—including one from the Theatre Guild to appear in *Porgy*—but I'd turned them down. Those plays never seemed quite true to life to me. The characters in them had been either created by white men or by Negro writers who had stopped thinking colored.

It was easy for me to visualize the staggering emotional impact *Mamba's Daughters*, written by a Southern white man and his wife, would deliver in the theater. In the theater it is the knockout that counts, and *Mamba's Daughters* was all knockout.

But even more exciting was its being a play ripped out of the life I'd always known and was still living. Even when I read it for the first time I understood instinctively that there could be no greater triumph in my professional career than playing Hagar. All my life I'd burned to tell the story of my mother's despair and long defeat, of Momweeze being hurt so by a world that then paid her no mind.

It was a tragedy and a story of courage, with Hagar, like Mom-weeze, meeting it all with her heart up, never once doubting her God, and furiously intent on staying a person no matter how tricked and buffeted and besmirched and bruised.

Now always the Heywards, Dorothy and DuBose, were fine people. They played straight and above the board with me. When the big theatrical firms, including the Theatre Guild (which had cleaned up on their *Porgy* and their *Porgy and Bess*), turned down *Mamba's Daughters*, they told me about each rejection.

For my part I had promised to steer clear of all long-term commitments so I could come to New York and start rehearsing whenever they sent for me. I just went on barnstorming with my unit and Eddie Mallory's band, barnstorming endlessly for buttons.

One main reason the moneybags men refused to put up the financing for *Mamba's Daughters* was because the Heywards insisted I play Hagar. "Ethel Waters, are you kidding?" was what they got whichever way they turned. "Ethel is a good singer, but no actress."

Mr. Gumm, my lawyer, was still handling my bookings, and he didn't like my turning down all the big movie-house offers. "That is where the big money is for you, Ethel," he said. I told him he was right, but I still had to play Hagar if I ever got the chance.

It began to look as if I'd never get the chance. A year passed, then a year and a half, and I started to get discouraged. I couldn't see how the Heywards would ever find their much-needed bank roll. Several twenty-five-hundred-dollar-a-week offers had come in from England, and I was considering taking them. The way things were going, I thought it might be best for me if I broke off clean and for good with Eddie Mallory.

My love affair was starting to go the way of my marriage and all my other love affairs. The unhappy ending was clearly in sight.

Eddie Mallory had talked me into investing a big slice of my savings in some Harlem properties he was interested in, including a bar and grill. I knew I was going to lose my money and I don't say I was beat out of it. All I knew was that whenever I mixed up romance and my bank account I seemed to end up with no dough and even less of a love affair.

And I was beginning to wonder if anyone could be so banged around and unloved during childhood days and still come out of it whole, a complete person.

I've always been a woman with normal physical appetites. But I'm also cold-natured. I never could learn to fuss over any man, sweet-talk him, and say, "I love you!" and all the rest of that stuff. Jack Johnson was right about that.

I want affection and tenderness desperately, but there's something in me that prevents me from handing it out. When you've been clubbed over the heart enough times you keep an eye out for the baseball bat. Every man seems to tote one with him, even though he might not let you see it for a while.

Now I had said nothing about the British offers I was considering or of my confusion about whether to split up with Eddie—when the big break came.

This was a wire from New York telling me to come in and start rehearsing for *Mamba's Daughters*, as the money man had been found. The wire came from Liebling and Wood, who are very reliable Broadway casting agents.

On my way East I stopped off, as usual, at Columbus to see Ruth Thompson. "It's interesting that you should come to see me right at this time, Ethel," she told me. "I've just been thinking a lot about you. Go upstairs and get relaxed. You never let me give you any readings. But today, when you come downstairs, I'm going to tell you something important."

When I had freshened up and relaxed I came down and she said, "Don't take those offers from England, Ethel. I know you've been toying with that idea. You have been unsettled in your domestic affairs and think that might be the best way to pull up stakes.

"And that deal in New York you are going to see about won't come through. But there is another deal you don't know about yet that is definitely going through. It is now May, yet your show won't go on until December. The man who will produce it has to go across the water first. He has to put on two other plays before yours. This man has two names in one. He's an auburn man, has a mustache and he is quick and energetic."

I was taken aback, of course, but I put no stock in her mystic predictions. On reporting to New York I found they were already casting. And who should our money man turn out to be but Maury Greenwald, who had put on the *Plantation Revue* in Chicago and wanted me to take it to its final death rattles in London.

It was May when I checked in. During the first week of June, Bill Liebling called up to say I had to go to a meeting at the Barbizon-Plaza. Everybody involved in the production, including DuBose, was there when I arrived.

They started hinting around, saying, "Now let me tell you this," and so on and thus forth. Without saying one damn thing, I looked around and remembered Ruth Thompson's prophecy.

"You are trying to tell me," I said, "that Mr. Greenwald can't finance *Mamba's Daughters*."

They were thunderstruck because they had hardly got started beating around the bush. I explained nonchalantly I had got the bad news in advance from a medium-friend and gave Ruth's description of the producer and how the play would go on in December.

DuBose Heyward—and he has since passed on, much to the sorrow of all who knew him—was a man of charm, great talent, absolute integrity, and deep-hearted sympathy for all Negroes.

Baffled that he couldn't get his play on, he next took it to an old friend, Guthrie McClintic, Katharine Cornell's husband and director. If there was anything wrong with the play DuBose thought that shrewd, smart showman would surely see what it was.

"Please read it, Guthrie," he said, "and give me your honest opinion. Don't spare my feelings."

The next day when DuBose again went to see him, McClintic had read *Mamba's Daughters*. "It's too long, DuBose," he said, "but what really worries me is what actress could give life to that stoic creature, Hagar?"

"I already have the Hagar," said DuBose Heyward. "That woman has given me her word not to make any commitments. Because of that she has been taking a terrible beating for a year and a half. She passed up one big-paying job after another so she'd be free whenever we called her. The actress is Ethel Waters."

"Ethel Waters!" said McClintic. "She could do it if any actress in the world could. All she'd have to do is give it the same underplaying and timing, the same repressed emotion she puts in her songs. I'd like to meet her."

DuBose arranged an appointment, and I went down with him and had a talk with Guthrie McClintic.

After that meeting Mr. McClintic told him, "DuBose, I'm going to do your play. But I won't be able to put it on for some time."

He explained he was leaving for London to direct a play there and when he came back he would have to stage his wife's new show. It was still June, and he said we'd have to wait until that winter to rehearse. "We'll open on New Year's Eve," he said.

On hearing the good news, we told McClintic of Ruth's amazing prophecy. She had batted one thousand per cent in describing Guthrie McClintic as an auburn man with a mustache, and quick and energetic. She had also said he'd be going over the water, would put on two plays before mine, and *Mamba's Daughters* would not get on the stage until December. She even said he would have two names in one, which he had—Mc and Clintic.

Mac was stunned with astonishment at Ruth's ability to call the turn on the future in such detail.

Guthrie McClintic didn't know much about colored actors and never minded my suggestions. I was able to get many of the performers who were good friends of mine into the show. And he got together a brilliant cast—Georgette Harvey as Mamba, José Ferrer as Saint, J. Rosamond Johnson as the Reverend Quintus Whaley, and lovely-looking little Fredi Washington as Lissa. Not to forget Ethel Waters as Hagar. I also got my accompanist, Reggie Beane, in the show as Slim.

But Mac didn't know who in the world to get for the vital role of Gilly Bluton, a cutie and a bastard if there ever was one. He said, "Now about this Gilly Bluton, Ethel?" and I said I knew the perfect actor, telling him:

"This person is like Gilly, cocky, egotistical, clever, but with all his faults he's a likable and lovable chap. I'm talking of a man named Willie Bryant."

Mac had never heard of Willie Bryant, who had been in the colored theater all his life. After starting as a dancer Willie became a wise-cracking master of ceremonies, at which he has now long been a fixture at the Apollo on 125th Street, in Harlem, and all other colored houses. Willie also has been for two years WHOM's all-night disc jockey. So the same brassy cheeriness that has made Willie so beloved a stage figure now comes over the air from him in the small hours.

I knew Willie wanted to get in the play because he'd asked me to speak for him. I also knew he would be right. Guthrie McClintic asked where he could see this ideal Gilly Bluton of mine. I said Willie Bryant was working just then in Philadelphia as master of ceremonies on a vaudeville bill which Bill Robinson was headlining. Mac told me he would go down there to catch him.

"I would like first to send Willie Bryant a wire," I said, "but it will say that only the show's casting agent is coming to see him. If Willie Bryant knew that Guthrie McClintic was in the audience he might freeze up, though it is possible he never heard of you either, Mr. McClintic. Your very name, on the other hand, might bewilder him. I want you to see Willie Bryant, gay and wisecracking, just as his colored audience sees him."

He said I should send the wire. In this I informed Willie, "This man will know how to sell you to his boss." And knowing Willie Bryant, I added, "Be yourself, Willie."

After catching the vaudeville show Mac sent word backstage that Stanley Gilkey, who was his general manager, would like to come back and talk to him. But it was, of course, Guthrie McClintic himself who went to Willie's dressing room.

Willie greeted him with, "Hello, Stan. Howya, Stan? I'll make it right with you if you put in the word for me with this bird McClintic."

When Mac got back to New York he told me he had asked Willie to call at his New York office. "He's wonderful, that Willie Bryant," he said. "I love him for the part."

On coming to the McClintic office Willie asked for his buddy, Stanley Gilkey. But when he was brought in to the general manager, he told him, "I don't want to see you. I wanna see Stanley Gilkey and nobody else."

"I am Stanley Gilkey," said the general manager of the same name.

"Don't give me that," snapped Willie.

"But I tell you I'm Stanley Gilkey."

"And I tell you you're not. I know Stan when I see him. You're not the man who came to Philadelphia to see me. *That* was Stanley Gilkey."

They were still at it and getting loud and hot when Guthrie McClintic himself came into Mr. Gilkey's office. "Hi, Stan," said Willie. "Will you please tell this bird here who I am? He's trying to tell me he's you."

Once he was straightened out, Willie got in a panic. He'd insulted the general manager and had been unduly familiar with the big boss.

Then they all enjoyed a good laugh and he was hired. Nobody

could have played Gilly Bluton—low-down, mean, and nasty—better. But all through the rehearsals I worried about the big fight scene in which I was supposed to choke Willie Bryant to death. We had rehearsed everything else to Mac's satisfaction. But each time we got to that scene I'd say:

"We'll just walk through this one."

Remember, I am a big woman, and a powerhouse, physically. I could tear down, brick by brick, the walls of a theater. And I was afraid I might kill Willie Bryant when we rehearsed that scene.

I was no longer Ethel Waters, blues singer. I wasn't even Ethel Waters, actress. I had become Hagar. And Willie Bryant had become Gilly Bluton, the blackhearted rogue who had seduced my daughter and was planning to blackmail and ruin her completely.

So I didn't trust myself. I didn't think I'd be able to control my hands once they closed around his throat. But naturally, I couldn't explain that to Guthrie McClintic, though he was the most sympathetic of stage directors. Even though Mac, having been an actor himself, breathed and sweated and suffered with me through every hour of rehearsal. By having Mac with me and for me every step of the way, I was able to cut myself free of other fears and concentrate on my work.

When he demanded I end my stalling, Willie and I went through the motions. "Oh no, *no!*" said Mac. "This has to be convincing. The whole play stands or falls on this one climactic, gripping scene. It has to be convincing, Hagar." As he talked he jumped up on the stage and walked over to me.

"Now, Hagar, you choke me. I want to make sure you'll put everything you've got into this scene."

"Oh no, boss," I told him, "I couldn't choke you."

But Guthrie kept telling me I had to. In the end he got me so nervous and excited that I grabbed him and shook the living hell out of him. I knocked the boss down. He was gasping and shaking when he got up, but he choked out:

"That's what I want you to do to Gilly."

Willie Bryant had watched us, his eyes big as basketballs. "You mean I gotta go through *that* every night!"

"Yep," said Mac. "She damn near choked me to death."

"Let me open," whispered Willie. "Just let me open in this show. That's all I ask."

Mr. McClintic, with a grim smile, made us rehearse that scene. After watching us do our knockdown-drag-out fight just once, he said the one rehearsal of the scene would be quite enough.

Playing opposite Willie was tense and exciting. Sometimes when I knocked him down Willie would get so mad he'd forget himself. He'd get up and keep coming at me.

Willie often said that when he looked into my eyes during that scene he would get paralyzed and unable to move. Out of terror. My eyes have pin-point pupils. Willie told me my eyes, full of hatred and rage, held him in such a trance he had to look at my forehead to avoid being hypnotized.

I'd got a kick out of being a one-woman employment agency for the Negroes in the cast of that show. It is always pleasant to be the helping hand. But my big thrill came when I was able to find spots in *Mamba's Daughters* for three of the little singers from the Holiness Church down in Lexington, Mississippi.

They were hired for the church scene. Mr. McClintic had told me he wanted the church scene to have true religious fire. "I would prefer, if possible," was the way he put it, "not to hire singers of organized groups. I want performers with less formal training and more natural religion."

I told him how I'd been swept away with emotion when I heard the girls sing in the Saints' School in Mississippi. "They would be just what you want, I think," I said. "I'm so sure of that I will pay their fares from Mississippi out of my own pocket. You can hear them sing, and if you like them you can make any financial deal with them you see fit."

It turned out there were a couple of those girls already in New York. So I only had to lay out the fares for two or three of them. Mac auditioned them and decided to use three of them—Ella Mae Lashley, Laura Vaughn, and Rebecca Champion. They were three good little girls who could hardly believe they were making so much money. They each got forty dollars a week and sent home every penny they could spare to help their poor folks down in Mississippi.

Mamba's Daughters had its preview opening on New Year's Eve and its regular opening on January 3, 1939, which I still remember as the most thrilling and important experience of my life as a performer. And my whole life, too, except for when I found God.

I was the first colored woman, the first actress of my race, ever to be starred on Broadway in a dramatic play. And we opened at the Empire Theatre, which has the richest theatrical history of any show-house in America.

And the Empire's star dressing room was mine on that opening night. While the carriage trade was arriving outside, I sat at the dressing table where all the great actresses, past and present, had sat as they made up their faces and wondered what the first-night verdict would be—Maude Adams, Ethel Barrymore, Helen Hayes, Katharine Cornell, Lynn Fontanne, and all the others, now dead, who had brought the glitter of talent and beauty and grace to that old stage.

Yes, there I was, the Ethel who had never been coddled or kissed as a child, the Ethel who was too big to fit, but big enough to be scullion and laundress and bus girl while still a kid. And I could have looked back over my shoulder and blown a kiss to all my yesterdays in show business. I had been pushed on the stage and prodded into becoming Sweet Mama Stringbean and the refined singer of risqué songs in Edmond's Cellar, and on and up to best-selling records, Broadway musicals, and being the best-paid woman in all show business.

That was *the* night of my professional life, sitting there in that old-fashioned dressing room that was a bower of flowers. The night I'd been born for, and God was in the room with me. I talked to God until the callboy came to say:

"Five minutes, Miss Waters."

Five minutes more to get ready to be Hagar and tell the story of my mother in front of the carriage trade. I asked God, "Oh, stay with me! Lord, keep Your hand on my shoulder! Please, God!"

Then I got up and started off on that terrifying last mile a performer has to walk every opening night. Into the wings, a pause there for a moment waiting for the cue—and then on, Ethel Waters, to glory or . . .

I was Hagar that night. Hagar and Momweeze and all of us.

Seventeen curtain calls that opening night for me alone.

I couldn't stand it. Half collapsing with joy and humility, I pushed through the kissing mouths and the slaps on the back to my dressing room where Elida was waiting.

"How do you feel now, Miss Waters?" she said. "And what are you thinking?"

"Elida, if I died here and now," I told her, "it would be all right.

For this is the pinnacle, and there will never be anything better or higher or bigger for me. I have fulfillment, Elida. At last, I have fulfillment."

And I burst into sobbing as I humbly thanked my God. Because even if no one else knew it, I had been no actress that night. I had only been remembering and all I had done was carry out His orders. And I had shown them all what it is to be a colored woman, dumb, ignorant, all boxed up and feeling everything with such intenseness that she is half crazy.

As usual, the newspapers came out next day. And the critics were like poets, saying things like Sidney Whipple's "In her moments of tenderness, she is heart-wrenching. In her moments of blind passion magnificent." And Burns Mantle's "Add the name of Ethel Waters to the list of the season's immortals." And Richard Lockridge's "In the playing of Ethel Waters, Hagar becomes magnificently like a force of nature." And Arthur Pollock's "Ethel Waters established herself as one of the finest actresses, white or black."

All were raves except the review of Brooks Atkinson in the New York *Times*. And Mr. Atkinson didn't like me or the play. That was bad, and I wondered if Mr. Atkinson didn't like us because he had forgotten his Carter's Little Liver Pills that night.

But for once I didn't have to get mad. My friends and admirers got mad for me, saving me the trouble and exhaustion. Carl Van Vechten rounded up a lot of them, and they all chipped in and bought a big ad in Mr. Atkinson's own paper, the *Times*, rebuking him for his lousy judgment. Stage scholars say nothing like this had ever happened before in all the long history of show business.

That ad read, and again I quote:

"We, the undersigned, feel that Ethel Waters' superb performance in *Mamba's Daughters* at the Empire Theatre is a profound emotional experience which any playgoer would be the poorer for missing. It seems indeed to be such a magnificent example of great acting, simple, deeply felt, moving on a plane of complete reality, that we are glad to pay for the privilege of saying so."

The names signed to it were:

"Judith Anderson, Tallulah Bankhead, Norman Bel Geddes, Cass Canfield, John Emery, Morris L. Ernst, John Farrar, Dorothy Gish, Jules Glaenzer, Helen Hall, Oscar Hammerstein, Ruth Kellogg, Edwin Knopf, Ben H. Lehman, Fania Marinoff, Aline MacMahon, Burgess Meredith, Stanley Reinhardt, Carl Van Vechten."

That ad so startled Mr. Atkinson that he hurried back for another look at our show. And he did a complete whirlabout. Yes, that second time he liked it.

Amidst all the opening-night to-do I had felt sorry for one little feller: Willie Bryant. After doing a great job, he stepped up to take his bow—only to be hailed by hisses and boos. The bewildered Willie almost burst into tears.

"They only hissed you, Willie," I told him, "because you're such a good actor. You convinced them you are Gilly Bluton."

"That good?" asked Willie doubtfully.

"It's terrific. You made them hate you."

And each night, just before I strangled Gilly, a sensational thing happened. The people up in the second balcony seemed to forget it was only a play they were watching. They'd yell, "Kill the sonofabitch, Hagar!" They used so much obscene language that the management sent men up there to replace the girl ushers.

I had to work on Willie Bryant a long time before I convinced him that those fruity catcalls and unseemly Bronx cheers he was getting at every performance were a supreme tribute.

Poor Willie told me that he felt in constant danger whenever he was up in his own Harlem. Lifelong buddies of his would tell him, "Willie, stay away from me! You are a no-good bastard. If I didn't know you, I'd cut your throat for what you are doing to Hagar."

In the end, however, Willie Bryant came to understand that he had established himself as a rat of distinction, and he could take great pride and gloat over that.

The reaction of the women who saw the play was also amazing. In their mind's eye I was transformed into Hagar. Each night they'd come back to my dressing room. Always I had to stay in my stage clothes until after they were gone. They had come to visit Hagar and would have resented finding Ethel Waters in her place.

After seeing the play friends would ask, "How can you do it, Ethel? How long can you continue to give out with all that pent-up emotion night after night?"

I could not convince them that the role gave me the sort of release I'd long needed. Being Hagar softened me, and I was able to make more allowance for the shortcomings of others. Before that I'd always been cursing outside and crying inside. Playing in *Mamba's Daughters* enabled me to rid myself of the terrible inward pressure, the flood of tears I'd been storing up ever since my childhood.

Canada Lee, who is now so widely admired as a serious actor, had a small part in that play. Before going on the stage this versatile man had been a successful jockey and also a good enough lightweight boxer to fight main events at Madison Square Garden.

Canada is a feller always full of fun. When he was in *Mamba's Daughters* he got his laughs by making difficulties. He'd make the other performers giggle by going on the stage with his shoes on the wrong feet.

In one of the fight scenes he was supposed to pull Ned, played by Hayes Proctor, out of the scrap. Instead Canada would push Hayes into the fight. Alberta Hunter, who was playing Ned's wife, stopped that bit of playfulness very simply. At one performance she brought her heel down hard on Canada's instep.

Canada would try to drive me crazy by using a string to hold up his stage pants. "If you don't put on suspenders or a belt," I kept telling him, "your pants will fall down someday."

"I believe in realism on the stage," he'd say. "And this character I play is too poor to buy a belt or suspenders."

The string did break one night and Mr. Lee's pants fell down, revealing the loudest pair of men's drawers ever seen on the American stage. Everybody else in the show got hysterical, but I couldn't laugh because Hagar was supposed to be a dumb creature without any sense of humor at all.

After a solid run on Broadway we took *Mamba's Daughters* out on tour.

Down through the years I'd been visiting my mother regularly. I had rented a little house for her on Catherine Street in Philadelphia, and she lived there with Vi. But her nervousness kept getting worse.

One night during the week we played Indianapolis I saw a man in a gray uniform crouching behind a counter on the stage. I got angry, thinking he was a stagehand who'd been caught on stage when the curtain went up. But when I walked out he'd disappeared.

Later, when I described the apparition to the backstage crew fellers, they told me that my description fitted exactly a man who had fallen to his death from the flies about a year before. He had not died immediately. He was an atheist, that man, and he lay on the stage, cursing God as he died.

I knew that seeing that apparition was a bad omen. And soon I got word that on that very same evening, almost at the same hour, my mother had got into bad trouble. Some newcomers to the neighborhood had sat on her stoop. When she ordered them away they just laughed at her. Momweeze then threw some hot coffee on them. The people went to the station house and signed an arrest paper.

When we moved to Detroit I was worried sick about Momweeze. And I had another omen there. During my stage fight with Willie I fell down in a dead faint. He had to shake me to make me come to.

At that very moment in Philadelphia the authorities were taking Momweeze to the hospital. I tried to get a plane to take me there the moment I heard about this. It was Christmas week, and a bad, bitter night. All passenger flights had been canceled, but I managed to get in a mail plane to New York and went on from there to Philadelphia by train.

The story I got from Genevieve shocked me. My mother had been handled very roughly by the ambulance people. She wasn't crazy, just eccentric. Yet they had forced her to go out with them—without even giving her a chance to get her coat—out into the cold and the biting wind. Vi had gone along with Momweeze in the ambulance to the Philadelphia General Hospital.

"Not the General!" I said. For what good was the money I was making if Momweeze could be hustled off like that, without a coat, to be thrown into some dirty, overcrowded ward?

I hurried to the hospital, where a nurse took me to the ward. It was the snake pit. Women who seemed no longer human leered and grinned and chattered all about us. Young women, old women, grimacing and making obscene gestures, women so far gone into mental decay they could no longer keep themselves clean or decently clothed.

And there sat my mother. She was in a corner, at a window, and looking out, her back straight as a rod and her head up.

"Louise," said the nurse, "here is your daughter."

Slowly Momweeze looked around at me. Her expression didn't change.

"Ethel," she said. "Who am I, Ethel?"

"My mother," I said, my heart turning, bursting.

Momweeze looked triumphantly at that nurse and said, "I told you my daughter would come and get me out of here."

I couldn't take my eyes off Momweeze. I'd never seen her looking so thin and undernourished. I learned the reason for that later on. It had been the work of Vi, my always mischievous and trouble-making aunt.

She had stayed on with Momweeze in the ward. When their first meal came Vi whispered to my mother, "Don't eat nothin', Louise. The food here is all doped. It puts you to sleep. If you eat any of it you'll never get out of here."

Vi had been eating all the food brought for both of them. After devouring her own portion, she gobbled up Momweeze's. Unable to reason with my mother, the hospital authorities had been feeding her intravenously.

I had the nurse take me to the doctor in charge of the ward. He proved to be a courteous and friendly man.

"Why was my mother taken here?" I asked. "You people must know she isn't mad. Her conduct may seem a little eccentric at times, but she's far from crazy."

"That's true," he agreed, "your mother is not demented. But she is very nervous, very high-strung. I'm very sorry to have to tell you that there was no other place we could take her."

"I take good care of my mother, Doctor——"

"We know that, Miss Waters," he said. "We investigated and learned you send her three hundred dollars each month. In fact, we discovered that three hundred dollars—two semi-monthly money orders for one hundred and fifty dollars each—are waiting for her right now. Nevertheless, we will have to send her to Norristown tomorrow."

"Norristown! Tomorrow!" Norristown is the state's mental institution. I tried to be calm. I tried not to cry. But the savage irony burned into my soul. Each night for a year many hundreds of white men and women had been acclaiming me for portraying my mother on the stage. These white people had sobbed and suffered with Hagar, who to me was the replica of my mother. I had broken their hearts and so blinded them to reality that I had stopped being Ethel Waters to them.

And there was the original of my stage portrait, thin, wasted, unfed. Tomorrow they'd take her from her place by the window, put her in a wagon, lock the back door, and cart her off to the state crazy house.

"Your mother had some terrible shock early in life," the doctor was saying.

"Me!" I thought. "The shock came when she brought me into the world."

"As a young woman," he was saying, "your mother withdrew from all normal living. She's always suffered from complete frustration. She's an introvert."

"I understand that, Doctor," I told him. "But you yourself say she is not crazy. I've investigated and I found that in the whole great state of Pennsylvania there is not one place I can send my mother as a patient. For one reason only: my mother is a colored woman.

"Can't I please take her home? You know she doesn't belong here, or in Norristown, or in any other institution like that. Genevieve, my half sister, would take good care of her, Doctor."

Thoughtfully he said, "I can do that, but only on one condition: someone must be with her at all times, night and day."

"That is something I can guarantee," I promised him.

Then I went back into that ward, that snake pit. Genevieve had brought some fried chicken for my mother, who fell on it, eating ravenously, like some wild animal long-starved. My mother, you see, had been starving, but she'd been strong enough to ignore the gnawing pain.

"Are you going to get me out of here, Ethel?" she asked.

"Yes, but only when you can walk out on your own two feet. To do that, you must eat. You must forget what Vi told you about the food here being poisoned. It's not true, Momweeze."

My mother promised to eat the hospital's food. She was not sent to Norristown the next day, or ever, in that locked-up wagon. Within a week I was able to get her out of the snake pit.

Some people around Philadelphia who knew my mother said she was crazy. But they were wrong. Whatever they thought, they never knew that when they saw Momweeze they were looking at a woman who had endured torment, long-sustained, that few human beings could have survived.

Momweeze was always as unhappy as Hagar, and as lonely. Playing that role gave me new insight into the depthless nature of her loneliness, and also the loneliness I've known ever since I was born.

Somehow or other, the things my mother wanted to do, the release in evangelism that she sought with such frenzy, were transferred to me. I think that through my plays and my pictures I have been able to get across the message she never had the chance to deliver.

That was her destiny—and my own. Our destiny, shared, lay in everything that my mother thought and felt about God in her heart being said—but not by her from a pulpit, but from me on stage and screen; me, her unwanted one, conceived in terror and violence, and against her will.

17

After a long tour *Mamba's Daughters* returned to New York for a second engagement. When it closed I went into the movie houses to pick up some more of those big checks.

While playing the movie-house dates I was asked to read *Little Joe*, the musical fantasy that was finally produced on Broadway under the title *Cabin in the Sky*. The role the producers wanted me to play was Petunia, the wife of Little Joe, a bad man. He is dying, and Petunia pleads with God to give him one more chance to live decently —so he'll be able to get into heaven. That was the plot.

I rejected the part because it seemed to me a man's play rather than a woman's. Petunia, in the original script, was no more than a punching bag for Little Joe. I objected also to the manner in which religion was being handled.

After some of the changes I demanded had been made I accepted the role, largely because the music was so pretty. But right through the rehearsals and even after the play had opened, I kept adding my own lines and little bits of business to build up the character of Petunia.

They had a first-rate all-Negro cast in *Cabin in the Sky*: Dooley Wilson, Rex Ingram, and Todd Duncan, not to mention Katherine Dunham and her whole troupe, complete with drums, which cavorted all over the stage, being very symbolic.

We got fine notices when we opened on October 25, 1940, and played on Broadway into the following March. Then we jumped to Los Angeles and closed in San Francisco.

While working there I got a special-delivery letter from my uncle Charlie that almost broke my heart. It said that my mother had just died and asked if I'd wire him enough money to buy a new suit that he could wear to the funeral.

But the letter, which came on a Saturday morning, seemed a little too clever for Charlie to have written all by himself. And I couldn't understand why Genevieve hadn't notified me.

Instead of sending Charlie the money, I wired Genevieve:

HOW IS MOTHER? IS EVERYTHING ALL RIGHT?

I phrased it that way so as not to alarm her if my mother had not passed on. No answer came over the week end. Twice that Saturday I had to do shows, go on and make the people out front laugh. Each time I came off the stage I burst into tears.

I got no sleep at all that night, nor the next. Then on Monday, Genevieve's answering wire came, saying that Momweeze was all right. Like a lot of other people, my half sister is terrified by telegrams. For two whole days she had been afraid to open that one of mine.

As I'd suspected, Charlie had not written that cruel letter himself. One of his bummy friends must have put him up to it. And if I'd sent the money for the suit, his bummy friend would have got it and would probably never even have told Uncle Charlie it had come.

However, Uncle Charlie had his own efficient system for getting a little extra money out of me. Whenever I played a white theater in Philadelphia he'd dress himself in the filthiest rags he could find and take up his post on the street, just outside the stage-door alley.

He'd stop the actors as they went in and would say, "I'm Ethel Waters' uncle. Please tell her I'm out here and ask her if she could send out just enough money for a cup of coffee."

The actors would give him a quarter or a half dollar and then come to me to ask if he was really my uncle. I'd say "Yes," and their eyes would fill with contempt. I didn't try to explain that I'd been supporting him and the rest of my family for years in a style they'd never before been accustomed to. I knew I wouldn't be believed.

Now Charlie, who died in 1949, was never vicious or cruel. In his last years he refused to live anywhere but at a mission. Each time I got to Philadelphia I'd go to the mission and pay for his board for weeks in advance. If Charlie heard about this he'd try to get the money from the mission, making such a fuss that he'd have to be suppressed, almost physically.

Uncle Charlie stayed woman-simple until the day he died. But his girl friend never became Charlie-simple. She only let him come into her house when he got his old-age pension check, not permitting him to cross her threshold until he'd passed it over to her. When the money was all gone she'd put him out on the street until his next government subsidy check came through.

I was playing at the Orpheum Theatre in Los Angeles when some movie men approached me, waving their checkbooks. They offered me ten thousand dollars—a thousand dollars a day for ten days' work —to star with Paul Robeson in an all-Negro sequence of an episodic picture called *Tales of Manhattan*. They had already lined up some of the biggest names in Hollywood for the other sequences.

I became interested only after they told me the story they were using for our episode. Realizing what a large part God plays in our daily lives, the producers were eager to inject religion in our part of the picture.

The story of the all-Negro episode begins with a suitcase crammed with money falling from a plane on a poverty-stricken colored community. Everyone living there has different ideas of how to spend this manna from heaven. Hester, the woman I was to portray, is the religious stronghold of the whole group, and she says:

"If that money isn't claimed by its legal owner, I think God meant for us to use it to build a hospital, a school, and the other things we need so badly."

I had my best scene in a hut where an old woman of over eighty lies dying. When she asks me to sing her across the River Jordan, I stroke her head and softly sing "Nobody Knows the Trouble I've Seen." They had the Hall Johnson Choir furnishing a musical background. As the old woman passes on to her reward a lovely light shines down on her head from above, and it is as though this light is the ladder that her soul can ascend to reach her Maker and the Lord of us all.

The scene was reverently and tenderly done, and all the studio executives raved about it. But when I went to the preview my heart broke. The entire scene had been cut out.

When *Tales of Manhattan* was released various Negro organizations picketed the theaters showing it. Their placards protested picturing us colored people as wretched, dirty, and poorly clad.

I didn't understand that. These same organizations were forever complaining that we Negroes in America are underprivileged. So why did they object to anyone showing us that way on the screen?

I realize, of course, that many of these organizations are led by men and women of the highest ideals. They've done a great deal in the fight to win the Negro equality. But they are making a mistake, I think, when they protest showing colored people as they really are.

There are thieves and murderers and wife-beaters among my people. There are also geniuses and saints and many Negroes who walk all their days down God's pathway. In other words, Negroes are human beings with exactly the same faults and virtues as members of the other races.

Now and always I will rest my case for the Negro as he is, gay and game, and with an ability to survive without a parallel in all the history of mankind. Yes, I'll take him with his music and his laughter, his love of God—and all his faults. I am proud of nothing as I am of being his blood sister.

Why some of us should want Negroes to be portrayed as neat, clean Elsie Dinsmores and Little Lord Fauntleroys baffles me. Those are white characters, brother, and damn bores. I'm for letting the white folks keep them for themselves.

About this time I worked in two more Hollywood pictures—*Cairo* and the screen version of *Cabin in the Sky*. M-G-M made both of them. I was happy in *Cairo*, largely because of the warm friendship of the star, Jeanette MacDonald. But when we made *Cabin in the Sky* there was conflict between the studio and me from the beginning. For one thing, I objected violently to the way religion was being treated in the screen play.

Eddie (Rochester) Anderson, Lena Horne, and many other performers were in the cast. But all through that picture there was so much snarling and scrapping that I don't know how in the world *Cabin in the Sky* ever stayed up there.

I won all my battles on that picture. But like many other performers, I was to discover that winning arguments in Hollywood is costly. Six years were to pass before I could get another movie job.

I got two big lifts that season, though. One day a letter came from the Mother Superior of St. Theresa's Monastery. It asked for a contribution to a fund of fifty-five hundred dollars the nuns had to raise to build a new sewerage system on their property. The cesspools they'd been using, the Mother Superior explained, had overflowed and, as a result, some of the sisters had come down with malaria and typhoid fever. Since the monastery was on private land, neither the local officials nor the state authorities could help them.

So I prayed and asked God to send in enough vaudeville dates to allow me to have the work done. And He did. And nothing I've ever done has given me more joy than the thought that I may have been able to save one or more of those sweet nuns from an attack of malaria or typhoid fever.

That was also the year I bought my house. Twenty-five years is a long while for a girl to live out of a trunk, and Uncle Albert Bauman, who was in the real estate business, for some time had been urging me to buy a home in California.

After looking over a few houses I fell in love with one located in Southwest Los Angeles. It had ten sunshine-filled rooms on three floors. There were two stately old trees in front and a neatly trimmed lawn, and some green stuff was growing over the door like a bower.

I had my furniture brought from New York, and it was moved in on December 12, 1942, which was about the time I started to work on the film version of *Cabin in the Sky*.

I shook with happiness that first evening when I walked into my house. During the day the moving men had brought my things, and when I saw that they had placed each chair and table exactly where I wanted it, I burst into tears.

"My house," I told myself. "The only place I've ever owned all by myself."

But 1942 was the year World War II gave sharks' teeth to the always hard-hitting internal revenue boys, and they took a sixteen-thousand-dollar bite that annum out of my bank roll.

Just the same, I felt I was sitting on top of the world. I had a home at last and plenty of cash reserve. With so many smash-hit revues, plays, and pictures behind me, it seemed apparent I would continue to get plenty of the kind of work I liked to do.

Shortly after finishing *Cabin in the Sky* I was co-starred with Frank Fay and Bert Wheeler in *Laugh Time*, a variety revue. It was while I was playing in *Laugh Time* that I had my most shocking experience with a man.

All the men in my life have been two things: an epic and an epidemic. Yet this man was no lover, but a young protégé for whom I'd got a job in a Hollywood studio as a dance director. I let him live in my home while I was on the road in *Laugh Time* and came back to discover he had robbed me.

That young man I'd befriended couldn't have been much more dear to me if he'd been my own son. In fact, I'd got in the habit of calling him "Sonny" and he called me "Mom." But now he'd robbed me of $10,150 in cash and $35,000 worth of jewelry.

The cold-blooded crime floored me. When I could no longer doubt he was the thief I asked him to come to my house. I sat with him and begged him to give me back my property.

He looked straight into my eyes and told me calmly, "Yes, Waters, I took your money and your jewelry. And there's not one thing you can do about it. If you dare to have me arrested I'll sue you for false arrest. And I'll win my case. You have nothing on me. It's just your word against mine."

Later he agreed to give me back my money and jewels—on two conditions: that I turn over my car and the deed to my house.

Being first robbed by a friend, then defied, threatened, and jeered at was too much. I went to the police. And, believe me, appealing to the authorities is always the last, desperate resort for a woman with my underworld background.

Sonny was arrested, tried, convicted, and sentenced to a year and a day in San Quentin. He got out on bail and kept on appealing the case for two whole years. Only after the highest criminal court in California confirmed the verdict did he have to serve his time.

While all that legal capering was going on my professional career came almost to a dead stop. Overnight my agents seemed unable to get me anything but dates in night clubs. And they were not always the best clubs, either.

What puzzled me was that whenever I appeared the public greeted me with all its old-time warm affection. But weeks, months, even years, passed without a sign that producers wanted me any more on stage, screen, or radio. What hurt worst was hearing that friends I had trusted and, in some cases, helped were saying:

"Old Ethel is washed up. She can't get a play, a picture, or even dates in the big movie houses. She's all through."

I never accepted the idea I was all through. I guess no person who has once been a star can do that, ever. But the years kept on rolling by with nothing happening.

Down and down I went, down and out of the public eye. It was as though I'd never been the star of *Mamba's Daughters*, *Cabin in the Sky*, *As Thousands Cheer*, and all the rest.

At one time I suspicioned that the Hollywood tycoons, angered by my outbursts of temper while making *Cabin in the Sky*, were using their power to blackball me out of show business. But later on I found out that was not true. Today I blame only certain agents for my long eclipse as a public entertainer.

Meanwhile, I didn't get enough night-club work to enable me to break even on any one year. I'd work four weeks, then lay off six, do one week, then lay off three more. I wasn't too eager to work the clubs, anyway. I could no longer think of myself as just a blues singer. I wasn't a Caledonia. No one in the world can beat Ella Fitzgerald as a riff singer. Away back in 1929 I'd done a lick in *I Got Rhythm*. But if I returned to that kind of singing I realized audiences would think I was imitating Ella. My big dream, of course, was to get another play.

That black period continued for almost the proverbial seven years. It wasn't until 1947 that I was offered a play I wanted to do. This was Ann Mercer's *I Talked with God*, a dramatization of the life of Sojourner Truth, the Negro woman who had been born into slavery in 1798 and lived to become one of the greatest preachers of all time. I felt I understood her passion for God because a similar emotion had so long been the biggest thing in my own life.

After reading the play and talking with me, Eddie Dowling, who was then appearing in *The Glass Menagerie*, said he'd put it on if Ann Mercer could raise half of the money he'd need to produce it. He estimated the production would cost between seventy and eighty thousand dollars. Ann raised her share very quickly, and Dowling promised to start rehearsals in the fall.

I was then living in a first-class mid-Manhattan hotel. For some years, whenever away from California, I'd lived in these good white hotels.

When I was traveling with a Broadway show there had never been any difficulty about getting accommodations, the company manager making the arrangements well in advance. But when playing independent dates or laying off I wasn't always successful in getting into such places.

It irked me that some of the hotels that couldn't find room for me were in towns where I'd been presented by the mayor with keys to the city. I figured out what to do about this one day when I was studying the set of rules pasted on the wall of a hotel room. Ever since, whenever I write for hotel reservations, I always enclose a set of rules I have made for the hotels.

These rules read:

1. I don't like to mix with white people.

2. I don't want to eat in your restaurant. I want all my meals sent up to my room because I don't care to dress up except when it is necessary or good for my business. I prefer to be comfortable when eating.

3. I don't have guests in my room, as I don't want to be bothered with them up there.

4. I am an isolationist and I will keep the key to my room with me. I don't like to walk across the lobby to get my key from the desk.

5. If you don't want colored people as guests, for Lord's sake don't write me that you're having some convention and, as a result, can't accommodate me. Just say you don't want colored people in your midst. I will understand. I may even sympathize with you because you are depriving yourself of so much good company.

I always have enjoyed the cleanliness, efficiency, and central location of these first-class white hotels. I didn't see any sense in jumping salty on the hotel managers. They are in business three hundred and sixty-five days in the year, didn't need my business, though I wanted the comfort they sold. Many of them wrote back that they would be delighted to have me stop in their hotels.

But today, as always, there are many Northern cities such as St. Louis, Indianapolis, Kansas City, and Cincinnati where no colored person can get a room in a first-rate hotel.

That summer my long idleness—broken only by occasional night-club dates—really began to press on my nerves and frighten me. Though I was enthusiastic about the Sojourner Truth play, it was not reassuring to think that my entire future might depend on the success of that one show. And long months would pass before I could even start rehearsing.

I began to spend more and more time up in Harlem. I had a driving desire to be with my own people again as much as possible. The walls of my neat, clean hotel room had become like the walls of a cell. I had to get away from those walls and the telephone that rang often but never said what I wanted to hear.

Many nights I'd eat in Mrs. Frazier's Dining Room on Seventh Avenue, between 123rd and 124th streets, where the cooking beats anything you'll find anywhere else in this whole world. I'd often go to Welles's to listen to the wonderful organists who play there. I'd get music-drunk, if such a thing is possible. I'd also relax, hour after hour, sitting alone in the Catholic churches.

Finally I decided to move into Mozelle's home, meanwhile keeping my hotel room downtown. But I quickly learned there are great disadvantages when you are prominent and try to live in a humble place.

Gossip spread around Harlem that I was broke and living on Mozelle's charity. People passing would point out the house and say, "Ethel Waters lives there now. She is down and out. She is living on the charity of a friend of hers."

I still had some money left, but I felt I was scraping bottom, professionally and emotionally. All I wanted was to be with the kind of people I'd grown up with, but I discovered you can't go back to them and be one of them again, no matter how hard you try. It is impossible for them to accept you. You've gone a long way up, and they can't forget that. Some of them can't forgive it, either.

That summer the Theatre Guild asked me to read Carson McCullers' *The Member of the Wedding*, adapted from her own novel and which they intended to produce. When I finished reading it I told the Guild people:

"No, I won't do it. Berenice Sadie Brown, the cook you want me to play, is a bitter woman. She's a chain smoker, drinks heavily, and has lost her faith in God. I won't deny there are characters like her in real life. I've met such women. But Berenice is sordid and ugly and she's not for me to play. I wouldn't work well in that channel."

The Guild people were looking for some Negro actress who resembled Berenice Sadie Brown. They asked me if I knew of some performer who looked like her. I said no. In the script Berenice is described as being short, stocky, with hardened features and with only one eye.

Anyway, I couldn't have taken the role as I was committed to do the Eddie Dowling play. Shortly after I rejected *The Member of the Wedding*, Dowling's secretary called up and said:

"Mr. Dowling can't put on the play because of illness."

That left me high and dry. I'd hoped so hard and waited so long for that show, that telephone call was truly a Sunday punch.

I played a short engagement at the Club Zanzibar in New York during December of 1947, and two Jewish benefits at Madison Square Garden early in 1948. Then I didn't hit one tap of work from February right through to July.

Sometimes I'd hear, but always too late, that managers had approached former agents of mine to find out if I'd work in their spots. These gentlemen would tell them I was booked up for months in advance and quite unavailable. That gave these unscrupulous agents the chance to push the Negro performers who were on their contract lists.

That sad summer of 1948 I thought I would lose my mind. One night burglars broke into Mozelle's apartment and stole some of my money and clothes. Fearing they'd come back, Mozelle became afraid to leave the house. So I moved into the home of another friend, who lived on 149th Street.

I was becoming a hermit and getting too shy to go out on the street at all. Whenever I did, somebody would come up to me and say, "Aren't you Ethel Waters? Sure never thought I'd see you up here."

The basement of the house on 149th Street was the only place I could find solitude, and I moved in down there. So once more I found myself living in a cellar. All night long I'd hear the cats fighting and each morning I'd be awakened by the symphony of the ash cans.

I was also back on the half-milk, half-cream diet and had to take sleeping pills. I had a stomach ulcer and would go mad whenever a bell rang in that house. My financial troubles were also piling up.

The Internal Revenue boys were demanding that I pay them back income taxes which they claimed I still owed for 1938 and 1939. I'd paid those taxes through an agent but couldn't get the receipts or canceled checks from him to prove it.

I was still getting $1,750 a week—when I worked—but those taxes, the long stretches of unemployment, the heavy cost of caring for my mother, paying the bills for my house in California, charities, and living expenses—trying to figure out how to cover all these had my brain jigging wildly and breaking wide open.

In the end I decided to go to California, feeling that out there in the sunshine I might get a new perspective on my career. But as it turned out, I wasn't even allowed to do that.

When I wrote to the agent I then had for a release from my contract, he filed a protest with the American Guild of Variety Artists, or AGVA, as it is sometimes affectionately called. The hearing of his protest was postponed month after month after month, which meant I had to stay in New York, waiting for my freedom.

I stayed in that basement because it did have its good side. I had my own things around me and could hibernate in peace there. I sat with the shades drawn and played all my old records. I could live in the past then, listening to "Dinah," "Cabin in the Sky," "Am I Blue?" and the others. I could remember how the name Ethel Waters looked in lights, the crowds and the excitement of opening nights. Best of all, I could remember how I'd always tried to give out love from the stage, in my singing and acting, and how I always got it back, a thousandfold, from the audiences.

My youth was gone now, and maybe my fame, I told myself as I sat in that cellar, reliving my past with all its glory and under-the-belt blows. And I tried to cheer myself up by remembering what a good life it had been, with the fine breaks always bigger than the bumps.

One day an agent called up and said I could have a week at a Buffalo night club at $1,750. He'd called before, but I had to turn down the chance because I had no accompanist. Reggie Beane, who had taken Pearl Wright's place in my act, was breaking in a new turn with a male partner on the road.

That second time I told the agent I'd have to call him back. I racked my brain. I didn't want to go on unless I had a suitable accompanist. Finally the name of an old friend, Herman Chitterson, occurred to me. I knew he would be fine for me. When I called Chitterson he agreed to go to Buffalo with me, and jubilantly I told the agent I was ready.

Pennies from heaven, and the first thing I did was dash down to Saks Fifth Avenue, where my credit, thank goodness, was still good, and bought two gorgeous gowns there. Chitterson and I rehearsed my repertory day and night.

But when we got to the club in Buffalo we were greeted by a manager who apparently had never heard of me before. He greeted me with polite indifference.

I felt that Buffalo might be a turning point, a crisis. But there had been lots of crises in my life. And there was plenty of spunk and battle cry still left in me. After praying in my dressing room I went out and sang all my old-time favorites—"Dinah," "Am I Blue?" "Heat Wave," and the others.

The town's white-tie and sable set were crowded into the club the night I opened. Each song I sang brought an ovation. When the first show was over, that manager knew who I was, all right, and I played to big business each evening.

On getting back to New York I found an offer to play an Indianapolis benefit. I didn't have to dicker much to get eight hundred and fifty dollars plus transportation for the one night. And I drove out to save train fare.

We had to sit all day long in that vast, cold auditorium, waiting to rehearse. A crumpled telegram was handed to me as I left. It was from young Bob Whitehead, of Whitehead and Rea, a new Broadway producing firm, and it read:

I MISSED YOU BY FIFTEEN MINUTES AFTER TRYING TO GET IN TOUCH WITH YOU FOR THREE WEEKS STOP HOW WOULD YOU LIKE TO DO THE ROLE OF THE NURSE IN MEDEA OPPOSITE JUDITH ANDERSON AND JOHN GIELGUD.

I got him on the long-distance phone at once and explained how his wire had been delayed for hours. "Oh, I'm sorry, Miss Waters," he said, "but at six o'clock tonight we signed Florence Reed for the nurse's role."

"Oh no. No!" I said.

I sat there for a long time, crying. Medea! And working with fine artists like Judith Anderson and John Gielgud in that classic! Such an opportunity was almost more than I'd prayed or hoped for in many years.

But that night I sang at the big benefit. Yet that was nothing new. Through good times and horror and hell I'd always had to go out with my heart jumping, or squeezed, or feeling all dead in my breast. The audience, as usual, applauded, and while I was bowing and smiling at them I thought, "And now, through someone else's carelessness, I've lost out on the biggest chance I may ever have again."

It was some satisfaction, though, on returning to New York, to get my release from the contract with my agent, after AGVA held its much-delayed hearing.

And there came a *big* lift for me a little later when Twentieth Century-Fox signed me for a small part in a Tyrone Power picture. Now I could walk down the streets of Harlem and tell everyone, "I've just signed with Twentieth. They're sending me to the Coast soon."

While waiting I was booked into St. Louis for two weeks, then into New Orleans. While I was working in New Orleans a call came through from a club in Las Vegas which wanted me for two weeks at thirty-five hundred dollars a week. That call came on my birthday, and I could have asked no better present than the chance to jump back to my top salary again with that one little date.

I told the Las Vegas man I'd have to clear the engagement with Twentieth, which had set no starting date for the Tyrone Power picture. "Sorry, Miss Waters," said Hollywood, "but unfortunately we'll need you here just at that time for costume fittings."

So bang like a bubble went that chance too. As though that wasn't enough, shortly afterward Twentieth called up to say the Tyrone Power picture had been postponed indefinitely. In movie language, that usually means postponed forever.

I had lost out on both big chances to get started again.

I felt awful.

I felt as low as you can get. I had a few more scattered weeks in the East, then flew to Hollywood for an engagement at Slapsie Maxie's.

For months after that there was no work at all. Nothing!

It was as though the entire theatrical world had forgotten there ever had been an Ethel Waters.

By that time I was so swamped with debts and unpaid bills that I mortgaged my house. That gave me a breather in my steady plunge toward bankruptcy. I'd paid only eighty-five hundred dollars for that house. But during the war real estate values had skyrocketed so that I was able to get a ten-thousand-dollar loan on it.

With that money I paid off my debts, and the few thousand dollars I had left over gave me a cushion against the immediate future. The problem of getting a suitable accompanist which had long worried me was also solved when Fletcher Henderson, my old musical pal of the Black Swan Jazz Masters days, agreed to be my pianist—if I ever got work again.

In New York some time before, Allen Adler, a member of the famous Jewish theatrical family, had suggested I try concert appearances of the type Maurice Chevalier was having great success with.

There seemingly being no other demand for my services, I did try out that idea up and down the West Coast. The recitals went over splendidly. Though I didn't get the money I thought I was entitled to, I did learn one important thing through this experiment: with just a backdrop and with Fletcher Henderson at the piano, I could hold an audience for two hours and a half with a repertory of my songs.

But a tour of the East—where the real money is—would take months to arrange, and I was glad when my agents told me they had five weeks of Midwest dates lined up for me. These included a week each in Cleveland and Columbus, a night each in Louisville and Detroit, and so on—but with too many long layoffs in between to help me even hold my own financially.

And that winter of 1948–49 I *hit* bottom. This time agents booked me into saloons without telling me what kind of places they were. It hurt. I don't think anyone who knows me would charge me with having an inflated idea of my own importance. But I was Ethel Waters who had starred in Broadway revues, dramatic hits, and million-dollar Hollywood pictures. Yet there I was back to singing in saloons.

I played the Click in Philadelphia and realized that the semi-innovations had just begun. They had a bar in the Click that ran the length of the block. There was a television set at each end. The performers stand on a platform behind the bar, and it was like being in a modernized stockade.

When you come on, they don't turn those television sets off. They just turn them down enough so the customers can keep on watching Hopalong Cassidy, the wrestling matches, or the fights if they want to, or they can listen to you.

For anyone who doesn't sing too good, this, of course, can be a big help. If the television lovers applaud for Hopalong, Ed Wynn, or the winnah and still champion, the performer can always bow and claim the applause is for him.

In the Tia Juana, in Cleveland, the platform you stand on revolves. The piano and the piano player go around with you. As that platform gets to a certain place it stops with a little jerk. You think and you hope the machinery has broken down, but no, after that first jerk it starts to turn again with another little jerk.

In the Pittsburgh place I played they had a much smaller thing for me to stand on. There was a flap in their bar, and you stood near the ladies' room until the time for you to sing. Then you pushed and elbowed your way to the bar. The bartender lifted the flap up after the customers who had drinks on the bar lifted them up. After all that you said "Excuse me!" and went through the flap.

The day I first saw that little thing I was to stand on I said to the manager:

"Heh! I'm a big fat woman. I can't stand on no little thing like that. I'll fall off."

"It's good and solid, Miss Waters," he told me.

It looked like an auction block to me. "I thought Mr. Lincoln abolished slavery a long time ago," I said. "Are you planning to raffle me off?"

You can't imagine the variety of noises that come up to you in places like that—phones ringing, people talking, doors opening and shutting, the waiters making a racket, fight fans at the bar arguing whether Jack Dempsey at his best could lick Joe Louis at his best.

Just the same, what happened in those saloons was pretty good. The customers there were used to small combos, bass and guitar and piano. They had had name performers before me. Good entertainers like Nellie Rose Lutcher, but they didn't sing in my style. My work has to be intimate. I should have quiet to work.

But I had to make good in those places or I was a dead duck. When I was first offered to the managers of those saloons they scratched their heads and they said:

"Ethel Waters? Oh yes, I remember her. I've heard of her."

But what they remembered was Ethel Waters, the blues singer of "Heat Wave," "Rhapsody in Black," Ethel Waters singing "Handy Man," "Summer Time." All the things I'd done since, the way I'd changed and grown, they knew nothing about. For the first two shows at each place the master of ceremonies would introduce me fast with:

". . . And now, Ethel Waters!"

No build-up. No nothing.

But after those first two shows the manager of each place would notice that I was drawing a different sort of audience than they had ever had before, including people who knew me and were awed by my reputation.

So he'd tell the m.c. to give me the big-star introduction, "And now we give you Miss Ethel Waters, star of stage and screen, who made history with her songs, and whose personality and talent . . ."

But the big compliment came from the beer drinkers who didn't know me. They wouldn't drink or move when I sang. If they had their glasses in mid-air, the glasses wouldn't come down. They'd hold them there until I finished my number.

And when I left each place, everyone there, from the porter and the hat-check girl on up, was sorry to see me go. And I felt I wasn't no dead duck if I could make that kind of impression.

When New Year's Day, 1949, came I was in Pittsburgh. I was lonely and more heartsick than ever over those layoffs which weren't getting any shorter.

I picked up the Bible, and where my hand fell it opened at the Seventieth Psalm. I read, and the last verse of that psalm is:

But I am poor and needy: make haste unto me, O God: thou art my help and my deliverer; O Lord, make no tarrying.

And then I read the Seventy-first Psalm, which begins:

In thee, O Lord, do I put my trust: let me never be put to confusion.

Deliver me in thy righteousness, and cause me to escape: incline thine ear unto me, and save me.

Be thou my strong habitation, whereunto I may continually resort: thou hast given commandment to save me; for thou art my rock and my fortress.

Those verses might have been written for me, I thought. I was so lonely that day in the hotel room. And for so many in the streets outside and in the little and big houses, that New Year's Day, I knew, was like the beginning of a new and better life.

And I wondered what I would do—I, the entertainer who had been acclaimed and beloved but now was labeled a has-been—if I didn't have my God to turn to and be able to read the Book He had divinely inspired.

Those psalms enabled me to go on, and I've read them every day of my life since, also the Thirty-fifth, from the first to the seventh verse, and the Thirty-seventh Psalm, from the first to the eighth verse. They made it possible, also, for me to go into a room where there were people who had knifed and betrayed me without checking first on the ugly, revengeful side of my nature. I could leave it to God, I believed, to avenge me.

I kept paying Fletcher Henderson seventy-five dollars a week while

I was laying off. One thing cheered and encouraged me: that was being on the Tex and Jinx program. Those two didn't think I was any has-been and they had such respect for me that it did my heart good.

After closing in Pittsburgh, I went to Chicago, which I was making my headquarters between my widely separated engagements.

I do think that winter was the very lowest period of my life. But always there was the one thing that keeps the hardest-pressed entertainer going. Today or any day that phone may ring and bring good news. And one day in January, God made my phone ring and I got a message that made my heart soar.

Twentieth Century-Fox wanted me to fly out to Hollywood to take a screen test for a picture John Ford was directing. I told Twentieth I'd fly but I'd have to come back to Chicago for a recital Jules Pfeiffer, an agent, had arranged. I had my hair dyed for the part. When John Ford saw me he shook his head.

"I wanted an old one," he said. "Give me a hint. I also have to have a woman who can speak without talking."

After making the test I flew back to Chicago for the recital, only to find out that Pfeiffer's creditors had taken over the box-office receipts. But people had paid to hear me, so I went out and sang for them, without pay.

I cannot remember ten tenser days than those I spent waiting to hear how I'd made out in that screen test. I felt that my whole future might depend on getting that part. Then, in answer to a thousand prayers, came the word:

"The part is yours, Miss Waters. You're to report to the studio on February 14. The test? Oh—it was swell."

I drove back to the Coast, hopes high again.

The picture was *Pinky*.

I had never pressed Twentieth Century-Fox to pay me for the Tyrone Power picture that had been canceled. This deal called for two weeks, and as they were picking up on the other commitment, my salary stayed at the same figure, fifteen hundred dollars.

I'd had a lucky break getting the role of Granny in *Pinky*. One of John Ford's closest friends was Ward Bond, the character actor, who had been a fan of mine for years. He was one of the actors who'd always followed my career with interest. He'd caught me every time I'd appeared in Los Angeles and had many of my old records.

So, being Ward Bond's baby, he suggested I be tested when John Ford started looking for a Granny. And Darryl Zanuck, now production head at Twentieth, remembered my working for him in *On with the Show* and enthusiastically okayed me for the job.

All I had to do to play Granny well was remember my own grandmother, Sally Anderson. The Granny in *Pinky* was much like her, being proud of her blood, hard-working, fierce-tempered, and devoted to her white employers. Jeanne Crain was my granddaughter, the Pinky, a colored girl who looked white enough to pass. William Lundigan was the white doctor in love with her. Ethel Barrymore played the aged mistress of the plantation. That great actress and I had several long scenes together.

I had always loved John Ford's pictures. And I came to love him, too, but I was frightened to death working for him. He'd never seen me on the stage and he used the shock treatment while directing me. That system has worked with a great many other performers, but it didn't work well with me. I almost had a stroke working for John Ford.

After four weeks, though, John Ford's doctor told him he'd have to quit directing for a while as he had overworked himself. Elia Kazan came in and replaced him. He remade the picture from the beginning. And Kazan, like Guthrie McClintic, had been an actor himself and he understood my problems. Mr. Kazan, God love him, was able to bring out the very best in me. I was able, through his help, to let myself go and live the part of Granny as I moved before the cameras.

Elia Kazan gave me credit for intelligence. Together we'd walk through the sets while discussing my role. Altogether I worked twelve weeks on that picture, three of them on half salary. I didn't finish my assignment until May.

On completing my work in the picture I went back to Chicago. I did a week in Montreal and one in Toronto. *Pinky* hadn't been released yet, and I was idle in Chicago all summer. I called my agents every day, and they finally got me two weeks at the Three Sixes, a colored place in Detroit.

But while I was in Chicago I heard from Bob Whitehead again. He wanted me to star in the Carson McCullers play, *The Member of the Wedding*, which the Theatre Guild originally had asked me to read.

Bob had been in Europe and he came to Chicago with the script. I read it and shook my head.

"There is still no God in this play," I told him. "Berenice, the cook, is nasty. She's lost her faith. I won't play such a character."

Bob Whitehead asked if I would come to New York and talk with Carson McCullers. I said I would if I got no engagement.

"But don't get the wrong impression," I told him. "I need the job and the money. Especially the money. I'm ten thousand dollars in debt right now, but I still can't be in a play without any God in it."

When I got to New York I told all that to Carson McCullers. I saw her in her home at Nyack, New York. She and Bob Whitehead finally agreed to let me give the role my own interpretation, and I signed a contract with Whitehead and Rea, the same firm I'd so narrowly missed the chance to work for in Medea. The arrangement permitted me to draw a thousand-dollar advance against my salary whenever I needed money.

So there I was, a good picture part behind me and a starring role on Broadway ahead of me, but I was still broke and couldn't get work.

And then came another break. An executive of the Fox theater chain asked me to make a week of personal appearances in neighborhood theaters to boost the picture. He said he could also put me in at the Roxy on Broadway for a run.

Bill Lundigan and Jeanne Crain had already been around to those neighborhood theaters. And now they wanted me to exploit their picture, Pinky.

"But I just can't go out there and talk," I told him.

The executive said I could sing, dance, do anything I wanted. He'd pay me a bonus and Fletcher Henderson's salary, he said.

Fox had got me a room in a first-class midtown hotel. And for a week I raced each night to seven or eight different neighborhood theaters all over New York.

My date at the Roxy proved one thing to everybody's satisfaction. At forty-nine, old and fat and gray, Ethel Waters could still go into one of those star-spangled Broadway presentation houses and stop the show, at every performance.

Bob Whitehead had got a first-class director, Harold Clurman, to put on The Member of the Wedding. He'd signed Julie Harris to play Frankie, the thirteen-year-old heroine, and little Brandon De Wilde to play the little boy, John Henry. But he still didn't know when he was going to start rehearsals.

Being pressed for money, I took a week at Blue Mirror, a spot down in Washington, D.C. That had to be the week they started rehearsing the play, and I arrived three days after they began.

Now no one was sure *The Member of the Wedding* would click. It is a peculiar play, having no big climaxes or sweeping movement. But it did capture a universal emotion in an adolescent, the feeling of being alone and wanting to belong to the world. And it was written with tenderness and great beauty.

My part of Berenice Sadie Brown, the colored cook, offered one hell of a problem. Though I was being starred in the show, I didn't have the star part in the play. Julie Harris had that, as Frankie. So my job, if I was to justify my star billing, was to pull and hold the play together, and thereby dominate it. But I also had to avoid distracting the audience's attention from Frankie, the central character.

Free to give my own interpretation, the character of Berenice satisfied me. She had been buffeted plenty, but now she was not without humor, and she had retained her faith in God. Besides this, she was moved and guided always by the memory of her one great love for a husband who was dead.

In the play Frankie, the little girl, wants more than anything else in the world to go on the honeymoon of her brother and his bride. Being left out of that honeymoon is too much for her to bear. And that was the play, all mood and loveliness, but not too much plot. Julie Harris and I fell in love with each other at first sight and got along fine. She is a magnificent little actress. Brandon was a perfect gem in his part too.

I was lousy, as usual, at the rehearsals.

No one could have done better than Harold Clurman in directing that fragile play. I'm grateful to him for the extraordinary job he did and welcome the chance to say that here.

Even though Mr. Clurman had been an actor at one time, during rehearsals I did not feel so strongly his sympathy and understanding. But the sympathy and understanding were there. His way of telling you when you are good is to say nothing.

The night we opened the out-of-town run in Philadelphia I said my prayers, as always. Then I told myself:

"I'm gonna walk out there and say everything just the way I feel it."

That's what I did. And that turned out to be just what Mr. Clurman wanted me to do. The Philadelphia papers came out with raves.

But the big test was ahead.

New York.

What would tough old New York say about *The Member of the Wedding?*

We opened at the Empire Theatre on January 5, 1950. And once again I sat before the dressing table in the room that had a star on the door and where so many other great stage ladies had trembled and powdered themselves and smiled into the mirror and cried. The same room where I had sat on the opening night of *Mamba's Daughters* eleven years before.

Could I make it? Could I do it all over again?

This time I was fifty years old and it was the end for me or a brand-new beginning. Once more the prayers said so humbly and earnestly. Once more I walked the last mile and out on that stage. But this time I was on-stage when the curtain went up.

On-stage with my whole future at stake and the past counting for nothing. For that's always the way it is in show business.

While I'd been in my dressing room the swells and the high hats, the carriage trade of New York, had been arriving. I didn't see them when the curtain went up.

I was trying too hard to be Berenice Sadie Brown to see, hear, or feel anything else. When the curtain came down there were ovations for all of us. The reviews next day were rapturous.

How the adjectives came tumbling out of those boys—"something rare and special" . . . "Ethel's terrific!" . . . "Miss Waters is giving her best performance in the theater" . . . and on and on and on!

There was a long line stretching from the box office next day, clear around the corner and up Fortieth Street. The house was sold out for weeks, then months, in advance, sold out solid!

And your Ethel was back!

Back, back, *back* on Broadway at last.

Now the record companies, the movie and television people were after me.

"Where the hell have you boys been the past few years?" I asked them.

I signed a contract with Bob Whitehead's firm to stay with the show until July 1, 1951. Julie Harris and Brandon got the same long-run deal.

I'm on the stage almost all the time in *The Member of the Wed-*

ding. That's a lot of work to do eight performances a week. But I also have signed to do Beulah on television once a week for Procter and Gamble, the soap people, and a nice clean firm it is, too.

In addition to all this I've been writing this book between shows. And I think that's been the toughest job of all, digging back into my tumultuous yesterdays, remembering Sally Anderson, my husband Buddy, the Hill Sisters, Momweeze, Vi, Ching, Charles P. Bailey, Earl Dancer, Eddie Matthews, the Prince of Wales, and all the rest. Whatever else the critics say about this book, they can't say it hasn't got one hell of a big cast.

I'd almost finished writing this book of my life the Sunday I decided to go back to Philadelphia and the little alley places where I grew up. I thought I would go to Chester, too, while I was at it and look at the house where I was borned.

Most of those jungle areas are unchanged. But some of the things I wanted to see weren't there any more. Clifton Street, of unholy memory, had been leveled to the ground. Fawn Street, too, was gone.

I drove down the little alleys in my Lincoln. The people came out to see me. Some of them were old neighbors and friends.

I was a star, but they didn't care. "Hello, Ethel, you old, fat thing," they said, and "My, Ethel, you're big."

And old Morton Street was now Yarnell Street. In Chester, where the shanties of Banana Avenue and Longbottom's Gut once stood in crumbling, tumble-down rows is a housing development for ofays!

But in other little streets my people still live with the privies in the back, the piles of rubbish and empty gin bottles and the smells that were there when I was a little girl.

In those alley houses I was borned and raised. Too big, always too big to fit or sit on anyone's lap. There I was shaped and formed with all my character and my faults and my good points. And I was still living there when I had the greatest experience of my life, finding God.

A long, hard way I've come indeed, but it's been a great life, and if I had it to do all over again I would choose no other path than that one I took—touring with the Hill Sisters as Sweet Mama Stringbean, singing in Edmond's Cellar and up to Broadway, London, Paris, and Hollywood. The pains and the heartaches were all part of that life.

And now I have told it all and it has been an ache and a joy both to look over this big shoulder of mine at all my yesterdays. And there are no regrets, not even sighs, only joy and thanksgiving to the Lord for this life He gave me.

For I was born naked and hungry and He fed me and clothed me and made me strong enough to make my way on my own. And there is no greater gift or destiny, I think.

Yes, I have told it all except one thing that I have been saving up until now, until the end.

And this was perhaps a greater event in my life story than the opening night of *Mamba's Daughters*. It was far greater than any of my nights in the theater—singing at Negro Day at the World's Fair or in Carnegie Hall or having Mrs. Eleanor Roosevelt, the wife of the President, come backstage one night in 1939, with Helen Hayes and Charles MacArthur, and throw her arms around me after watching me play Hagar.

Except for finding God, I think this which I tell now was the greatest thing that ever happened to me. And it happened three years ago, when I was so low and people said I was beaten and through in show business.

That day I was playing in a hinky-dink night club in Philadelphia and I went to see Momweeze, who was living with Genevieve. I opened the door and there she was, sitting in a chair, and she stared at me. Then she laughed.

"Mother," I said, "Momweeze, it's Ethel."

"But you are so big, Ethel. You were so thin before. I never saw you so big. Are you sure you aren't pregnant, Ethel?"

"No, Momweeze, I'm not pregnant."

And my mother looked at me with love in her eyes and she said, "Ethel, I'm glad you've come. I want you to know that, even if you never see me again. You've been a good girl, Ethel. You know God, and He has His arms around you. And you'll come back, Ethel. Those men can't stop you.

"You really have took a beating. But don't you worry none, because you're coming back. Once again you'll be top of the heap. And do you know something, Ethel?

"You're pretty. You're pretty, Ethel, and you're a good daughter. He'll bring you back."

And that was it.

That was the acceptance and the fulfillment I'd been dreaming of winning all my life. And my heart filled up, and my eyes. For the first time I knew then that Momweeze loved me. I knew then that she had loved me and cherished me for many years in her storm-tossed, buffeted heart.

But she had been unable to say it, any of it, until then, when she sensed I was down and needed her simple words of praise as I'd never needed them before and never might again.

And I bless the Lord and thank Him for building that bridge between us and getting Momweeze to hold out her hands to me, her unwanted one, whom she had borned so long ago in such great pain and sorrow and humiliation.